EVERYDAY
CONVERSIONS

NEXT WAVE: New Directions in Women's Studies
A series edited by Inderpal Grewal, Caren Kaplan, and Robyn Wiegman

ATTIYA AHMAD

EVERYDAY
CONVERSIONS Islam, Domestic Work,

and South Asian Migrant Women *in* Kuwait

Duke University Press—Durham and London—2017

Library of Congress Cataloging-in-Publication Data
Names: Ahmad, Attiya, [date]—author.
Title: Everyday conversions : Islam, domestic work, and South Asian migrant women
in Kuwait / Attiya Ahmad.
Other titles: Next wave.
Description: Durham : Duke University Press, 2017. | Series: Next wave | Includes
bibliographical references and index.
Identifiers: LCCN 2016041936 (print) | LCCN 2016043714 (ebook)
ISBN 9780822363330 (hardcover : alk. paper)
ISBN 9780822363446 (pbk. : alk. paper)
ISBN 9780822373223 (e-book)
Subjects: LCSH: Household employees—Kuwait. | Women immigrants—Employment—
Kuwait. | South Asians—Employment—Kuwait. | Conversion—Islam—
Social aspects. | South Asian diaspora. | Belonging (Social psychology)
Classification: LCC HD8039.D52 K89 2017 (print)
LCC HD8039.D52 (ebook)
DDC 305.48/891405367—dc23
LC record available at https://lccn.loc.gov/2016041936

Cover art: Azra Akšamija, *Flocking Mosque,* 2008. Installation view. Details of line drawings of *Flocking Mosque* also appear on the title page and chapter opening pages. Courtesy of the artist.

To Rifat Jahan Ahmad *and* Syed Ishtiaq Ahmad

CONTENTS

When I started this project, I had little sense of what it would all entail. Many years later I am acutely aware that I would not be here were it not for the generosity and support of so many.

First, I would like to thank a tangled network of people in Kuwait and South Asia—"interlocutors" including domestic workers, employers, Islamic *da'wa* and reform movement members, and actors affiliated with the domestic work sector—who gifted me so generously with their thoughts, time, and energy. With hindsight I have come to appreciate how odd and in many cases presumptuous my presence and requests were, and how necessary their kindness, curiosity, playfulness, and dedication were to making this research possible. Most especially I would like to thank (*shukriya, mashkura, shukran, dhanyabad, merabani*) the women, "domestic workers," with whom I spent much of my time in Kuwait and parts of South Asia. They shared with me so much—challenging conversations, teasing comments, worlds-within-stories, jokes, advice, hugs, snacks, fashion tips, solicitous phone calls and visits, and above all their companionship—for which I will forever remain humbled and in their debt. Given the density of social connections in Kuwait, concerns about privacy, and the often-sensitive nature of our conversations, with few exceptions my interlocutors asked me to maintain their anonymity, something that I have respected in this book. Although I have assigned pseudonyms, and use numerous categories and terms to refer to my interlocutors in this book, I ask that you, gentle reader, please bear in mind that these pseudonyms and terms only gesture at individuals of extraordinary complexity. Their utterances and experiences are rich and textured in ways that far outstrip any rendering of them.

This project was conceived and initially developed in a space I can only describe as ideal. I was fortunate enough to undertake this work as a doctoral student in the Department of Cultural Anthropology at Duke University, where mentors, fellow graduate students, faculty, and staff members fostered a vibrant, collegial, and generative intellectual environment. Katherine Ewing, Diane Nelson and Deborah Thomas—advisors, mentors and friends—have shaped, challenged, and enabled my intellectual development and work (and overall well-being) in ways both great and subtle. Kathy's nimbleness of thought, unrelenting ability to surprise and discover the singular, and unfailing kindness have made so much possible. Diane's irrepressible ways of being/knowing have pushed me to (at least try to) think in 3D, if not multiverses, beginning with where I stand. Deb is an extraordinary scholar and role model who inspires me in ways that resonate more strongly every day. All three exemplify living, embodied forms of learning that move me to no end. Special thanks to Bianca Robinson, Wang Yu, Aaron Thornburg, Netta Van Vlliet, Mara Kaufman, Brian Goldstone, Leigh Campoamor, Neta Bar, Duane Dixon, Alvaro Jarrin, Yektan Turkyilmaz, Jatin Dua, Youshaa Patel, Holly Francis, and Pat Bodager, from whom I learned so much. While at Duke I also benefited greatly from the generous advice and support of Charlie Piot, John Jackson, Ebrahim Moosa, and Anne Allison. While they may not necessarily remember them, snatches or sustained conversations with Rebecca Stein, miriam cooke, Ellen McLarney, Tina Campt, Kathi Weeks, and Ranjanna Khanna pushed my thinking on this project in a myriad of ways that I am very thankful for.

My work has benefited from several institutions that offered me the time, space, and resources to grow as a scholar, including Kuwait University's College of Social Studies; the Center for International and Regional Studies at Georgetown University; and the Religion Department and Feminism, Gender and Sexuality Studies Program at Wesleyan University. In Kuwait, I would like to thank Prof. Zahra Ali, Anfal Al-Awadhi, Dr. Nasra Shah, Dr. Lubna Al-Kazi, and Dr. Yaqoub Al-Qandari for their much-needed support. In Qatar I would like to thank Zahra Babar, Suzi Mirgani, Rogaia Abu Sharraf, Judith Tucker, Amira Sonbol, Abdullah Al-Arian, Younis Mirza, Mehran Kamrava, and Rehenuma Asmi for their suggestions and comments on this project. In Middletown, I am grateful to have worked with scholars who invigorated my work in so many ways, including Courtney Fullilove, Tami Navarro, Mary-Jane Rubenstein, Peter Gottschalk, Justine Quijada, Elizabeth McAlister, Anu Sharma, Jennifer Tucker, Gina Ulysse, Christina Crosby, Gillian Goslinga, Annelise Glauz-Todrank, Jill Morawski, and Kehaulani Kauanui. Earlier versions of parts of chapters 1 and 4 appeared in an edited volume *Labour Migration in the Persian Gulf* and the *Asian and Pacific Journal of Anthropology*. Work on this project was further supported with funding from the Columbia College Facilitation Fund, Institute of Middle

East Studies, and the Global Humanities Program at the George Washington University; Advanced Research grants and UISFL grants at Wesleyan University; the Bass Award, Franklin Humanities Center Dissertation Fellowship, Boone Advanced International Fellowship, Graduate Student Travel Award, Women's Studies Travel Award, Center for South Asian Studies Research Award, and the Center for International Studies Research Award at Duke University.

Drafts of chapters were presented at talks, workshops and conferences at Stanford, UC Berkeley, Yale, Columbia, William & Mary, Texas A&M, Georgetown, Qatar University, NUS Singapore, Rutgers University, NYU, Kings College London, Exeter University, Keele University, the Rockefeller Bellagio Center, and UC Irvine. I am grateful to my hosts and colleagues for their questions, comments, and critiques, in particular Lila Abu Lughod, Ayca Alemdaroglu, Sara Friedman, Jonathan Glasser, Zareena Grewal, Nadia Guessous, Sherine Hamdy, Humeira Iqtidar, Mark Johnson, Maia Ksenia, Karen Leonard, Saba Mahmood, Annelies Moors, Gul Ozyegin, Krishnendu Rai, Ronit Ricci, Sara Shneiderman, Sharika Thiranagama, Pnina Werbner, and Sibel Zandi-Sayek. One of the greatest pleasures of conducting research in the Greater Arabian Peninsula and Persian Gulf region has been working alongside wonderfully collegial and gifted colleagues, in particular Neha Vora, Farah Al Nakib, Fahad Bishara, Ahmad Kanna, Filippo Osella, Andrew Gardner, Mai Al Nakib, Noora Lori, Pardis Mahdavi, Michelle Gamburd, Noor Al Qasimi, Sharon Nagy, James Onley, Gwenn Okruhlik, the late Mary Ann Tetreault, and Matteo Legrenzi. Caroline Osella, a kinetic and indefatigable scholar, has been a steadfast source of encouragement and generative conversation, for which I thank her wholeheartedly.

Thanks to my supportive colleagues at the George Washington University's Department of Anthropology, Institute of Middle East Studies, and Women's Studies Program. From our first conversation, Joel Kuipers "got" this project, and with tremendous acuity matched only by unfailing generosity has been instrumental in helping me move it forward. Sarah Wagner, Alex Dent, Chet Sherwood, Ilana Feldman, Richard Grinker, Steve Lubkemann, Bob Shepherd, Hugh Gusterson, Mona Atia, Dina Khoury, Shana Marshall, Nathan Brown, Marc Lynch, and Melani McAlister model the tricky balance of being talented, productive scholars and generous colleagues. I am also thankful to Jonathan Higman, Kristina Short, Cortney Cogan, and their multifarious crew who make it possible for our department to function. I am grateful for the thoughtful comments and encouragement that Jennifer Nash, Libby Anker, Ivy Ken, Sam Pinto, and Dara Orenstein provided during our writing group meetings—and the pleasure of reading their works before others do!

In the midst of busy semesters and even busier lives, Inderpal Grewal, Nicole Constable, Mandana Limbert, and Melani McAlister not only took the time to read an earlier draft of this manuscript, but to travel to Washington, DC, to share their critiques, suggestions, and advice in a workshop setting. Their generosity and commitment to supporting a junior colleague speak volumes about the scholars they are. Incisive and comprehensive, their comments have improved this book immeasurably. This project also owes so much to Duke University Press, especially to Ken Wissoker, Jade Brooks, Susan Albury, Amy Ruth Buchanan, and the three anonymous reviewers whose insightful and challenging questions have pushed me to think about the book in greater focus and depth. All remaining errors are entirely my own.

The bulk of the revisions for this book were undertaken while I was in residence at the Stanford Humanities Center. I am grateful to Carolyn Winterer, Roland Hsu, Bob Barrick, Susan Sebbard, Najwa Salame, Patricia Blessing, and other members of the center's crew for making possible a truly blissful haven for thinking and writing. My fellow fellows enlivened and enriched this project in ways that make me smile and sigh longingly for our lunch conversations. In particular I would like to thank Stephanie Hom, Fred Donner, Erika Doss, Joseph Boone, Thomas O'Donnell, JP Daughton, and Bruno Perreau for their wit, wisdom and ever-playful spirits.

Since meeting Azra Akšamija, I continue to be moved, iinspired, and often stunned by her brilliant and powerful work. I am honored beyond words to have her *Flocking Mosque* grace the cover of this book and suffuse its discussion. An always-shifting geographical configuration of relatives and kindred spirits has supported this project with care and cheer. My aunts, uncles, and cousins' gentle inquiries and hints about gaps on their bookshelves remind me how fortunate I am to be part of such an encouraging and loving family matrix. In particular I would like to thank the women I know as Ruqayya Bobo and (my late) Nani Umma, two largely unsung heroes. To my great delight I discovered a new branch of my family in the form of Jennifer Nash, Amin Ahmad, and Naima Nash in Washington, DC. Their joy is infectious, as is their tremendous generosity of spirit. Michelle Syba, friend and confidante extraordinaire has shared, commiserated, and counseled me during every step of this journey. In Kuwait, I would like to thank Ebtehal Ahmad; Muhammad Muzaffar; Sakina Al-Kout; Abdel Aziz Ahmed; the extended Muzaffar, Al-Kout, and Ahmad families; Abeer Tebawi and her family; and Fatouma Ali and Zahra Ali for their support and friendship. In particular I would like to thank Ebtehal, a woman of extraordinary charisma, courage, and unfailing generosity. Ebtehal and her remarkable family not only made it possible for me to function in Kuwait, but to function well. Her friendship is an immeasurable gift.

Syed Ishtiaq Ahmad landed in Montreal over forty-five years ago in the dead of winter without a coat and a missing ride. Books and trousseau in tow, Rifat Jahan Ahmad joined him a few years later. With quiet determination and integrity the two have endured so much and made so much possible for our family, both in Canada and the always-connected elsewhere. I am grateful to them for *sab kuch*, not least of which are Syed Zulfiqar Ahmad and Salma A. Ahmad, wondrous beings who (mostly) let me share in their adventures, including some recent forays with Khadija Mahmood, Mustafa Thomas, Noor Ahmad, and Soraya Thomas. Ummi and Aboo are the soul of generosity and grace. They have never pretended that hard things are easy, and they have never allowed for complacency of thought or deed—yet they smooth so much in their wake. I have asked and continue to ask so much of them, and they always respond with consideration and unstinting love. This book is dedicated to them both.

The female intellectual as intellectual has a circumscribed task which she must not disown with a flourish. —GAYATRI C. SPIVAK, *Can the Subaltern Speak?*

———————

Whatever its other aspects, the everyday has this essential trait: it allows no hold. It escapes. It belongs to insignificance, and the insignificant is without truth, without reality, without secret, but perhaps also the site of all possible signification. The everyday escapes. This makes its strangeness—the familiar showing itself (but already dispersing) in the guise of the astonishing. It is the unperceived, first in the sense that one has always looked past it; nor can it be introduced into a whole or "reviewed," that is to say, enclosed within a panoramic vision; for, by another trait, the everyday is what we never see for a first time, but only see again, having always already seen it by illusion that is, as it happens, constitutive of the everyday. —MAURICE BLANCHOT, *The Infinite Conversation*

EVERYDAY CONVERSIONS

A Moment

An ethnography of South Asian migrant domestic workers' adoption of Islamic precepts and practices in Kuwait, this book begins with a moment of everyday conversion, one leading me to research a reconfigured set of issues I had long been focused on. It was a searing hot July day in 2004. I was seated in the backseat of a taxi on my way to the home of Auntie Anjum, a new contact and potential interlocutor from Pakistan. Jose, a taxi driver from the Philippines and one of my de facto guides was swearing softly under his breath. We were late. The emir's impromptu decision to visit his favorite palace, a sprawling seafront compound on the outskirts of Kuwait city, had left Jose and me idling behind a hastily erected roadblock. Part of an ever-lengthening queue of cars, all we could do was wait. I did my own cursing in the backseat. A couple of weeks into my first trip to Kuwait, I was en route to attending a *dars* (lesson) organized by women participating in Al-Huda, a Pakistani Islamic women's movement. My research on the movement's transnational spread into the Gulf was beginning in earnest—that is, if I ever got to Auntie Anjum's home.

Anxious yet resigned, I looked out my window. A few meters ahead of us in one of the other lanes was a white minibus emblazoned with the logo of one of the largest construction companies in Kuwait. The men inside, wearing identical blue work suits, looked to be South Asian. Sweat-stained, most were slumped in their seats, or sleeping with their heads pressed against the windows, the backs of their seats, a friend's shoulder, or any supportive surface they could find. "They are probably coming back from a construction site," Jose told me. "Look at them, poor devils; look how tired they are! And for what?" Behind the bus was a gleaming SUV. The driver, a stylishly dressed Kuwaiti woman, was using the rearview mirror to adjust her *hijab*. In the backseat a diminutive Indonesian woman was holding a toddler. "Probably going shopping before lunch, and taking her maid," Jose explained, "or maybe on her way to a family member's home. She looks dressed up, but," he added, "I guess they always do." Immediately to our right was a group of young Kuwaiti men who were listening to music and gesticulating animatedly. I could feel their insistent gazes. "Don't look," Jose warned, "they will get the wrong idea. I don't want to have to deal with that. You don't want to have to deal with that." We didn't. The police officers, who, Jose had informed me earlier, were primarily Bedouin, the underclass of the citizenry, had gotten back into their cars. The highway was opening up again.

As we made our way into the labyrinthine streets of Auntie Anjum's neighborhood, I was thinking about what I had just seen: a street scene-cum-microcosm of Kuwait. There was the emir, the sovereign, who generally directed the country from afar, but occasionally, and often unpredictably, punctuated the everyday with his exceptional presence.[1] Then there was the police, an integral part of Kuwait's state apparatus charged with regulating the movements of citizens and noncitizens, whether across roadblocks or borders. And stalled or speedily moving along, citizens and foreign residents, who comprise the majority of the population, were trying to go about their daily lives. As suggested by their dress, activities and vehicles, they shared the road in ways indexing the deeply entrenched asymmetrical political, economic, and gendered relations that comprise Kuwaiti society.

Before traveling to Kuwait, I had read numerous reports juxtaposing the privileges Gulf citizens enjoy with the difficulties the region's labor migrant and foreign resident populations endure. Seeing the politics of the region's migration, labor, and citizenship regimes playing out firsthand through the mundane yet quintessential act of navigating Kuwaiti traffic was striking. Yet at the same time, as I scanned the lettered and numbered street signs looking for the coordinates Auntie Anjum had given me, I was cognizant of how these issues are often examined in isolation from another set of issues that define the Gulf externally. In addition to its petrodollars and vast populations of migrant workers, the Gulf is commonly depicted as a place where puritanical forms of Islam (often glossed as *Wahhabi*) are practiced, traditions of Islam that have become globally pervasive due to the region's oil wealth. Rather than conceiving of these two sets of issues as separate, I had developed an acute sense of their interrelationship through my experiences of living and working in different parts of South Asia and the Middle East, and of growing up in the thick of Canada's diasporic Muslim networks. In these spaces, what was commonly referred to as "Gulf influences" were not only marked by migrants' remittances, conspicuous displays of consumer goods, newly built or enlarged family homes, and their plentiful commentaries about the Gulf.[2] So too were Gulf influences marked by religious changes, including shifts in veiling practices, everyday language practices, gender relations, and religious gatherings.[3] These shifts were not simply unidirectional in nature, marking the ascendancy of "Saudi" or "Wahhabi" forms of Islam, but embedded in longer-term transnational circuits of Islamic reforms movements crosscutting the Gulf, South Asia, and Indian Ocean regions.

Mapped onto broader historical and transnational fields, the interrelation between the Greater Arabian Peninsula and Persian Gulf Region's (Gulf's) religious movements and its regimes of migration, labor and citizenship, animated my interest in researching Al-Huda's spread into the region—beginning with Auntie Anjum's dars. Finally finding myself in front of her complex, I was relieved to note that other women were also arriving late. Introducing myself hurriedly, I joined them as we made our way up the stairs and into the room in which everyone was assembled. It was large and beautifully appointed: striped silk sofas ringed the walls, the dark wood tables were intricately carved and inlaid with mother-of-pearl, and the tiled floors were strewn with plush carpets and even plusher cushions. Once seated and taking in my surroundings, I became increasingly perplexed with what I saw. Was this an Al-Huda dars?

Whether in Islamabad, Dubai or Toronto, the other Al-Huda dars I had previously attended were conducted in Urdu, almost exclusively attended by women of South Asian background, and centered around the recorded lectures of Dr. Farhat Hashmi, the founder of Al-Huda. The scene playing out in front of me was markedly different. In the far corner of the room, seated on a hard-backed chair, a tall spare woman dressed in a dark blue hijab and matching *abaya* (long cloak) was addressing the other women present. Sister Hawa, a woman I later learned was from Egypt, spoke in an English heavily inflected with Arabic, and she was leading the group in Qur'anic exegesis (*tafsir*). Judging from their attire and appearance, the women listening were of diverse backgrounds. A couple of younger women wore floor-length tunics decorated with embroidery that was distinctively North African. Next to them was a blond-haired, blue-eyed woman who looked to be Lebanese or Syrian. Several other women—who I was to later learn were from Sri Lanka, Canada, Egypt, and the UK—wore black hijabs and *abayat*, or jeans and shirts. Seated on the sofas were numerous South Asian women wearing *shalwar kameez* (Urdu: tunic and loose trousers). And closer to where I sat was a Filipina woman dressed in a lavender and white domestic worker's uniform, and an Indonesian woman wearing a bonnet-like hijab and matching tunic.

Towards the end of the halaqa, an affair at times serene or spirited, Sister Hawa called for the other women's attention. "Sisters," she began,

> today is a day of great *baraka* [blessings]. I know many of you have to get back to your families or pick up your children before the lunch hour, so my words will be short, but *inshallah* [God willing], we can talk of this more, and celebrate this great news next time.
>
> As you know Sister Rosa, may Allah be pleased with her, has been attending our *halaqa* for, *alhumdullilah* [praise be to God], many months now. A few weeks ago she approached me about taking *shahada* [Islamic testament of faith] . . . [*quiet murmurings in the room*] . . . I told her to wait, think about it some more, and talk to her family.
>
> And *mashallah* [God willed it], she is persistent: she asked me about this again two weeks ago. I told her again to wait, think about it, and talk to her mother and father in the Philippines.
>
> And *mashallah* sisters, she is persistent: Last week, she came to me again after class and told me she wants to take *shahada*, and rather than going to the women's center [of Kuwait's largest *da'wa* movement] she wants to take it here with you. And so sisters . . .

She gestured to Rosa, the Filipina woman in the domestic worker's uniform. Rosa approached Sister Hawa and raised her right hand and index finger. Without any further preamble, she recited the Islamic testament of faith, the speech act through which she became Muslim: "La Illah a illullah Mohammedan rasul-ullah."[4]

When most of the other women had left, I introduced myself to Auntie Anjum, a fixture of Kuwait's diasporic South Asian Muslim community. Still a little confused, and obstinately clinging to my initial research lead, I asked Auntie Anjum whether she and Sister Hawa held these halaqa regularly, and whether they were influenced by the lectures of Dr. Hashmi, the leader of Al-Huda. Auntie Anjum wrinkled her brow slightly and paused. Then, realization dawning, she exclaimed, "Oh-ho! Sorry, sorry Attiya-*beti* [Urdu: daughter]. Naureen told me you wanted to come when we listen to Dr. Farhat's lessons. No, no—today is the day of Sister Hawa's *halaqa*." More than any other moment, my going to Auntie Anjum's home, ostensibly on the wrong day of the week, and attending Sister Hawa's *halaqa* rather than Dr. Hashmi's recorded *dars*, defined the course of my subsequent research. It was the first of what was to become many instances in which I witnessed or learned of migrant domestic workers' conversion to Islam.

Over the next several weeks as I continued with my research on Al-Huda, Rosa's story traveled with me. While meeting with long-standing members of Kuwait's South Asian Muslim community, interviewing members of Al-Huda, attending *durus* (lessons), mapping out the group's networks, and developing relations with Kuwaiti families and academics, the issue of domestic workers' Islamic conversions insistently poked its way into our conversation. Many had heard of Rosa's situation, and knowing that I was present when she had recited the shahada, they asked me a series of questions I was in no real position to answer, yet keen to establish connections and credibility as a scholar, that I gamely discussed with them:

- How did she learn about Islam?
- Was she pressured, or did she recite the shahada sincerely?
- Did her salary increase? Did the women who were present give her money or gifts, and if not then, at that moment, perhaps later?
- Can she go back to her family, or will she now stay in Kuwait?
- Will she remain a practicing Muslim when she returns home?

Initially I found these conversations to be an interesting sidenote, if sometimes irritatingly long sidetrack, to my research on Al-Huda. As I was in the thick of learning, migrant domestic workers' conversion to Islam is a widespread phenomenon in the Greater Arabian Peninsula and Persian Gulf region. Over the past twenty years, tens of thousands of domestic workers—migrant women of diverse ethnonational, linguistic, educational and religious backgrounds—have converted to Islam. Among the region's vast population of noncitizens, groups often referred to as migrant workers, expatriates, and foreign residents, domestic workers are by far the largest group of converts. These women's experiences in the Gulf also contrast with those of migrant domestic workers in other parts of the world, where religious conversions are little reported in what is now a robust body of policy reports and scholarly literature focusing on the feminization of transnational labor migration.

In Kuwait, most people directly knew of or had heard of domestic workers' Islamic conversions—and everyone had an opinion about the matter. Scrawling down my interlocutors' comments and my own scattered impressions—and, later seeing these suffused throughout my notebooks—my fascination grew. Slowly but surely, a new research field was starting to form. Witnessing Rosa's recitation of the shahada was leading to the gradual conversion of my own research. The issues animating my interest in Al-Huda—how transnational processes are reworking gendered geographies of religious piety and belongings crosscutting the Middle East, South Asia and Indian Ocean region—were taking on a new and unexpected configuration, one encapsulated by a question whose constant refrain would weave its way through my subsequent research: Why are South Asian domestic workers converting to Islam in the Gulf?

In this book I argue that understanding the circumstances through which South Asian migrant domestic workers adopt Islamic precepts and practices in Kuwait requires us to bring into focus a realm—the everyday—that is often relegated to the background.[5] The particularity of domestic workers' experiences in the Gulf constitutes a form of everyday conversion, a form of transnational relations marked by emergent subjectivities, affinities, and belongings that complicate conventional understandings of both the feminization of transnational migration and religious conversion. Domestic workers' everyday conversions develop through their gendered experiences of transnational migration and their relations and work centered on household spaces, ones marking the confluence of Islamic ethical formation, the reworking of domestic workers' subjectivities through their affective laboring, and a South Asian gendered discourse of women's malleability (being *naram*). They experience religious conversion not as an eventful moment, but as an ongoing process rooted in the everyday where differences between their preexisting and newfound religious practice, and the outcomes of the conversion process, are not evident at the outset. Their adoption of Islam is not characterized by the rejection or renunciation of their preexisting lives, but as a gradual reworking thereof. Domestic workers' experiences foreground a particular gendered space of the everyday—household relations and activities—as not only productive and reproductive of their existing familial networks and ethnonational belongings, but as also engendering newfound possibilities and transformations marked by their Islamic conversion. These women's everyday conversions constitute a form of transnational subjectivity and belonging that does not supplant but develops alongside and reconfigures their existing familial and ethnonational belongings. Their experiences underscore how transnational processes are marked not simply by the diffusion or extension across borders of kinship networks, ethnonational forms, and religious movements, but how transnationalism constitutes a dynamic field in which gendered, religious, occupational-class, and ethnonational differences are invoked and reworked, configured and reconfigured together, a field generative of everyday conversions. Here the everyday functions not just as a space of routine and continuity, but of contingency, emergent possibility, and ongoing conversion.

The Question of Conversion

Religious conversions beget questions, and religious converts are beset by questions. Why all this questioning? To begin addressing this issue—what I will call the question of conversion, and how to develop an approach attuned to everyday conversions, let me begin by making a general observation: questions are rarely simple matters, not just in terms of the answers they insist upon, but for what they simultaneously reveal and conceal in their formulation. We feel the prick of a question when something surprises or puzzles us, often when it disturbs our taken-for-granted understandings and hegemonic expectations. We pose questions for phenomena that need an explanation, yet under the pretext of wanting to learn more—a projection outward of our not knowing—we rarely examine the underlying reasons why these phenomena need to be accounted for. This is particularly the case with religious conversions. As Talal Asad incisively notes, "religious conversion appears to need explaining in a way that secular conversion into modern ways of being does not."[6] Religious conversions constitute one form of what Hussein Ali Agrama refers to as an "an emergent religiosity . . . seen within social theory as a problem to be explained."[7] Countering and complicating discourses of modernity that posit the decline of religion,[8] as well as secularist discourses that seek to delimit the public and political role of religion,[9] religious conversions underscore the continued salience and spread of religious practice in our world, prompting the need for explanations.[10]

The question of conversion is perhaps most acute with respect to Islam, where hegemonic discourses of modernity and secularism bleed into and are buttressed by Orientalist and Islamophobic ones, particularly in the aftermath of 9/11, the subsequent invasions of Afghanistan and Iraq, and the recent rise of ISIS.[11] These discourses promulgate a generalized understanding of Islam as intrinsically nonmodern, and pious Muslims as recalcitrant toward and inimical to the trapping of modernity, in particular liberal democracy, individual freedom, and the rights of women.[12] Hegemonic expectations of modernity and secularism produce an incitement to questions about religious conversion, in particular Islamic ones, placing the burden of explanation on their occurrence, not on why they are deemed to need an explanation, or the terms through which they are to be explained.[13] In so doing, the question of conversion insistently (and insidiously) ensures the ongoing reproduction of discourses of modernity, secularism, and Islam.

My research on migrant domestic workers' everyday conversions does not elude this incitement to discourse about religious conversion. Ultimately, I have found it impossible to do so, and trying to do so misses an important point. Discourses of modernity and secularism, and the questions of conversion they give rise to, are tacit and globally pervasive. They shape my interlocutors' experiences and utterances in myriad ways that are difficult to disentangle from other dimensions of their lives. As a scholar who is situated within an academy that has developed through and continues to be subject to these discourses, they also shape my renderings of my interlocutors' experiences. Although subject to them, domestic workers' everyday conversions and my research are not determined or reducible to these hegemonic discourses. Both my research and the circumstances by which domestic workers convert to Islam are configured in complex and often contradictory ways in relation to these discourses as well as to other histories, political-economic processes, and interregional relations. Acknowledging what animates the question of conversion rather than taking it for granted, and scrutinizing the terms through which these conversions are to be accounted for rather than reinscribing them, makes it possible to begin examining these configurations.

Discourses of modernity and secularism do not just incite scholarly explanations of contemporary expressions of Islamic piety, they also inform them. To provide an analysis of Islamic practice without recourse to concepts that reproduce discourses of modernity and secularism, one trajectory of ethnographic work has tended to identify their interlocutors and field sites in juxtaposition to these discourses. These works, in particular Saba Mahmood's brilliant study of Cairene women who participate in a mosque-based piety movement,[14] focus on interlocutors who experience their pieties in radically different and incommensurable terms, ones stemming from traditions of Islamic practice. By excavating these terms and painstakingly differentiating them from hegemonic discourses of liberalism, secularism and modernity, these ethnographic accounts help us to better understand expressions of Islamic piety while simultaneously underscoring the misapprehensions and limitations of studies that fail to do so.

Examining phenomena while simultaneously problematizing the concepts through which they are analyzed constitutes a predominant tradition of anthropological work. Rooted in the discipline's formation, this approach is predicated on the positing of binary difference. Anthropology emerged in the nineteenth century tasked with making comprehensible peoples and places that were considered fundamentally different from the Modern West.[15] Although the categories of analysis have changed—the Modern West replaced by hegemonic discourses of modernity and secularism (among others) that are associated with but not tethered to the Modern West, and non-Western others replaced by other discursive traditions such as the Islamic discursive tradition—the underlying binary framework of analysis persists. This approach is characterized by a particular dynamic: the constant tacking back and forth between hegemonic discourses and other discursive traditions; of documenting and making legible other possibilities, and often marginalized ways of being in the world while simultaneously demonstrating that the truths deemed to be self-evident by hegemonic discourses are in fact sociohistorically specific sets of understandings and practices, and not neutral or universal as they are often assumed to be. Contemporary anthropological studies of Islamic pieties link this tradition of anthropological analysis to a broader postcolonial critique. These works not only relativize and provincialize secular modern understandings of subjectivity, agency, and embodied practice. Their critiques also point to how these discourses are universalizing in nature: that their projected universal nature masks the very processes through which these concepts and understandings spread and become the self-evident basis by which Islamic pieties are apprehended and assessed.

This ethnography of domestic workers' everyday conversions develops through yet differs in significant respects from this trajectory of anthropological work. While I seek to examine domestic workers' Islamic conversions in ways that are faithful to their experiences and that are attentive to the hegemonic and universalizing nature of modern secular and liberal understandings, I do so using an alternative framework of analysis. Rather than identifying and juxtaposing differences between discursive traditions, and emphasizing their incommensurabilities, examining the circumstances of domestic workers' everyday conversions to Islam pushes us to consider the complex ways in which discursive traditions are interrelated and historically situated. My analysis draws from transnational scholarship that points to how discursive traditions—both hegemonic and forms designated and differentiated as "other"—have developed through processes of colonial modernity and are the products of entangled rather than distinctive historical trajectories. Anthropological approaches based on the positing of binary differences account for how power relations are produced and perpetuated when differences are obfuscated, yet they elide the processes and power relations through which differences are themselves produced, maintained, and reinscribed.[16] These approaches often conceive of interrelations in terms of hegemony or hybridity; where a particular discursive tradition becomes dominant and naturalized, or two discursive traditions blend together. By contrast, other forms of their interrelation remain little examined, including mutual constitution and self-constituting othering, as well as the sociohistorical circumstances through which discursive traditions become interrelated and are configured together.

Religious conversions constitute one site of interrelation between discursive traditions. Subjects' experiences of conversion involve transformations in their understandings, practices, relationships, sense of self, and sociopolitical belongings that are brought about through their simultaneous engagement, negotiation, and shifting between discursive traditions. As I discuss through an examination of migrant domestic workers' experiences of everyday conversions, processes of religious conversions do not simply entail the rejection or supplanting of one religious discursive tradition in favor of another; rather, they are sites through which similarities and differences between religious discursive traditions are reworked and reconfigured.

Competing Explanations

Debates about why domestic workers are converting to Islam are widespread and vociferous in Kuwait. As a newcomer to the country, I was often struck by the affect animating these discussions. From the cadence and tenor of people's comments, to the emphatic hand gestures and sharpened gazes that accompanied them, it was clear that Rosa and other domestic workers' conversions mattered, yet the reasons why they mattered were not always so clear. While many in Kuwait knew of domestic workers who had converted to Islam, as far as I could discern, these conversions did not affect them in any overt or significant way. In learning more about Kuwait—in particular the country's complex social, political and religious terrain, one shaped by its interregional past and transnational present—I gradually began to understand why. Domestic workers' conversions channeled discussions about some of the region's most contentious issues, providing migrant workers, foreign residents, and citizens alike with an oblique way of addressing them. These groups analyzed domestic workers' conversions in ways inflected by their own understandings, experiences, and often-pointed opinions about the region, in particular migration policies, citizenship rights, gender relations, labor politics, and the role of religion in everyday life and governance.

A proxy for different groups' political preoccupations, discussions about domestic workers' conversions center on two competing explanations for why these women are converting to Islam. In contrast to domestic workers' experiences of everyday conversion—a gradual process rooted in their everyday household activities and relations, a process characterized by a complex configuration of continuity and change—these competing explanations view domestic workers in terms of a linear process of transformation brought about through a subset of factors. These explanations can be seen as similar to materialist versus ideational approaches to the study of religion and Islam that emphasize either political-economic or religiodiscursive factors to account for domestic workers' conversion to Islam.[17] Articulated in relation to the region's politics of belonging and exclusion or its politics of Islamic reform, both explanations are predicated on radically different and incommensurable understandings of subjectivity, agency, religion, and households. These explanations index two distinct visions of political practice: those of liberal-secularists and of Islamic reformers. For groups espousing liberal-secular discourses, domestic workers convert to Islam because of the deeply hierarchical and dependent relationships that exist between themselves and their employers, relationships that index the region's politics of belonging and exclusion. Muslim reformers attributed domestic workers' "becoming Muslim" to the expanding influence of Islamic movements in shaping everyday life, a cornerstone of the region's politics of Islamic reform.

LIBERAL-SECULAR EXPLANATIONS

Liberal-secular explanations circulated among Kuwait's diverse noncitizen populations, members of the country's self-styled liberal movement, local and international human rights organizations, labor agencies, and foreign embassies.[18] These groups analyzed domestic workers' conversions in terms of the region's politics of belonging and exclusion, a framework that underscores the hierarchical relations that exist between domestic workers and their employers. A significant percentage of the Gulf consists of populations who are not citizens and who are unlikely to ever become naturalized citizens. In several states, including Kuwait, noncitizens comprise the majority of the country. State discourses depict these populations as "migrant workers" or "foreign workers": a temporary presence whose status is contingent upon, and whose experiences in the region are limited to, their capacity as workers. These discourses are echoed by international news media accounts and human rights reports that largely focus on labor migrants, in particular male construction workers and female domestic workers' experiences of abuse and exploitation. These hegemonic and popular discourses gloss over a more complicated sociopolitical landscape, one requiring us to place the region's politics of exclusion and belonging in a broader historical and geographical context.

The Gulf countries are situated in the Greater Arabian Peninsula and Persian Gulf, a region at the crossroads of the Middle East, Africa, Asia, and part of the Indian Ocean. Long before the discovery of oil, the Gulf was enmeshed in interregional relations with the peoples and places of these regions through pearl diving and merchant trade networks, as well as colonial and imperial systems. Gulf citizens comprise a dynamic mix of peoples from throughout the Middle East, the Indian subcontinent, and East Africa.[19] Sailors, traders, functionaries, and others contracted marriages among families and communities to bolster and perpetuate the relations that constituted this ecumenical interregional realm. With the advent of the region's petrodollar-driven economies and concomitant state formation, the extent and density of these kinship relations diminished and became publicly downplayed through processes of Arabization, and citizenship in the region became more exclusionary.[20] Gulf citizens began conceiving of national belonging in increasingly racialized terms.[21] For instance, being a Khaliji (term that means "of the Gulf") became synonymous with being Arab.[22] This process was an integral means through which many Gulf ruling families, descendants of migrants from the Najd region of present-day Saudi Arabia, entwined their family mythos with the city-states and nations they had come to rule.[23]

Similar to other Gulf states, in Kuwait citizenship became restricted to those who could prove their residency prior to 1941, those who could trace patrilineal descent from this group, and to women who married into this group.[24] Effectively excluded from these requirements are the vast majority of peoples who have migrated to the region from the early 1950s onward, a population that has played a crucial role in the country's post-oil development. Kuwait's first wave of migrants was predominately Arab. Most came from Egypt, or were Palestinian refugees who had been displaced from their homes after the *Nakba* and creation of Israel. Better educated and trained than the majority of Kuwait's population at the time, they became the teachers, doctors, nurses, and administrators of government-sponsored social institutions, and they were integral to the development of the country's rapidly growing state institutions and oil industry. In the mid-1970s the demographic composition of Kuwait began shifting with increasing numbers of migrants from South Asia, Southeast Asia, and East Africa moving to the region. Within the span of two decades, Kuwait went from being predominantly Muslim and Arab to becoming religiously and ethnonationally diverse.

Noncitizens have been, and continue to be, disciplined into becoming "migrant workers" and "foreign workers." This disciplining is achieved through a vast assemblage of laws, policies, and institutions.[25] The *kafala* system, the sponsorship system of most states in the Greater Arabian Peninsula—one similar to systems of migrant sponsorship in other parts of the world, most notably Southeast and East Asia—anchors this labor assemblage. In order to work and reside in the Gulf, foreign residents require a residency permit, which they can only obtain by entering into a kafala arrangement with someone who has the right to act as their *kafeel*, or sponsor and guarantor. Gulf states conferred this right upon citizens in good civic and legal standing, and to a far more limited extent, well-heeled foreign residents. A citizen-devolved system of governance, the kafala system has become the primary means of managing and policing the Gulf's burgeoning population of noncitizens.[26] Focused as they are on maintaining the political and economic status quo, and on redistributing their countries' oil wealth to their citizens in the form of services and subsidies, the governments of the Gulf states treat foreign residents as though, with the exception of policing their cross-border movements, they fall outside the ambit of their activities—a further means through which noncitizens' exclusions are enacted.[27]

Developing out of the Gulf states' concerted strategies of simultaneously managing and excluding large swathes of its population, the kafala system constitutes a set of relationships and agreements that fundamentally shape noncitizens' experiences in the Gulf. No matter how long they reside in the Gulf, or whether they are born in the Gulf, or are part of multigenerational families who consider the Gulf home[28]—and regardless of the role they play in these countries' development and prosperity[29]—noncitizens are only allowed to reside in the Gulf on a temporary basis. Their presence remains contingent upon, and policed by citizens or by comprador and well-heeled noncitizens.[30] Noncitizens are allowed to stay in the Gulf for periods of time delimited by the labor contracts they enter into with individual citizens and institutions: their kafeel. Emerging in tandem and parallel to the Gulf countries' state institutions, the kafala system plays an integral role in producing hierarchized differences between citizens and noncitizens and in ensuring the impermanence of the region's noncitizens.[31] This system, coupled with the perception that Kuwait's police and judiciary are favorably disposed toward the country's citizenry, suffuses foreign residents and migrants' everyday experiences with an acute sense of uncertainty and vulnerability with respect to their status.

In relation to that of other noncitizens, the position of domestic workers is precarious in the Gulf. Unlike labor migrants who typically live in dormitories or shared accommodations with fellow migrants, and foreign residents who establish their own households, domestic workers both work and reside within their employers' households, where they are subject to intense forms of surveillance and policing that permeate the most mundane details of their lives. Tasked with cooking, cleaning, caring for children and the elderly, and other work associated with the social reproduction of Kuwait's citizenry, domestic workers are intimately imbricated in Kuwaitis' everyday lives yet they are excluded from kinship and citizenship ties that confer rights. Like domestic workers in most other parts of the world, at the time I was conducting research they did not fall under the purview of the country's labor laws.[32] Few have established networks of family and friends when they first migrate to the country. These factors, coupled with the fact that domestic workers obtain their work and residency visas from their employers, creates a situation of domestic workers' acute dependence upon their employers.

Many groups in Kuwait attributed domestic workers' Islamic conversions to these women's precarious position in the Gulf, and the hierarchical relations that exist between them and their employers.[33] These groups frequently questioned the sincerity of domestic workers' conversions given their marginal status in Kuwait. They maintained domestic workers converted in order to wrest better remuneration and treatment from their employers, or because of the pressure, implicit or explicit, brought to bear upon them by the families with whom they work. The issue of sincerity is important to these groups' determination of whether or not domestic workers' conversions constitute a political issue. Predicated on secular-liberal understandings of governance, in which religious belief and practice is subject to individual choice, and is relegated to the private sphere, these groups regarded religious conversion as an intrinsically private matter, one that becomes a political issue only insofar as it is brought about through pressure or coercion. In such cases, they looked to state or statelike institutions, as neutral moral arbiters, to adjudicate and uphold the rights of domestic workers to their religious beliefs and practices. These groups recognized, however, how difficult this is in Kuwait given the region's politics of exclusion and belonging in which state intervention would necessitate the expansion of state authority and the fraught reconfiguration of governance between citizens and state institutions.

MUSLIM REFORMIST EXPLANATIONS

The second set of explanations for why domestic workers convert to Islam is one espoused by members of Kuwait's myriad Islamic revival and reform movements. They attributed domestic workers' "reversion to Islam" or "becoming Muslim" to the region's Islamic movements, in particular these groups' widespread attempts to promote everyday religious piety and social reform.[34] These groups' understandings of Kuwait, as a space requiring their constant effort at religious reform, contrasts markedly with popular news media reports that depict the region as awash in fundamentalist or Wahhabi forms of Islam that have persisted and spread due to the region's vast oil wealth. These popular accounts gloss over a more dynamic and contested religious landscape, one that can only be understood in relation to historical and transnational processes. Under Ottoman rule from the late seventeenth century through until the early twentieth century, Kuwait was subject to the empire's Majellat al-Ahkam al-Adliya, a codification of Islamic civil law according to the Hanafi school of jurisprudence; however, local Sunni rulers adhered to the Maliki school, Shiʻa Muslims followed the Jafari school, and Kuwait's minority Christian and Jewish populations had relative juridical autonomy over their communities' internal affairs.

In the late nineteenth century, other groups sought to introduce new juridical and religious orders into the area. The British, who began administering Kuwait as a protectorate in 1899, introduced their own judicial system, one that was primarily used to adjudicate their own officials and subjects. Another group, the Ikhwan, under the leadership of Ibn Saud from the Najd region of the Arabian Peninsula, also sought to gain control over Kuwait. These fighters were followers of the teachings of Muhammad ibn Abd al-Wahhab, a school of thought popularly referred to as Wahhabism, which would become the dominant school of Islam in the state of Saudi Arabia.[35] The intellectual tradition of this revivalist Islamic movement was founded in the mid-eighteenth century.[36] Its fundamental precepts are found in the writings of Abd al-Wahhab, in particular his books *The Oneness of God* and *The Removal of Doubts*. Abd al-Wahhab was greatly influenced by the work of medieval jurist Ahmad al-Din Ibn Taymiyya, who argued that religious judgments should derive from the Qur'an, the sunna, or prophetic tradition, and the *ijma'*, or consensus of the first generations of Muslims. Abd al-Wahhab favored direct interpretation of sacred texts over *taqlid*, or following the canonical schools of Islamic jurisprudence.[37] Followers of Wahhabism sought to purify Islamic precepts and practice from what they deemed to be innovations, and return to orthodox Islamic forms as practiced by the first generation of Muslims. In particular they sought to reestablish the primacy of *tawhid*, the oneness of God, and end practices they considered polytheistic in nature, including the veneration of saints and the excessive veneration of the Prophet, which they associated with Sufi and Shiʻa forms of Islamic practice.

The Ikhwan were ultimately defeated during the Battle of Jahra in 1920, a turning point in Kuwaiti history marking the country as distinctive and separate from what would become the Kingdom of Saudi Arabia. In 1961, the British protectorate period ended, and Kuwait's ruler Sheikh Abdullah al-Salim

Al-Sabah began a widespread process of legal and judicial reform. He enlisted the services of Abd al-Razzaq al-Sanhuri, a renowned Arab jurist, who developed a secular legal system based on Egyptian and French civil law.[38] This system of law applied to all matters except with respect to family law, which followed systems of Islamic jurisprudence.[39] This period is marked by the rising influence of liberalism, secularism, and leftist groups, which developed not only through North American and European influence, but also through Kuwait's deepening transnational connections with Egypt, the Mashreq, Iran, and the Indian subcontinent, all of which had developed distinctive trajectories of secular, leftist, and liberal practice. The Communist Party, the Bath Party, and Nasserist groups, as well as pan-Arab movements, spread to the Gulf through Arab and South Asian foreign residents and migrants, and Kuwaiti students who were increasingly being sent abroad for training and education.[40] The influence of these movements was widespread in society, marked by the loosening of gendered segregation, changes in clothing styles (e.g., men wearing suits, women wearing styles inspired by Lebanese and Egyptian fashions), and the spread of discos, of clubs, and of the consumption of alcohol.[41]

Islamic movements also began developing in the mid-twentieth century, and they became increasingly well organized and influential from the 1970s onward. Scholars attribute their rise to several interlocking factors, including the migration and exile of Islamic reformers and leaders from Egypt, Syria and Iraq; transnational networks established by Kuwaiti students and entrepreneurs throughout the region; the Kuwaiti leadership's support of Islamic groups as a bulwark against existing political opponents; and the population's growing disenchantment with pan-Arabism, Nasserism, and leftist movements.[42] Three Islamic movements became particularly prominent. The first, the Islamic Guidance Society, later renamed the Social Reform Society, was established in 1952.[43] This movement developed as an offshoot of the Muslim Brotherhood (Ikhwan Muslimin), a transnational organization founded in Egypt by Hassan al-Banna. Influenced by the Islamic reformist teachings of Muhammad Abduh and Rashid Rida, members of the Muslim Brotherhood believed that the end of Muslim societies' colonial subjugation and a broader sociopolitical awakening (sahwa) would only occur through these societies' return to the teachings found in the Qur'an and sunna. Unlike Wahhabis, members of the Brotherhood do not believe the Islamic discursive tradition is antithetical to processes of modernization and traditions of modern Western scientific thought, philosophy, and education. Members of Kuwait's Shi'a community, who comprise one-third of Kuwaiti citizens, established the second Islamic movement: the Cultural and Social Society.[44] This movement developed in relation to Hezb al-Daʻwa al-Islamiyya, a group founded in Iraq in 1958. To counter processes of secularization in the region, al-Daʻwa sought to develop new modes of religious authority and forms of organizing, one that drew from yet were distinct from traditional forms of Shiʻa clerical authority: the *marjaʻiyya*.[45] The movement developed a party system, and programs of social reform and political activism inspired by the Muslim Brotherhood, in particular the writings of Hassan al-Banna and Sayyid Qutb.[46] The third Islamic movement, the Ancestral or Heritage Society, is associated with the *salafiyyun* (commonly referred to as salafi), a movement that is often conflated with Wahhabism.[47] The two share marked similarities; however, whereas many Wahhabis are followers of the Hanbali school of Islamic jurisprudence, salafiyyun reject *taqlid*, the following of any *madhhab* completely, preferring to interface directly with the Qurʼan and sunna.[48] Salafi refers to a distinctive theological group that goes back to the Ahl al-Hadith of the Abbasid period, who concentrated on the study of the hadith, and the example set by the *al salaf al-salih*, the first three generations of Muslims who are regarded as exemplary in their practice of Islam, in order to purge Islamic practice from non-Muslim innovations.[49] Because the movement does not subscribe to or follow traditions of Islamic jurisprudence and scholarship, it is relatively easy to become an authority figure among the salafi. They are relatively open and democratic in their interpretive practices.[50] As a result, the movement is fluid and widespread, with different groups, often with distinctive and contradictory features, developing in different regions of the world.[51]

Kuwait's Islamic movements are doctrinally diverse, and they have different political objectives and projects. Although varied, they share a common underlying goal: promoting Islamic piety and social reform. Cumulatively, their influence has permeated every facet of Kuwaiti life. Members of these movements have been elected to the Kuwaiti Parliament, and have played a significant role in drafting legislation and legal codes.[52] They have become influential in different government ministries, most notably the Ministry of Education and Islamic Affairs and Endowment.[53] In the finance sector, they have developed banks that eschew *riba*, the charging of interest, as well as charitable institutions that collect *zakat* and *sadaqa*. Members have also become influential in Kuwait's education sector, social organizations, including teachers' associations, labor unions, food co-ops, and voluntary associations.[54]

Within this context, many in Kuwait attributed domestic workers' Islamic conversions to these movements' overall success in promoting Islamic reform. Members of these movements viewed domestic workers' "reversion to Islam" or "becoming Muslim" as indexing their movements' success on two fronts crucial to the development of a rightly guided *umma* (community of believers): their success in reaching out to Kuwait's diverse non-Muslim population and in reforming Kuwaiti families and households, two sites Islamic reformers consider to be of paramount importance to the production and reproduction of Muslim subjects.[55] Domestic workers' "reversions" are seen as both resulting from and further encouraging Islamic practice within the household.

Alternative Explanation: Everyday Conversions

The politics of the region's belonging and exclusion, and its politics of Islamic reform, informed much of my thinking when I first began research in Kuwait. As the initial contacts I established with South Asian domestic workers through friends, neighbors, and colleagues snowballed into a network of two dozen domestic interlocutors, and as polite small talk deepened into sustained conversations and visits, I started to develop a textured sense of my interlocutors' everyday lives.[56] Yet, I was impatient about what I was learning—what I often dismissed as tidbits of household gossip and details about their everyday routines. To me this was merely background information. I suspected my interlocutors were prevaricating about the circumstances surrounding their Islamic conversions. With time, as I developed more trusting relationships with them, I hoped they would begin opening up to me in earnest and that our discussions would be more frank and forthright.

I attributed what I took to be South Asian domestic workers' silence about the reasons for their conversions to the different factors that each explanatory frame emphasized. Far from being conspicuous, domestic workers' silence was readily assimilable to the logics of these explanatory frames. Both liberal-secularist and Islamic reformers understood domestic workers' silence as further evidence of the veracity of their respective explanations. For groups who analyzed their conversions in terms of the region's politics of belonging and exclusion, it was clear why domestic workers would not want to discuss their conversions: such discussions would raise uncomfortable questions about the sincerity and motivations for their conversions. Domestic workers' conversions and their silence were both read as symptomatic of the hierarchical relations that existed between themselves and their employers. In this view, they converted because of their precarious positioning, which also accounted for why they would be loath to discuss their conversions. The reason for domestic workers' silence was also obvious to Islamic reformers. These women's becoming Muslim was understood to be an act with its own justification. They had come to understand the truth of Islam, to recognize and return to their *fitra*, a God-given ability to distinguish right from wrong that marked them as Muslim, for which explanations were superfluous.

When I began my research I was looking for materials—responses, comments, stories and observations—that would confirm or counter these two explanatory frames, yet what I was learning from South Asian domestic workers seemed to evade them altogether. It took me some time to realize that in the repetitive folds of their utterances about everyday work, experiences of migration, and transnational networks of family and friends, domestic workers were not being silent or evasive about their Islamic conversions. Rather, they discussed and experienced their religious conversions in a register that was more muted and subtle, one that is easy to overlook, particularly amidst the din of public debates undergirded by liberal-secularist and Islamic reformist explanations. Both these explanatory frames emphasize a particular set of factors to account for domestic workers' Islamic conversions, namely, their precarious positioning and hierarchical relations with their sponsor employers in Kuwait, or the influence of Islamic reform movements in Kuwait. The alternative explanation domestic workers were pointing to pushes us to consider how these factors are embedded in their everyday activities and relations. Migrant domestic workers' Islamic conversions do not develop because of, in spite of, nor do they mitigate the hierarchical relations that exist between themselves and their employers. Their Islamic conversions also do not develop through the direct outreach of Kuwait's Islamic da'wa movement. Though related to these factors, domestic workers' conversions are not reducible to them. These women's precarious positions and hierarchical relations with their employers, and the activities of Islamic da'wa movements in Kuwait tell part of the story of their everyday conversions, but not in the ways envisioned by liberal-secularists or Islamic reformers. Domestic workers' conversion experiences point to how these factors come into confluence and are configured by their everyday gendered experiences centered on household spaces and routed through longer histories of interregional connections between the Gulf and South Asia. More succinctly put, domestic workers' experiences foreground a realm—the everyday—as crucial to their Islamic conversions. Their conversions are inextricable from their everyday experiences in ways that necessitate a more expansive understanding of both "conversion" and the "everyday." Their conversions are not marked by an eventful moment, or by an abrupt, radical transformation. Rather, their conversions develop through ongoing processes of transformation, a gradual reworking of their lives embedded in the everyday where the outcomes are not clear at the outset. Domestic workers' experiences push us to consider how the everyday is not just a space of habit, routine and continuity—a space through which discursive and disciplinary regimes are produced and reproduced—but how the everyday also constitutes a space of contingency, emergent possibility, and ongoing conversion.[57]

Domestic workers' Islamic conversions were inextricable from their everyday activities and relations, ones centered on their households—both those in Kuwait and more remotely mediated through letters, phone conversations and occasional visits, the households in the places they had migrated from. Although radically different from one another—one focusing on political-economic factors, the other religious processes, one positing a self-interested, cost-benefit maximizing subject, the other a subject shaped through pious practice—both liberal secularist and Islamic reformist explanations of domestic workers' conversion or "reversion" to Islam emphasize the importance of the household. For groups promoting secular-liberal forms of governance domestic workers' conversions underscore an important yet fraught gendered limit point to state authority and intervention. Among members of Kuwait's Islamic movements, households are considered to be sites of paramount importance to the production and reproduction of pious Muslim subjects. Domestic workers' utterances and my own observations of their experiences in Kuwait highlight the importance of their everyday relations within Kuwaiti households to their Islamic conversions, but in ways that resist reduction to self-interest, pressure or simple assimilation, and that are not accounted for by general public discourse. Households constituted dense and vital spaces of everyday work, intimacy, economic exchange, affect, and hierarchical gendered, aged, raced, and kinship relations through which these women came to convert to Islam—sensibilities and practices through which they then came to reexperience and rework their lives.[58] Routed through the household, domestic workers' Islamic conversions mark the confluence of two realms often assumed to be distinct and separate: the everyday ethical formation of religious subjectivities related to their engagement with Islam,[59] and the reshaping of their comportment and personalities related to their undertaking of affective labor.[60] Their experiences mark the interrelation of political-economic and religious processes without eliding or fetishizing the importance of each to the other. Undergirded by gendered logics and relations, in particular a gendered discourse of South Asian women being *naram*—a Hindi-Urdu word denoting malleability—these processes are reshaping domestic workers' subjectivities, affinities, and transnational social networks. Rather than marking a rebirth or abrupt change in their lives, they experienced conversion to Islam as a gradual process through which they came to reengage and rework their lives. This process was neither unidirectional nor linear, but cyclical and recursive: they apprehended, approached, and actualized Islamic precepts and practices in and through the stuff of their everyday lives, which included their hierarchical and often fraught relationships with their employers; the gendered labor they undertake; and their preexisting languages, religious traditions, familial relations and other forms of belonging, including those based on ethnicity and nationality. Domestic workers' conversion to Islam were marked by emergent relationships and affinities, ones that did not supersede or subsume their existing familial and ethnonational belongings, but developed alongside them, in tandem, and reconfigured them.

Domestic workers' everyday conversions resonate in significant ways with a large body of work in religious studies, history, and anthropology that emphasizes the processual nature of religious conversion. These works challenge the prevailing idea of religious conversion as an abrupt and radical change involving a subject's total transformation and the abandonment of previous modes of living and association. They underscore how this understanding of conversion is, in particular, one associated with Modern Western Christian thought—especially charismatic forms of Christianity—that belies most conversion experiences.[61] Rather than a sudden and dramatic transformation, these works discuss the gradual, ongoing process through which converts' lives are transformed in relation to the religious tradition they are adopting, whether it be Christians in twelfth-century Western Europe or Scandinavian women who are becoming Muslim in our contemporary period. Instead of constituting a qualitatively different type of religious experience involving divine intercession, individual revelation, or visions, religious conversion falls along a spectrum, and is similar to processes of everyday piety; or, otherwise put, everyday piety constitutes ongoing conversion. As Karl Morrison succinctly states: "In fact, all of life, rightly lived, was conversion."[62] In the Gulf, the Islamic reformist discourse of fitra similarly draws a correlation between the cultivation of Islamic piety and processes of Islamic conversion. A universalizing discourse that posits everyone as having the capacity to distinguish right from wrong—a form of moral reasoning that guide's people's actions—this discourse of fitra accounts for why Islamic reformers believe all human beings are latently Muslim, a potential that is realized through constant effort, a constant striving or becoming in relation to Islamic precepts and practices.

This processual form of becoming Muslim resonates with what Gilles Deleuze refers to as an "ontology of becoming." Deleuze's philosophy—or, as he puts it, his "nomadic thought"—is premised on the idea that there are no fixed Platonic forms, ultimate foundations, or original identities. In contrast to this "ontology of being," which assumes the sameness of these forms, foundations and identities across space and time, and that treats difference or variation in them as a deviation or lack, Deleuze's "ontology of becoming" treats differ-ence as primary, and draws our attention to the processes through which forms, foundations and identities are striven for, instantiated, and become a shared or common project. Rather than a fixed state of being, these forms, foundations, and identities are said to be in a constant state of becoming. Or, as Deleuze ex-plains, "it is not being that returns but rather returning itself that constitutes being . . . it is not one thing which returns but rather returning is the one thing which is affirmed of diversity or multiplicity."[63] Similarly, an approach attuned to everyday conversions does not treat or conceive of being Muslim as a tran-scendent or fixed state; rather, it is something the subject constantly strives at becoming and instantiates through her or his very belief and practice.

This processual understanding of conversion informs Michel Foucault's work on ethics and technologies of the self, theoretical writings on subject forma-tion that underpin recent scholarship on Islamic movements and piety.[64] Ac-cording to Foucault, techniques or technologies of the self are what "permit in-dividuals to effect, by their own means, a certain operation on their own bodies, on their own souls, on their own thoughts, on their own conducts, and this in a manner so as to transform themselves, modify themselves, and to at-tain a certain state of perfection, of happiness, of purity, of supernatural power, and so on."[65] As his continuous use of the possessive and reflexive pronouns *own* and *themselves* underscore, Foucault's focus is not on subject-formation as conventionally conceived. The subject here is not merely the product, but also the agent of her subjectivization and subjection. Foucault's deployment of the term *technology* further underscores this point. Usually associated with some-thing external to the individual, here *technology* is used to refer to methods by which the individual acts upon herself. Individuals do not construct these methods by themselves.[66] In an interview he makes it clear that these practices of the self are not "something that the individual invents by himself [sic]. They are patterns in his culture and which are proposed, suggested and imposed on him by his culture, his society, and his social group."[67]

Works on religious conversion and ethical self-formation emphasize embod-ied practice and iterative performance in the cultivation of pious dispositions, affects, acts, and modes of thinking. Individuals undertake these practices and performances in relation to a set of precepts they aspire to and actualize. This process is characterized by a particular trajectory—repetitive performance in relation to a set of principles and goals whose forms are not predetermined but immanent to apt performance. Domestic workers' experience becoming Muslim through their everyday Islamic practice in relation to Islamic precepts yet like other converts and pious Muslims, they enact and actualize their pieties through their everyday understandings, activities and relations, which for them necessarily include their preexisting religious traditions, languages, familial relations and other forms of belonging, most notably those based on ethnicity and nationality. Their experiences of Islamic conversion underscores the importance of examining the everyday not simply as the raw materials or as an inert and undifferentiated mass through which pieties are enacted and actualized, but as substances with their own particularities and vitality that shape the development of piety.[68] Processes of everyday conversion point to how ethical formation not only develops in relation to the religious tradition the convert is being socialized into and striving toward, in this case the Islamic discursive tradition, but also in relation to other discursive traditions and socioeconomic and historical processes. They push us to consider what Eve Sedgwick refers to as that which "lies alongside" or "beside" Islamic ethical formation. In her discussion of how Judith Butler's theory of gender performativity draws from J. L. Austin's work on performative utterances, Sedgwick argues that Butler unmoors "Austin's performative from its localized dwelling in a few exemplary utterances or kinds of utterance and show[s] it instead to be a property of language or discourse much more broadly."[69] Butler places temporal emphasis on the repetition or iteration of gender performance rather than considering what Sedgwick refers to as the ecological field through which it develops.[70] Sedgwick highlights the irony of Butler's antiessentialist project of gender performativity: that it is itself predicated on a reductive essentializing of the process of performativity.[71] Rather than a "paranoid reading" or "strong theory"—that is, an emphasis on one set of factors in our analysis[72]—Sedgwick proposes that we should also be attentive to elements that "lie alongside" or "beside" these factors.[73]

Sedgwick's approach resonates strongly with transnational feminists—and the genealogies of feminist, critical race, postcolonial, historical-materialist, poststructural theories they develop through and contribute to—who have developed modes of analysis that examine the interrelations between discursive traditions, capitalist and colonial hegemonies, and relations of gender, race, class, and sexuality.[74] In contrast to anthropological frameworks that are predicated on the positing of binary difference, transnational feminist analyses attend to how situated differences complicate and challenge universalizing discourses and globalizing processes while simultaneously examining how these differences are themselves produced. An approach that does not reify or fetishize difference, transnational feminism examines how discursive traditions, and categories of identity and belonging, do not just precede but are also produced through their historical interrelations. A transnational feminist approach that eschews "strong theory" raises questions about a dimension of religious conversion often glossed over. Works on religious conversion typically assume existing bases of differences between religious traditions and belongings, and focus on how religious converts reconstitute these forms of difference through their socialization or striving in relation to their adopted religious tradition. The focus is on converts' shift and replacement of one set of religious precepts and practices in favor of another. Except for the fraught liminal period of transition at which the boundaries between religious traditions and belongings become permeable, these works focus on how conversions reconstitute and in many cases reinforce differences between religious traditions. By attending to how religious conversion is informed by other religious and discursive traditions and historical processes, a transnational feminist approach draws attention to the interrelation between these discursive traditions and processes, and to how processes of conversion both presuppose and are a site through which differences are themselves produced. Domestic workers' experiences of everyday conversion were not simply marked by their shift from one religious tradition to another, or by their rejection of their previous lives. Their conversions constituted a more complex process, one characterized by changes as well as by continuities and uncertainties. Instead of reading these continuities and uncertainties as evidence of the incomplete nature of their conversion, as a sign of "bad faith," or as marking a syncretic or heterodoxical form of religious practice, through a transnational approach that does not presuppose difference, this ethnography examines everyday conversion as a site through which similarities and differences are produced. Rather than conceiving of the process only in terms of a shift or transition, this book highlights how religious conversion also constitutes a complex site of interrelation through which religious traditions are configured and reconfigured together.

This approach to religious conversion resonates with works that examine rather than assume the sociohistorical processes through which religious traditions, including what Masuzawa refers to as "world religions,"[75] become differentiated from one another, and that examine the porousness and plurality of practice of religious traditions in the Indian Ocean region.[76] Several domestic workers whose everyday conversion are discussed in this book come from families and communities with histories of religious conversion and whose members' religious practices, subjectivities, and identifications crosscut what are often depicted as distinct "world religions." Their experiences underscore how migrant domestic workers' experiences of everyday conversion index and are shaped by a subterranean stream of South Asian and Indian Ocean history, one examined by a wide range of scholarship, including works on material culture,[77] elite and court culture of premodern India,[78] healing traditions,[79] and instances of women's refusal of, reluctance at, or forcible "recovery" and "rehabilitation" back into what state laws dictated as their "own" communities (i.e., religious and ethnonational groups) in the wake of the subcontinent's partition.[80] These works all point to the porousness and fluidity of the boundaries existing between religious groups and traditions in the subcontinent, whether in the form of intermarriage, shared genealogies, or overlapping ritual practices, religious sites, and religious figures. South Asian domestic workers everyday conversions in the Gulf emphasize a related yet distinct dynamic. These women's experiences are shaped by an underlying gendered discourse of South Asian women being naram—that animates their household relations and work, religious learning and practice, and transnational affinities and belongings, which in turn mark their everyday conversions. South Asian domestic workers' transnational experiences of everyday conversion in the Gulf underscore the importance of not reifying, flattening, or glossing over religious differences, but examining how complex configurations of commonality/contrast, identity/alterity, and resemblance/distinction develop through particular sets of gendered sociohistorical processes, ones situated within and indexing broader currents of regional and interregional histories.

Everyday Conversions as a Mode of Transnational Relations

Domestic workers' conversion to Islam develops through their everyday transnational experiences centered on household spaces, a gradual process that not only complicates our understanding of religious conversion, but also of the everyday. Here, everyday activities and relations are not just spaces through which hegemonic discourses, disciplinary apparatuses, and sociohistorical processes are reproduced or resisted,[81] but where they configured together in complex and contingent ways, leading to newfound possibilities and ongoing transformation. Domestic workers' adoption of Islamic precepts and practices brings into focus the importance of a particular space of everyday gendered relations and activities—the household—as not only productive of ethnonational belongings (including diasporic forms thereof), but also of newfound transnational ones. Everyday conversions complicate our understanding of the feminization of transnational labor migration, in particular the experiences of migrant domestic workers. Cumulatively, scholarship focusing on these migrant women provides an extensive and textured account of transnational domestic work in the late twentieth century and early twenty-first century.[82] I discuss these aspects in more detail throughout this book, in particular chapters 1, 2, and 3.

Domestic workers' everyday conversions contribute to this literature by underscoring another dimension of these migrant women's experiences: how they develop emergent forms of transnational subjectivities and belongings that are not articulated in terms of diasporic forms of ethnonationalism—forms existing scholarship has largely focused on.[83]

To understand the transnational forms of subjectivities and belongings that domestic workers develop through their everyday conversions, we need to situate their experiences by interrogating—rather than assuming—the household as a site of analysis. As feminist political theorists, historians, and geographers all underscore, households—and the family structures, social reproduction, and gendered roles and relations that comprise them—are often depicted as "private" spaces outside of politics, realms existing prior to, and outside the jurisdiction of modern nation-states.[84] Households are portrayed as the primordial building blocks of the nation, and at the same time, as realms within which states are reluctant to intercede. These depictions naturalize households, placing them, and their constitutive gendered relations and activities, outside of historical and political processes. These accounts do not simply omit or "leave out" households, but obfuscate their social, economic, and political importance to the formation of modern nation-states.[85]

Households are co-constitutive of modern nation-states, emerging in tandem with them through processes of colonial modernity. They are vital biopolitical spaces crucial to the disciplining of individual bodies and the regulatory control of populations that are central to modern forms of governance. Nation-states exercise biopower—the power to administer, secure, develop and foster life, or disallow it to the point of death—through households. Households were, and continue to be, the primary sites in which the citizenry is biologically reproduced; where children are reared and receive their formative moral and intellectual training; and where workers and citizens are fed, sheltered, and cared for, thus ensuring their broader contributions to other economic and political spheres.[86] Colonial/imperial powers as well as anticolonial/anti-imperial nationalist forces throughout the Indian Ocean regarded households as fundamental to their state and national building projects. Through an assortment of welfare, health care, family and educational policies and programs, households have become sites of reform and regulatory control through which modern, orderly, healthy and developed nations are built, and through which other bases of sociopolitical organizing and belonging, in particular familial and tribal networks, are integrated into the nation-state.[87]

The widespread transnational migration of domestic workers throughout the Indian Ocean has redoubled rather than unsettled households as sites of ethnonational formation, indicating how global processes can reinscribe rather than undo national and local ones. Since the mid-1970s, the number of female migrants has risen dramatically throughout the Indian Ocean region. Today, women constitute almost half of the region's overall migrant population, the vast majority of which are domestic workers.[88] The largest destination site is the Gulf region, where migrant domestic workers are a ubiquitous presence. In Kuwait, they comprise one-sixth of the total population and are employed in over 90 percent of citizen households. Marked by the presence of "foreign maids" within Khaliji households, the absence of mothers, sisters, daughters, and other family members in South Asian households—and the cross-border circulations of capital, goods, knowledge, and information—domestic workers' migration may have transnationalized the composition and economies of households through the Gulf and South Asia, but it has not undermined or weakened the household as a site of ethnonational formation and reproduction. The feminization of transnational labor migration has resulted in new territorial configurations of these processes. These processes have been reconfigured and redoubled through, not despite, transnational processes.

The continuity of familial and ethnonational forms does not confirm their primordial quality, or the naturalness of the bonds and loyalty that exist between migrant domestic workers and their families and nation-states; rather, it requires us to examine how households are interrelated with processes of globalization and how states and nationalist discourses are configured into this interrelationship. Similar to how the role of households has been elided in analyses of the formation of nation-states, so too have they been disregarded in accounts of globalization. Numerous feminist scholars, most notably Carla Freeman, have pointed to the gendered nature of existing scholarship on globalization.[89] These works depict gendered subjects, activities, and spaces as being passive, reactive, or incidental to processes of globalization. They do not account for how gendered phenomena such as households are integral to and productive of global processes.

Globalization, most notably huge global disparities in wealth and the international division of labor that have developed through processes of neoliberalization, has not simply caused the feminization of transnational labor migration. These gendered migrations also develop through the complex and often conflicting demands of household labor, childcare responsibilities, and shifting gendered roles and familial relations. In Kuwait, the growing demand for domestic workers is not simply due to the oil boom, but to a concatenation of factors including the shift from extended to nuclear family households, changing patterns of hospitality that are central to Kuwaiti social life, and increased numbers of youth entering into secondary and higher education, as well as greater numbers of women joining the waged labor market. Similarly, the migration of South Asian women to the Gulf does not just come about due to their countries' and communities' impoverishment brought about through the oil crisis, national debt, and structural adjustment programs. They are also spurred by changing patterns of marriage, shifting tastes and consumption patterns, and new understandings of and aspirations to middle-class respectability. Though related, these factors are not reducible to global political-economic processes.[90] They are processes that prefigure and shape domestic workers' transnational migrations, and are not just the effect of them.[91]

State policies and nationalist discourses play an important role in the interrelationship between households and global processes. Although state institutions in the Indian Ocean often represent themselves as having no jurisdiction over migrant domestic workers—either because they are citizens abroad, or are noncitizens who work and reside in private spaces—they do shape these women's migration in multiple ways.[92] State institutions channel who migrates and where through their implementation of partial or full labor migration bans, though not always in the ways ostensibly intended.[93] Government cuts to subsidies and public services (e.g., to public education), and the distribution of welfare services in the form of family or child bonuses, affect household economies, divisions of labor and long-term financial strategies, all of which impact the demand and supply for migrant domestic workers.[94] Immigration and citizenship laws, work and residency visa programs, and migration-processing systems also produce domestic workers' status as temporary transnational migrants. This status positions domestic workers as pivot points in the ongoing reproduction of two sets of households simultaneously—those in their countries of origin and in the countries they migrate to. Their temporary status produces (not merely reflects) differences between domestic workers' "home" and "work" households, and differences between domestic workers and their employers—differences that are articulated in familial and ethnonational terms.[95]

State policies and programs do not simply express but are generative of ethnonational differences between domestic workers and their employers. This includes state mandated predeparture orientation and reentry sessions that emphasize differences between domestic workers and their employers, instructing these migrant women through professionalization discourses "to maintain a 'safe distance' from their employers."[96] Nationalist discourses of moral panic related to migrant domestic workers—of children being reared and sons or husbands being seduced by "foreign maids," or of families falling apart because women are overseas, away from their "rightful" homes and families—do not just index the decline of family values or the dismantlement of households as sites of national reproduction and belonging,[97] but mark attempts to reconstitute and consolidate households in these forms. These attempts are further buttressed by nationalist discourses that hail migrant domestic workers as victims in need of rescuing by the state, or as heroes whose self-sacrifice sustains the nation.[98]

Migrant domestic workers' activities and relations within their work households do not unsettle ethnonational subjectivities and belongings, but further reinscribe them. Their sustained, intimate interactions with their employers do not break down differences, but are constitutive of them.[99] Differences are not only produced through what a domestic worker does—that is, through her laboring, which is socially reproductive of her employers' household members—but in domestic workers' very doing of it—that is, the fact that it is she, the domestic worker, who is undertaking this work, and not her employer.[100] As Adams and Dickey explain, "both domestic workers and employers create opposing identities out of their experiences with one another," with "notions of self and other constructed in relation and opposition to one another."[101] The relations between domestic workers and employers are sites through which hierarchized gendered, classed, and racialized differences are produced—differences that are articulated and mapped onto ethnonational ones.

Domestic workers are crucial pivot points in the ongoing production of ethnonational forms in both the countries they migrate from and migrate to. They are dual agents of reproduction. Yet, they experience their own ethnonational subjectivities and belonging ambivalently. As Nicole Constable incisively points out, domestic workers' transnational migration engenders experiences of "being at home but not at home" in both the states they migrate to *and* from.[102] Their transnational dislocation may redouble their maintenance of familial connections and ethnonational belongings through visits to their families and home communities;[103] maintaining regular communication through letters, phone calls, and social media; engaging with diasporic media forms such as magazines and satellite television;[104] and participating in diasporic community activities and events.[105] At the same time, Manalansan, Constable, and others have highlighted how migrant domestic workers throughout the Indian Ocean and Inter-Asian regions are often hailed in gendered, familial, and ethnonational forms that they do not identify with or experience mixed feelings and misgivings.[106] They may have or develop alternative forms of subjectivity and belonging—ones elided given the hegemonic nature of discourses of gender, sexuality, family, and nation that configure households as ongoing sites of eth-nonational production, and domestic workers as transnational nodal points in this process. In the face of the hegemonic nature of these discourses, domestic workers may disavow or avoid discussion of these alternative forms of subjec-tivity and belonging—for example their attachments to the families they work with or countries they migrate to, "illicit" relationships they develop, their re-luctance to return home—out of concern of seeming disloyal, improper, or immoral. Given the equally hegemonic nature of discourses treating migrant domestic workers as a temporary transnational population, others may assume these alternative forms to be fleeting, provisional, and of no long-term signifi-cance. Among South Asian domestic workers in the Gulf, the reconfiguring of their subjectivities, affinities and belongings and, concomitantly, their reluc-tance to overtly demonstrate or "show" these forms also relate to an underlying gendered discourse of South Asian women being naram—the expectation of, and their own enactment of malleability, softness, and adjustment in the face of their changing circumstances—that animates their transnational experi-ences.[107] South Asian domestic workers enact what they consider to be proper forms of womanhood not only by seamlessly developing newfound disposi-tions, capabilities and learning in the Gulf, but also by not making these appar-ent when they visit or "adjust back" to their families and home communities in the subcontinent.

Domestic workers' adoption of Islam in the Gulf constitutes one such alter-native and oft-overlooked form of transnational subjectivity and belonging, an alternative that points to households as sites of everyday conversion as well as ethnonational reproduction. Everyday conversions are not character-ized by domestic workers' rejection or subversion of their existing familial and ethnonational belongings in favor of Kuwaiti or Khaliji ones. By becom-ing Muslim, domestic workers do not become more Kuwaiti, either formally through citizenship or, more informally, by becoming part of the families for whom they work. Their sociopolitical situation in the Gulf continues to be shaped by their ethnonational background, occupational status, and status as noncitizens. Their everyday conversions constitute an alternative form of transnational belonging not by supplanting or subverting their existing famil-ial and ethnonational belongings, but by developing alongside and reconfig-uring them. The overlapping—rather than antithetical—nature of everyday conversion underscores how households have become spaces of confluence of ethnonational formation, secularization, and Islamic reform in the Gulf. Households are crucial to processes of everyday conversion not because they are sites where domestic workers are pressured or coerced to convert to Islam as liberal-secularists in the region maintain, or because they are natural sites of religious practice as Islamic reformers aver. Through processes of colonial modernity and globalization, households have not only become spaces for the reproduction of national citizens and populations. Concomitantly, through processes of secularization, households have also become designated as part of the "private realm"—the proper locus of religious belief and practice—and through Islamic reform movements, as spaces vital to the development of the umma. While colonial governments and postcolonial states often depict personal status laws (including family laws) as the heart of religious doctrine and practice, a realm within which they are reluctant to interfere, as Talal Asad has noted, this understanding of religion as an intrinsically private matter "is precisely a secular formula for privatizing 'religion.'"[108] These processes are redoubled by Islamic movements' focus on everyday gendered activities and relations centered on household spaces as foundational to their reform efforts.[109]

Moments

Domestic workers' everyday conversions marking their migration experiences underscore incipient transnational subjectivities, affinities, and belongings that develop through an unexpected space—the household—and that take an unexpected form—articulated in relation to Islamic precepts and practices—rather than in terms of liberal subjectivities and globalizing human rights discourses, or diasporic forms of ethnonationalism, forms existing work on the feminization of transnational labor migration focuses on.[110] These women's experiences of everyday conversion are situated at the confluence of two transnational processes—the feminization of transnational labor migration and Islamic reform—that crosscut and knit together the Middle East and South Asia. Their Islamic conversions develop through their everyday experiences within Kuwaiti households, spaces of gendered activity and hierarchical relations that reshape their subjectivities and affinities, and that mark the confluence of processes of ethnonational formation, Islamic reform, and secularization. Domestic workers' everyday conversions index the emergent and contingent forms of subjectivity and affinity that are developing in our unevenly globalizing world, ones marked by the interrelation and complex configuration of gendered, religious, and political-economic processes.

Analyzing domestic workers' experiences in terms of everyday conversion constitutes an alternative explanation not just in terms of the factors that are given explanatory weight for their adoption of Islam, but also in terms of the framework of explanation itself. To fully understand how everyday conversions come about and what they entail, a shift in our underlying conceptual approach to analyzing processes of transformation is necessary. We need to shift from a linear understanding of transformation—with two points at the outset, and a precipitating factor or set of factors leading to a shift from one point to the other—to a more decentered and fluid concept of transformation, one that accounts for the reconfiguration of what are always a dynamic and shifting constellation of factors. Analyzing everyday conversions necessitates an expansive conceptual approach that accounts for possibility as well as continuity within discursive traditions, and for multiplicity and hegemony within sociopolitical groups. It is an approach that is attentive to ongoing transnational interrelations between differentiated discursive traditions and sociopolitical bodies. It does not assume sameness or difference at the outset (whether as ontology or heuristic), but looks to how complex configurations of difference and sameness are produced within particular historical conjunctures—and how these are reconfigured.

Examining the fluid and multidimensional phenomenon of everyday conversions raises a number of epistemological and analytical conundrums: How do we attend to, much less analyze, experiences that are often expressed in an affective register, that slip between and undo distinctions between binarized categories such as the religious and political economic? How do we account for forms of subjectivity and affinity that are fluid and emergent? How do we analyze the slipperiness of everyday experiences, the realm of the seemingly inconsequential and ordinary? In developing an ethnography attuned to entanglements rather than juxtaposition, of confluence and complex configurations rather than binary difference, of the everyday as a site of contingency and possibility rather than just continuity, this book focuses on moments. An emphasis on moments is far from novel or unprecedented in anthropological works. From being pursued by the police on the heels of a Balinese cockfight;[111] having one's father negotiate one's entry into Bedouin life;[112] being told by one's interlocutors who the real cannibals are[113]—ethnographic vignettes have long eased readers into explorations of unfamiliar worlds and have long been used by anthropologists to illustrate and instantiate their arguments. My description of moments is firmly situated within this tradition—and also points to other possibilities. Moments punctuated my fieldwork, moments that were neither marking the ongoing continuation of routine and habit, nor were they of the magnitude of life-altering events. They constituted something else, something in-between, something familiar and strange, blurring the line between continuity and change. These moments intertwined the unexpected with the ordinary. They pointed to how experiences, encounters, situations, utterances, or pauses are not just structured by discursive traditions, disciplinary practices, and ongoing political-economic relations, but also mark instances of everyday conversion, of newfound possibilities, ones just glimpsed, or barely grasped at the time.[114] Moments push us to be as attentive to possibility and contingency as we are to process and continuity, an approach that enables us to account for the novel forms of subjectivity and belonging that are being configured by transnational processes today, everyday conversions that might otherwise elude, or be elided by, our scholarship.

My own research began with one such moment of everyday conversion, the unexpected witnessing of Rosa's recitation of the shahada, which pushed me to begin analyzing a different configuration of issues I had long been thinking about. Like the transnational spread of Al-Huda, domestic workers' Islamic conversions in the Gulf involves South Asian migrant women's pious Islamic practice, pieties that mark the complex interrelation between middle-class aspirations, gendered labor, transnational diasporic formations, and Islamic reform movements that crosscut the Indian Ocean. Yet domestic workers' Islamic conversions raise a further series of questions, ones pushing us to consider the ways in which everyday relations, activities, and laboring centered on household spaces are vital to the production of Muslim pieties, subjectivities, and belongings. Domestic workers' experiences of everyday conversion necessitate our rethinking of how the everyday and the most ordinary of spaces and activities are not just sites of continuity and process, but also of contingency and possibility. Their experiences underscore how transnational processes do not simply mark the diffusion or cross-border expansion of kinship networks, ethnonational forms, and religious movements, but how transnationalism constitutes a dynamic field in which differences are configured and reconfigured, a site generative of everyday conversions. This book maps these transnational processes through moments. Each chapter begins as this introduction does: by narrating and unfurling important moments that comprised, or were recounted to me during my fieldwork, ones that piece together different dimensions of domestic workers' everyday conversions.

The first three chapters map key dimensions of South Asian domestic workers' experiences of transnational migration and everyday conversion. Chapter 1 examines the assemblage of processes, policies, and systems of governance that designate and discipline South Asian migrant domestic workers into a "temporary population" in Kuwait, one that positions domestic workers as dual agents of reproduction. This chapter underscores how domestic workers' "temporariness" is produced amidst—and belied by—ongoing transnational connections. These connections stretch from the past to the present and future, and knit together the Gulf region and the Indian subcontinent. Chapter 1 also examines the gendered juridicopolitical aporias that characterize the transnational domestic work sector, ones placing domestic workers into precarious juridopolitical positions that further reinscribe their "temporariness" in the Gulf. South Asian domestic workers' experiences of migration are further characterized by "suspension"—of their being a part of, yet apart from their "work households" in the Gulf and their "family households" in South Asia. Chapter 2 examines how domestic workers' experiences of "suspension" are produced through a number of macro- and microlevel socioeconomic processes that tether them to household spaces and that further position them as dual agents of reproduction. Yet, as this chapter further explores, South Asian domestic workers' suspension also engenders forms of everyday conversions marked by the development of emergent affinities, connections, and belongings. Chapter 3 focuses on a gendered discourse of South Asian women's malleability or "being *naram,*" the intrinsic capacity and learned capability of South Asian women to circulate between and accommodate themselves seamlessly to different sociocultural circumstances. Being naram not only enables these migrant women to be involved in the reproduction of subjects, households, and ethnonational formations in both the Gulf and South Asia, but to simultaneously develop newfound abilities, dispositions and subjectivities, forms of everyday conversions that, as chapter 3 discusses, they try not "to show." Cumulatively, these chapters provide a textured sense of the everyday understandings, activities, relationships, and concerns characterizing South Asian domestic workers' transnational migration experiences in the Gulf. The chapters show how their experiences position them as dual agents of reproduction while simultaneously engendering emergent forms of affinities, subjectivities, and belongings that constitute everyday forms of conversion.

Domestic workers' adoption of Islam constitutes one form and trajectory of everyday conversion. It is an expression and culmination of reconfigurations taking place in these migrant women's sense of self, relationships, and belongings. Chapter 4 examines domestic workers' "housetalk"—how their emergent Islamic pieties develop through their relations and work within Kuwaiti households. Domestic workers' Islamic conversions mark the reworking of their subjectivities, a process that develops through the confluence of affective labor, Islamic ethical formation, and a gendered discourse of South Asian women being naram. To learn more about Islam, many domestic workers obtain learning materials and take classes at Kuwait's Islamic da'wa movement's women's center, the focus of chapter 5. Taught in their first languages, by teachers of similar ethnonational backgrounds, these classes effectively reproduce domestic workers' ethnonational belongings—yet these belongings are suffused with new Islamic sensibilities, understandings, and practices. Emphasizing fluid, student-centered pedagogies, these classes intertwine discussions of domestic workers' Islamic conversions with other changes taking place in their lives, ones existing prior to but further spurred by their migration and everyday life in Kuwait. The epilogue reprises the major themes of this ethnography and, by briefly revisiting the situations of some of my interlocutors, underscores the ongoing nature of their everyday conversions and the fluid forms of subjectivity and affinity they are developing—forms of everyday conversions that are incipient, tenuous, but significant still.

ONE

TEMPORARINESS

Atti-*beti* [daughter], you came a year ago?
I was like that
I came thinking I will stay two, maybe four years
But life has been such that I have been here over thirty years
Oh God, so many years!
—Mary/Maryam

Temporary Connections?

Saad, the four-year-old grandson of Geeti's employer Mama Lulua, followed Geeti around constantly when he visited. He often perched himself on a stool as she cooked, watching as she sliced onions or stirred pots of rice. When she conducted her rounds of the house, scrutinizing the work of the other domestic workers she supervised, Saad trailed after her, adjusting cushions and tracing his fingers along surfaces to check for dust. His ease and familiarity with Geeti was telling. Around others—including strangers to the house like myself, or even his uncles and aunts—Saad kept a wary distance.

During one of my visits, I was therefore not surprised to find Saad sitting at the kitchen table. He had snuck down from the family sitting room, coloring book and crayons in hand, and was babbling happily at Geeti as she washed up after lunch. To the side of the sink, a line of pots dripped into the dishtowels she had placed underneath. She was in the midst of stacking clean dishes into the cupboard when Saad's mother Al-Anoud, walked in. Smiling past Geeti and me, she came up behind her son, inspecting his coloring.

AL-ANOUD: Good job. . . . Now let's go up and rest. You can do more [coloring] later.

SAAD: No. Don't want to.

AL-ANOUD: Saad, it's time to rest.

SAAD: No, I want to stay here and color.

AL-ANOUD: Geeti will be resting soon as well. We should let her finish and rest.

SAAD: Ok. I'll rest with her.

Having finished her work, Geeti impassively watched the back and forth between mother and son, an exchange that ended abruptly when Al-Anoud took Saad by the hand and marched him out of the kitchen. Geeti said nothing after they left, but gestured for us to go to her room.

Over thirty years earlier, when Geeti first arrived in Kuwait from India, her employer Mama Lulua put her cooking skills to use, assigning Geeti the task of preparing the family's everyday meals. Geeti was also responsible for some childcare duties. At the time there was only one son, who was followed in quick succession by two daughters and a few years later, by another son. Geeti played an integral role in their upbringing: preparing a mushed concoction she rather wryly called "oil" and changing diapers when they were babies; cooking their meals and walking them to school when they were children; and now that they were adults—the daughters with families and homes of their own, the eldest son and his growing family taking up a wing of the family home, and their youngest son abroad studying—Geeti was someone they would go to for a comforting meal or conversation in the kitchen.

I had always been curious about Geeti's relationship with Mama Lulua's children. Their interactions were familiar, easy, sometimes teasing and tender and, for Geeti, also laced through with another quality, one I found difficult to discern and describe, evident only in fleeting facial expressions and a sometimes restrained clip in her voice. That afternoon I had glimpsed the expression again. Later in her room I tried again to probe at this inchoate issue, asking her what it was like to see and interact with the children of the children she helped to feed and raise. She responded:

That is how life is, no? Children grow.
It is the same when I visit my brother in India.
His children are big now, with their own children.

They [Mama Lulua's children] are also big now, with their own children.
Life it is like that for them, but for us . . .
Life, life [*repeats in Urdu and Hindi*], it cannot happen like that;
for us it is difficult, for us it is not possible.
We help, we watch, we stay in between

Geeti's words and gestures are telling. Embedded in a moment that conveys the texture of her everyday experience as a migrant domestic worker—the cooking, cleaning, caring for children, and dealing with employers that occupies her days—her comments provide an acute sense of how domestic workers understand and situate their experiences in relation to broader social and temporal trajectories, what she described as "life." Drawing a parallel between her family's and her employers' households, Geeti points to them both as places where a certain kind of life is possible. Geeti not only contrasts this type of life with the ones she and other migrant domestic workers lead, but she also draws a specific connection—in the form of domestic workers' activities and relations—between these two types of life. Geeti's comments emphasize her position in relation to both her brother's household in Pune and to Mama Lulua's household in Kuwait, a position of being "in between," a part of *and* apart from both households. She underscores how domestic workers "stay" there, how their lives remain suspended as the lives of others—brothers, employers, nephews, employers' children—unfold and develop while domestic workers such as herself are relegated to the supportive sidelines, helping and watching.

With subtlety and acuity, Geeti's words not only attest to the importance of migrant domestic workers' role in the ongoing reproduction of subjects, households and sociopolitical bodies in both South Asia and the Gulf, but they also highlight the temporal cast of migrant domestic workers' experiences of displacement. Existing work on labor migration, diasporic communities, and interregional Indian Ocean relations—works that partially chart Geeti and other domestic workers' experiences—all revolve around the issue of displacement. They do so both in terms of mapping the transnational migrations that have developed through petrodollar economies, late-stage capitalism, and the feminization of transnational labor migration, and in terms of deepening our understanding of the circumstances and implications of these movements to emergent forms of economic relations, sociopolitical belonging and political governance that comprise and crosscut our unevenly globalizing world. Scholarship on migrant domestic workers has pointed to how these women constitute a provisional diaspora, occupying liminal sociopolitical positions due to a concatenation of factors, including their subordinate position within the global economy, separation from their families, contradictory social mobility, and the politics of exclusion and belonging in relation to their fellow ethnonationals and to the populations of the countries they migrate to.[1]

In my discussion of domestic workers' experiences of transnational migration in this chapter and the next, I also focus on the issue of displacement but I shift the terms of analysis somewhat. Drawing from Geeti and my other interlocutors' utterances and experiences, I examine displacement not just in terms of change or movement across geographical space and sociocultural place. I also foreground the temporal cast of my interlocutors' experiences of displacement. Characterized by a sense of being out of place *and* time, their experiences of displacement are shaped by two processes: first, an assemblage of policies and systems of governance that define and discipline them as a temporary population, what I refer to in this chapter as their "temporariness"; and, second, the everyday gendered relations and activities of their households, in both the subcontinent and Kuwait, that precipitate and manage their migration experiences, leaving them suspended or staying in between these households (an issue I examine in chapter 2).

Similar to other foreign residents and migrants, domestic workers are subject to processes that seek to produce their temporariness in Kuwait and the other Gulf countries. Although domestic workers often conceive of and discuss their presence in Kuwait as temporary, the moment I witnessed between Geeti and her employers in Mama Lulua's kitchen belies their temporariness and illustrates the limits of discourses and disciplinary practices that produce them as such. Far from transient or provisional, domestic workers have become an integral, widespread, and long-standing presence in the Gulf. In Kuwait, domestic workers are employed by over 90 percent of Kuwaiti households, and constitute over 16 percent of the total population. Their work is crucial to the social reproduction of Kuwaiti citizens, the maintenance of Kuwaiti households, and the ongoing functioning of the Kuwaiti economy and public life. Many domestic workers such as Geeti develop long-term, close-knit relationships with their employers in the face of the hierarchical relations that exist between them. Migrant domestic workers constitute an essential and established presence despite regimes that attempt to depict or discipline them otherwise.

Discourses and disciplinary practices producing domestic workers' "temporariness" are predicated on several assumptions: namely, that these women work in Kuwait for short durations of time, and that they are away from, and will return back to, families and communities in the places from which they have migrated—peoples and places to which they are assumed to belong permanently. Reinscribing national and familial forms of belonging, these assumptions elide the ways in which South Asian domestic workers are part of long-standing cross-Oceanic connections that knit together the Gulf and Indian subcontinent, and they obfuscate the long-term effects of domestic workers' intimate imbrications with Kuwaiti families and households. Assumptions of domestic workers' temporariness naturalize the processes through which domestic workers reproduce existing forms of familial and ethnonational subjectivities and belongings, and do not account for the other forms of subjectivity and affinity that these women develop through processes of everyday conversion that mark their transnational experiences.

This chapter examines two sets of interlocking processes that produce domestic workers' temporariness in Kuwait. The first set is one that all noncitizens are subject to. It includes the ongoing but changing relations between peoples of the Indian subcontinent and the Arabian Peninsula, the emergence of increasingly exclusionary understandings of national belonging and citizenship in Kuwait, state policies and practices that produce Kuwait's resident noncitizen population, and Kuwait's sponsorship, or *kafala*, system, a citizen-devolved system through which noncitizens are governed on an everyday basis. Domestic workers are further subject to gendered features of the transnational domestic work sector that place them in precarious juridicopolitical positions, which further compound their experiences of temporariness in the Gulf region.

From Interregional to National Imaginaries

Long before she arrived at the port in Kuwait City and was struck by heat as implacable and heavy as a wall—a heat so different from the swirling monsoons of Southern India where she had grown up—Geeti, short for Gertrude, had associated Kuwait with a large burlap bag. Heavy and crunching with rice, the bag was given to her grandmother by her uncle during one of his summer visits to India. After cycles of hand sifting, washing, cooking, and eating—cycles Geeti had been an integral part of as that was the summer when the loose training of her childhood had tightened into adolescent duty—the bag became a crumpled heap on the lower shelf where it was kept. Once emptied, her grandmother repurposed it. The bag's heft was good for holding heavy wooden spoons and a rolling pin; later, its smoothened, aerated weave became ideal for keeping dried ginger roots.

The bag caught Geeti's eye many years later as she was preparing tea in the kitchen. Her uncle's wife had moved it, placing it under a large earthenware pot in which she had begun growing some flowers. Though faded from soil and water, Geeti could still make out the bag's Hindi and Arabic markings. In the adjoining room she could hear the low hum of the discussion between her uncle and parents. Staring at the bag, waiting for the tea to boil, and listening to her family's murmurings, Geeti started to reconcile herself to what was becoming increasingly likely, if not inevitable. Several months earlier, her fiancé had broken off their engagement. Her family's attempt at finding another match was proving fruitless. Geeti had been an indifferent student, and fully expecting her to marry, her parents had not encouraged her in her studies or to pursue the vocational training offered by a local nongovernmental organization. Her brother's wife was expecting their first child, and with more certainly to follow, Geeti knew their already crowded family home would soon become uncomfortable for her—where she would be constantly working yet feeling underfoot all the time.

Her uncle had proposed a solution, one he had first raised with her parents, then with her, then with her brother, paving the way for a discussion that had begun in earnest that evening. She was apprehensive, but staring at the bag, it gave her a sense of familiarity and possibility that smoothed over, at least for a while, her anxieties and disappointments. As her uncle suggested, she would go to Kuwait and "help," or work, in the households of members of a Kuwaiti family whose lives and fortunes were loosely intertwined with her own family. Former traders residing in Pune, the Kuwaiti family had employed her grandmother as their cook for over thirty years while they lived in India. When they settled back in Kuwait, one of the sons hired Geeti's uncle as his driver. Geeti's migration to Kuwait, where she would work for almost forty years, marked the third generation of their families' interrelation.

Several months later, a new passport in hand and the necessary visas procured, Geeti embarked on a ten-day long voyage across the Arabian Sea. Her journey was at the cusp of profound changes transforming the nature and scope of interrelations between the two regions. The Indian Ocean had long supported travel and trade.[2] This trade occurred not just between the subcontinent and the Arabian Peninsula but more expansively among communities in Persia, East Africa, and South-East Asia.[3] Port cities along the coasts—including Zanzibar, Aden, Muscat, Bahrain, Surat and Calicut—were home to cosmopolitan networks of merchants, pearlers, financiers, shopkeepers, and artisans. As the presence of the Kuwaiti traders in Pune points to, these networks were dense and well established, often involving the intimate and intricate imbrication of languages, cultural traditions, marriages, and kinship bonds. Relations were articulated not just through trade, but overlapping ties of gifting, loans and debt bondage, blood ties, social reciprocity, and legal systems.

Geeti's migration was facilitated by these enduring connections; however, her experiences also point to a series of transformations taking place in their nature and form. This was apparent upon her arrival in Kuwait. When she disembarked, spoke to immigration officials, and met her new employer, Mama Lulua, and her son Muhammad, they all identified her as *Al-Hindiyya* (Indian, feminine), an appellation that no longer referred (simply) to locality and place (i.e., where she was from), and to concomitant associations of language and cultural practice, but increasingly denoted nationality—*jinsiyya*—a form of belonging understood in homogenous and mutually exclusive terms, one that increasingly articulated relations among Kuwait's citizenry and its foreign migrant and resident populations. As a noun indicative of a type of nationality/*jinsiyya*, rather than an adjective referencing a region and its attendant sociocultural forms, *Al-Hindiyya* smoothed out differences among the people of India, and effaced the historical connections between the subcontinent and the residents of Kuwait. Although many of Kuwait's residents had migrated from and maintained familial and trade connections interregionally, they turned inward toward Kuwait City and the Arabian Peninsula in articulating their national identity and mythos.

In the decades prior to Geeti's arrival, a robust national imaginary had been developing in Kuwait, one that centered on the experiences of city residents who had migrated from the Najd region of the Arabian Peninsula, and on the city-state's emergence and endurance in the face of numerous historical challenges faced by its residents. These challenges included accounts of the region's perennially harsh environment, the drying up of the city's water reservoirs leading to the importation of water from the Shatt al-Arab, plagues and epidemics that devastated the population, the collapse of the pearling industry, and the threats posed by foreign powers, whether these be attacks, trade embargoes, or the all-too-looming interest of the Ottomans, the Qajars, the al-Saud-backed Ikhwan, or the British. Nationalist narratives extolled the city-state residents' resilience and hard-won autonomy in the face of these challenges. This autonomy, rather than residents' transregional connections, became the cornerstone of Kuwait's nationalist ethos. Unlike the far-flung, overlapping networks of the Kuwaiti family in Pune, Kuwaitis' horizons of belonging were increasingly articulated in national terms, a localized, Arabized, and increasingly exclusionary form of belonging.

These nationalist narratives emerged in tandem with shifts in Kuwait's political economy, governance, and sovereignty—shifts brought about through the advent of oil. Prior to the development of its petrodollar economy, Kuwait's rule was notable for the overlapping, often competing efforts of its elite.[4] The city consisted of an assortment of ethnic (Arab, Persian, East African, Turkish, Kurdish, from the subcontinent, etc.), linguistic (Arabic plus Urdu/Hindi, Gujarati, Hyderabadi, etc.), and to a lesser extent religious groups (Sunni, Shi'a, Christian, Jewish, Zoroastrian) ruled by a Sunni Arab elite, descendants of tribes that had migrated to the region in the eighteenth century from the Najd region of the Arabian Peninsula. Kuwait's governance was characterized by the interdependence of two groups of elite: the large merchant families and the Al-Sabah family. As employers, financiers, creditors, and patrons, the large merchant families held sway over large segments of the population. They also played an integral role in developing the city-state's public infrastructure and resources, including the establishment of schools, health clinics, and a municipal council responsible for overseeing the day-to-day operations of the public market, for building roads, and for supervising traffic, zoning, and the construction of new buildings in the city.[5] In addition to improving the well-being of the city's residents and promoting industry and trade in the region, these projects provided an important means through which the merchants cultivated the support and loyalty of the populace. Although they commanded a great deal of authority in Kuwait, the merchant families were focused on their trade and were uninterested in undertaking the day-to-day adjudication and military protection of the city, unless it directly related to their sphere of activities. These responsibilities were vested in the Al-Sabah family, whose activities were largely financed by the merchants. Relations among the merchant families, the Al-Sabah, and the rest of the populace were mediated through a series of *majlis* and *diwaniyyat* (colloquial Kuwaiti: *diwawin*). Forums of sociopolitical coordination and consultation attended primarily by men and organized along familial, trade and sectarian lines, these majlis and diwaniyyat were gendered sites of intense political jockeying that both reflected and buttressed hierarchies among Kuwait's residents.

The late 1930s through the 1950s marked a time of tremendous political contestation and change in Kuwait. The advent of oil transformed the country's decentered hierarchical system of governance, and shifted the balance of power among its elite. As the group charged with Kuwait's foreign relations, the Al-Sabah were the intermediaries with whom the British negotiated oil concession and treaties and, as a consequence of this, the group who controlled and channeled the revenues generated by the rapidly burgeoning oil industry. This eventually ended the family's financial dependence on the merchants, and provided them with the resources to achieve political ascendancy in Kuwait. Through a series of complicated political maneuvers, and their resounding defeat of political factions led by prominent members of the merchant class that sought to unseat them and challenge their control over the country's oil wealth, the Al-Sabah established themselves as the sovereign rulers of Kuwait.[6] The family was led by the Jabir and Salim branches of the (now royal) family—descendants of Mubarak the Great (1896–1915), whose carefully redacted personal history became a cornerstone of Kuwait's national mythos.[7] The Al-Sabah consolidated their rule through two major strategies.

First, they centralized existing state functions, and further developed and expanded the reach of the state. Drawing on Arab intelligentsia and functionaries that were recruited primarily from Egypt and among Palestinian refugees, Kuwait developed into a generous welfare state. The state provided citizens, such as Geeti's employer, Mama Lulua, and her children with access to public education (from primary to higher education levels), universal health care coverage, generously paying public-sector jobs, retirement plans after twenty and fifteen years of work for men and women respectively, periodic bonuses dependent upon the country's oil revenues, child allowances, and subsidies for marriage expenses, housing, utilities, and foodstuffs.[8] State institutions became an ever-present and necessary part of the citizenry's lives. As political historian Jill Crystal notes: "to get married and receive housing, to have children and receive money, to get an education, a job or a prescription filled, to walk down the street, you went through the state . . . the state was apparent everywhere in the new streets and houses as well as the ministries."[9] State formation was the means through which the Al-Sabah redistributed Kuwait's oil wealth, and in so doing established clientelistic and disciplinary relations with the populace.[10] The nascent Kuwaiti state functioned through biopolitical, disciplinary, and sovereign forms of power. In the form of education, health, housing, infrastructure and jobs, citizens' lives were enabled, shaped, and ordered through the state. With these state resources and services "came the eyes of the state, now everywhere and nowhere. The gaze it cast was less a controlling gaze than an ordering one. . . . Sets of very ordinary rules and norms came to order all aspects of life. Constant but diffuse scrutiny, not fear, kept people in line."[11] Citizens' everyday experiences were inextricably bound to the state, a state controlled and ordered by the Al-Sabah, whose rule came to be seen as historically determined, inevitable, and beneficent.

Through these state-making ventures, the Al-Sabah supplanted the merchant elite as the primary financiers, employers, and patrons of the Kuwaiti populace.[12] In the wake of attempts by some members of the merchant class to challenge the ruling family—by developing broad-based coalition movements organized around the Majlis al-Umma, or by organizing political groups allied with pan-Arab movements in the Middle East[13]—and in order to stave off further such challenges, the ruling family made a tacit agreement with the merchant families.[14] The merchant families ceded control of state functions and institutions, as well as the National Assembly to the Al-Sabah, largely absenting themselves from formal political spheres.[15] In return the Al-Sabah vested control of certain realms of economic activity, ones outside state distribution networks and services, to the merchant families.[16] The Al-Sabah not only agreed to keep out of Kuwait's private sector, but through state policies and laws, they created conditions for the merchant class to dominate and prosper in this sector. Direct aid and protection were given to the merchants to create enclave economies through state grants of land, money, and concessions.[17] This arrangement was cemented through protective commercial laws, which restricted property and business ownership rights to nationals.[18] Through these favorable conditions, the merchant class came to monopolize trade, construction, and commercial services in Kuwait, spaces of authority and economic wealth that were complementary to the oil industry and state-driven petrodollar redistribution networks.[19]

Preferential access to Kuwait's private sector, and access to resources provided by the Kuwaiti state, were predicated on having Kuwaiti nationality and citizenship, the criteria for which became increasingly exclusionary in the mid-twentieth century. Kuwaiti nationality codes date from the late 1940s, but were only loosely applied until the late 1960s.[20] In 1948 two decrees were issued defining who were to be considered originally Kuwaitis" (*Kuwaiti bil-asl*; Kuwaiti by "origin"), a group that included any member of the ruling family (i.e., the Al-Sabah), those residing in Kuwait since 1899, children of Arab or Muslim men born in Kuwait, and the children of Kuwaiti men.[21] These decrees further stipulated that naturalization (*Kuwaiti bil-tajanus*; Kuwaiti by "naturalization") was possible for those who had resided in Kuwait for at least 10 years, were employed, and spoke Arabic.[22] In 1959 a further "Nationality Law" was adopted in which the category "originally Kuwaiti" was expanded to include descendants of those residing in Kuwait since 1920 and where the category of children born to Arab or Muslim men was dropped as a criterion for citizenship.[23] Naturalization also became more limited—requiring residency for fifteen years, and the total number limited to a maximum of fifty cases annually.[24] From the 1960s through to the early 1980s, the state adopted special policies that led to the naturalization of thousands of Bedouins, who had previously lived nomadic lives, crossing between the borders of Kuwait, Saudi Arabia and Iraq, but who had increasingly been settling in Kuwait.[25]

These state decrees, laws, and policies alternated between and blended the principles of jus soli (nationality/citizenship predicated on residency) and jus sanguinis (nationality/citizenship predicated on blood). Kuwaiti nationality initially encompassed and was extended to peoples based on their residency in the city-state. Elite families as well as the general populace; city dwellers as well as the Bedouin (*hadar* and *badu*); Sunni, Shi'a, Christians, and Jews (until most migrated/fled to Israel); Arabs, Persians, and Indians were all granted citizenship and the rights and entitlements citizenship conferred.[26] The city-state was diverse, fragmented, and intensely hierarchical. As a basis of identification and belonging, being "Kuwaiti" did not necessarily have more purchase than did any others. This situation changed with petrodollar-driven state-making processes, the consolidation of the Al-Sabah's rule and the nationalist mythos they promulgated, the emergence of a merchant-led private sector that gave special privileges and entitlements to Kuwaiti nationals, and the increased migration of populations that would come to be referred to as "foreign workers" and "expatriates." Such populations, though integral to the development of the Kuwaiti nation-state, were "workers of the nation" rather than "nation builders." A concerted sense of national belonging was emerging, one based on two overlapping understandings. Nationality was understood in terms of *jinsiyya*, from the root words *jns*, meaning "to make alike, to assimilate, to naturalize," and the word *jins*, translating as "species, class, category, race, and recently, nation."[27] It was also understood in terms of *taba'iyya*, from the root words *bay'a*, meaning pledging oneself to a higher power, and translated as following or allegiance to a leader.[28] Kuwaiti nationality was thus understood in both horizontal and vertical terms—where nationals were parts of and subject to the nation-state, a nation-state ruled by the emir, who was often presented in patriarchal terms as the beneficent father of the nation.[29]

During the 1960s, the principles of Kuwaiti nationality shifted from jus soli to jus sanguinis. Naturalization became increasingly restricted, and with few exceptions, citizenship was extended only to the descendants of existing nationals.[30] This extension was an intrinsically gendered process, where only the children of male citizens were permitted to become citizens, a process based on the patrilineal understanding that belonging and citizenship are channeled through the father.[31] Kuwaiti nationality also began to carry racial overtones; that is, Kuwaiti became synonymous with being "Arab." This is evidenced by the national Constitution, which proclaims: "Kuwait is an Arab State, independent and fully sovereign . . . the people of Kuwait are part of the Arab nation."[32] A concerted process was underway whereby interregional pasts were elided and

Arab genealogies emphasized.[33] This process was an integral means through which Kuwait's ruling families, most of whom were descendants of migrants from the Najd region, entwined their family mythos with that of the Kuwait city-state and nation, thereby further consolidating their hegemony over Kuwait. Emphasizing Kuwait's Arabness might also have reflected the Al-Sabah's attempts to wrest authority and legitimacy away from the merchants—a group linked as much to far-flung interregional networks as they were to the interior of the Arabian Peninsula. Arabization might have also been part and parcel of a broader intellectual and political shift in which Kuwait's intelligentsia began to look Westward, to the rest of the Arab world, in articulating their aspirations and modernization-development projects. This process reflected the expanding circulation and currency of Arab print media in Kuwait, elite Kuwaiti families sending their children to study at universities in Cairo and Beirut, and the fact that many Kuwaiti educational institutions were developed and initially run by teachers and administrators from Egypt and the Sham region.[34]

Exclusionary Citizenship and the Production of Temporariness

Gendered, racialized, Arabized, both horizontal and hierarchical in form, entailing access to a general welfare state, and preferential treatment in the private sector, Kuwaiti national belonging and citizenship gained greater currency among residents of the city-state over the course of the twentieth century. It also became increasingly exclusionary. By the early 1950s and late 1960s, when Geeti's uncle and Geeti were migrating to Kuwait, naturalization was no longer possible for migrants, a population that was increasing in number and scope at the time. Large-scale migration to the region had begun several decades prior in the 1930s, a process spurred by the advent of the oil industry and related infrastructural projects and by the limited pool of educated, skilled workers available in Kuwait at the time. British officials were initially the ones involved with recruiting and managing migrant workers. They had been granted this right based on the terms of the oil concessions; however, their decisions were still subject to the political approval of Kuwait's ruling elite. The British brought in workers from the Indian subcontinent, a group consisting of semiskilled manual workers, skilled artisans, and clerical staff.[35] The migration of these workers was channeled through a system of labor recruitment that had developed through the British colonial presence in the Indian subcontinent.[36] In some parts of the Arabian Peninsula, most notably Bahrain and Qatar, the local population protested against the higher salaries given to the Indian migrants, and to the higher-status occupations that they held.[37] Based on existing research, it is unclear whether a similar situation developed in Kuwait. What is known is that in Kuwait the British constructed a racially and ethnonationally stratified system of labor in which workers' wages and working conditions varied according to their race and ethnonationality. Reports indicate that the situation of workers from the subcontinent was a largely difficult one.[38] In August 1948 the Kuwait Oil Company (KOC) Indo-Pakistani Employees Association was formed.[39] The association organized labor strikes to improve workers' wages and living conditions.[40] Attributing workers' activism to "unrestrained nationalism," the British deported the striking workers. This act in turn prompted the newly independent Indian government to send a "Goodwill mission" in December 1948, comprising the Indian secretary general and Indian representative to the UN General Assembly to investigate the conditions of their compatriots working in Bahrain and Kuwait. The reports they produced were highly critical of the living conditions and the discriminatory attitudes toward Indians among the British staff, especially as experienced by those working with the KOC.[41]

In the 1940s, in response to the labor strikes, and linked to the country's project of Arabization, Kuwait increasingly began to turn to Egypt and the Sham region for labor. Arabic-speaking intelligentsia from these regions were key to the development of the Kuwaiti state, especially with respect to the country's public educational system. From primary to higher education levels, Egyptian and Palestinian teachers educated a generation of Kuwaitis. Many of the country's doctors, shopkeepers, restaurant managers, office clerks, and bureaucrats were also from the broader Arab world, and Egyptian and Yemeni men predominated in semiskilled trades. The demographic composition of migrants in Kuwait shifted again in the 1970s, when increasing numbers of workers from South and Southeast Asia were recruited, primarily for semiskilled occupations (e.g., construction work), and then again in the late 1970s, a period that witnessed the wide-scale migration of women from South Asia, most of whom worked as domestic workers within the households of Kuwaitis and well-to-do foreign residents. From 1975 to 1996, the number of Arab foreign migrants and residents in Kuwait fell from 80 percent to 33 percent.[42] The reasons for this shift are greatly debated. Some argue that Kuwait and other Gulf Cooperation Council (GCC) countries began hiring non-Arabs because they "were perceived to pose less of a political threat and to be less inclined to interfere in their host country's internal affairs."[43] Rulers of these countries were concerned that pan-Arab ideologies and movements might destabilize the authority of existing systems of governance in the GCC, a concern exemplified by the support and collaboration among Palestinians within Kuwait of the Iraqi occupation of Kuwait during the first Gulf war. Other argue that after the rise of oil prices in 1973, the GCC states found themselves flush with capital, and embarked on large-scale infrastructural and building developments that were "labor-intensive" in nature. Arab markets were already exhausted, and the mobility of these workers was restricted. As a result, companies turned to South and Southeast Asia labor markets.[44] Workers from these countries were also perceived as being a cheaper, more docile laboring population than were Arabs, and because they lacked linguistic or cultural affinities with Kuwaitis, it was assumed they would be reluctant to settle in the country permanently.[45]

In addition to changes in the composition of its migrant population, the early 1970s also marks the beginning of the period when Kuwait's foreign resident and migrant population began to exceed that of its citizenry. For almost forty years, noncitizens have comprised the majority of the country's population.[46] Today, it is estimated that foreign residents and migrants comprise two-thirds of the country's total population. Although a long-standing, widespread and integral part of Kuwait, this population has been regarded as and concerted attempts have been made to discipline them into a temporary, transient population.[47] Whether they are recruited as domestic workers, construction workers, doctors or engineers, migrants usually hold limited term contracts (typically two years), and come on two-year residency and work visas subject to renewal. They can only obtain these visas through a *kafeel*, a Kuwaiti or well-heeled foreign resident who acts as their sponsor and guarantor. Their work contracts usually include health and dental insurance (universal coverage is available in Kuwait, though employers have to pay initial fees), housing, in-country visa costs, and return flights to the places from which they have migrated. Noncitizens are not permitted to invest in land or housing, or have majority ownership in businesses. Their work contracts and living circumstances in Kuwait are structured in a manner that encourages saving (there are no income or sales taxes in Kuwait), and the accumulation of easily portable and transferable forms of capital—all to ensure their return migration or further migration to other more permanent destinations, such as North America, Australia, and Europe.

This assemblage—supporting impermanence rather than residence—is further bolstered by restrictions hindering foreign residents and migrants' ability to sponsor family members and establish their own households in Kuwait. In the early 2000s, foreign residents and migrants needed to earn a minimum of 250 Kuwaiti dinars per month (well above the average of 50–145 KD domestic workers earn per month) to sponsor a family member's residency in Kuwait.[48] This salary threshold effectively bars working-class and service industry migrants from bringing family members to Kuwait, and it ensures the production of large populations of the country's so-called bachelor workers and single lady workers. Family sponsorship systems are also highly gendered: parents and daughters of foreign residents and migrants can be sponsored; however, sons over the age of eighteen cannot be sponsored. Women may not sponsor their spouses unless their spouses are able to find their own employment. In addition, unless paid for or subsidized by their employers, the cost of sending children to private schools is higher for foreign residents and migrants in Kuwait than are similar costs in their home countries, a difference that has effectively discouraged many from moving their families.[49]

Kafala System

Foreign residents and migrants' temporariness are further produced through the kafala system, the sponsorship system of Kuwait and other countries of the greater Arabian Peninsula.[50] It is a system that is often analyzed as being exceptional to the region, but is in fact resonant with migrant sponsorship systems in other parts of the world, in particular Southeast and East Asia (e.g., Singapore, Malaysia, and Hong Kong). At its core the kafala system is a set of triangulating relationships, agreements, and procedures between domestic workers, citizens, and the state. Foreign residents and migrants are granted the right to reside and work in Kuwait through a kafeel, a term often translated as "sponsor,"[51] but which also carries the meaning of "guarantor."[52] The kafeel is able to procure the necessary visas by adhering to a set of conditions and stipulations set by the state. Most notably, the kafeel must (1) employ the noncitizen who they are sponsoring for the duration of their stay in Kuwait; (2) repatriate noncitizens at their own (kafeel's) expense upon the termination of the contract; and (3) monitor and inform the Ministry of Interior if there are any changes in the noncitizen's labor contract, place of residence, or civil status.[53] If the person they sponsor should abscond or "run away," by law it is incumbent upon the kafeel to report this to the police station in his or her district within twenty-four to forty-eight hours. Foreign residents and migrants, in turn, are not allowed to change their kafeel until the completion of their contract, or unless mutually agreed upon by them. Within this arrangement, the kafeel becomes economically and legally responsible for those she sponsors, and those being sponsored are in turn dependent and beholden upon their kafeel for the right to stay and work in Kuwait.

State institutions play a purposefully limited role within this context. In addition to issuing work and residency visas to the kafeel and civil identity cards to foreign residents and migrants, Kuwaiti state institutions can also be called upon to ensure that the kafala arrangements are fulfilled. They can be brought in to intervene if the terms of the foreign residents and migrants' contracts are not upheld, either through Kuwait's judiciary or, in rare cases, through legislation, direct arbitration, or decrees issued by the executive branch (i.e., cabinet and/or the emir). The police and Ministry of Interior can also undertake procedures to deport foreign residents and migrants if they are found to be in breach of their kafala arrangement, most notably if they abscond from their employer.

The development of the kafala system has generated a great deal of debate among scholars of the Arabian Peninsula. Although there are varying perspectives on why this system has emerged and continues to persist, these debates are predicated on the general agreement that the kafala system is fundamentally related to processes of state making and governance, and the normative assumption that the state should play the primary role in the adjudication and governance of foreign residents and migrants. Some argue the kafala system's predominance relates to the Kuwaiti state's capacity. The large-scale migration of much-needed workers from throughout the Arab world and Asia began in the 1950s, a period during which the Kuwaiti state was beginning to develop its own institutions of rule and, it is argued, did not have the institutional apparatus necessary to oversee this population. Consequently, the state devolved the responsibility of the adjudication and governance of migrants to its citizenry in the form of the kafala system.[54] While this may have been the case during the early stages of state development, in the aftermath of the 1970s oil boom and of the Gulf War in the early 1990s—when, respectively, state capacity expanded greatly and the governance and policing of noncitizens became an acute and pressing political issue—the argument that the kafala system continues to exist because of limited state capacity has become less convincing.

A more compelling argument is that the kafala system has developed into a strategy deployed by the state to buttress and consolidate overlapping systems of rule and privilege in Kuwait. As several scholars and rights groups have long documented,[55] the kafala system reinscribes differences between citizens and noncitizens, produces power asymmetries between the two, and reinforces the existing system of rule and division of power among Kuwaiti citizens. As mentioned, beginning in the 1960s Kuwait's naturalization policies became increasingly restrictive, effectively making it impossible for foreign residents and migrants to become citizens. Without citizenship, foreign residents and migrants were excluded from the state's petrodollar redistribution networks, and fell largely outside the purview and disciplinary practices of Kuwait's state infrastructure. To redress the potential political problems that might ensue— most notably foreign residents' and migrants' demands for enfranchisement, especially given that from the mid-1970s onward, Kuwait's population of non-citizenry began to exceed that of its citizenry[56]—the state conferred daily control and disciplining of foreign residents and migrants to individual employers and kafeel,[57] who are overwhelmingly but not exclusively citizens.[58] With foreign residents' and migrants' presence in Kuwait being contingent upon, and policed by, their kafeel, the kafala system has become an important means through which asymmetrical power relations between citizens and Kuwait's resident noncitizens are produced and reproduced. The delegation of everyday governance of migrants and foreign residents to their kafeel is not marked by absence of state power, but marks a doubling of authority, kafeel and state institutions working in tandem and bolstering one another.

With the exception of the early years of Kuwait's development, foreign residents and migrants have overwhelmingly been employed in Kuwait's private sector. Today it is estimated that foreign residents and migrants comprise over 95 percent of Kuwait's private sector and that over 92 percent of Kuwaiti nationals are concentrated in the public sector.[59] State institutions have become the means through which the Al-Sabah have distributed the country's oil wealth—over which they maintain primary control—and have established their rule over the city-state's population. In doing so, the Al-Sabah came to a tacit agreement with the other members of Kuwait's ruling elite, ceding control of the private sector to the merchant families and the rest of the citizenry, and establishing policies ensuring their privileged position within this sector. The state passed legislation stipulating majority ownership of private businesses needs to be held by citizens, and granting generous subsidies and contracts to these businesses.[60] The governance of foreign residents and migrants through the kafala system is another means of ensuring citizens' advantageous position within this sector. Foreign residents' and migrants' labor is an important means of capital accumulation in sectors falling largely outside Kuwait's oil industries and public sector, an alternative source of wealth from which Kuwaiti entrepreneurs and businesses profit.[61] The kafala system encourages the development of economic realms relatively autonomous from those dominated by the Al-Sabah and Kuwaiti state, parallel and interlocking realms of activity that both consolidate Kuwait's body politic, and actively produce and reinscribe status distinctions between citizens, foreign residents, and migrants.

Developing through concerted strategy rather than limited state authority, the kafala system constitutes a set of relationships and agreements fundamentally shaping migrants' experiences in Kuwait. No matter how long they reside in Kuwait, or whether they are born in Kuwait, and regardless of their contribution to the country's development and prosperity, migrants are only allowed to stay in Kuwait on a temporary basis. Their presence remains contingent upon and policed by their kafeel. Migrants are allowed to stay in Kuwait for periods of time delimited by the labor contracts signed with individual citizens and institutions—their kafeel—who act as both their guarantor and sponsor. Emerging in tandem and parallel to the country's state infrastructure, Kuwait's kafala system plays an integral role in bolstering the existing division of power among citizens, and in ensuring the impermanence of the country's migrant population.

It is in both citizens' and foreign residents' and migrants' interest to fulfill the terms of their agreements. Contravention has consequences for both, but, perhaps not surprisingly given that the kafala system systematically ensures citizens' privileged status, penalties are weighted toward foreign residents' and migrants' disfavor. The kafeel, who is responsible for her employees' visa and travel costs, medical health care coverage, and recruitment agency fees, incurs costs and invests capital in those she sponsors at the beginning of the contract cycle, and it is in her interest to have those she sponsors complete their contracts. If her employees abscond, the kafeel not only loses her return and potential dividends on the money she invested, but she can also be held liable should those she sponsors engage in any illegal activity.[62] Citizens can also have their right to sponsor migrants revoked if they are found to be negligent in their duties as guarantor and sponsor, and if they do not report employees who have absconded within twenty-four to forty-eight hours. As a result of this, and although it is illegal, many kafeels confiscate and hold onto the passport of those they sponsor, thereby making it difficult for these foreign residents and migrants to abscond, leave the country, or find other employment opportunities in Kuwait.

There are several reasons why migrants abscond, or in Kuwaiti common parlance "run away." Some do so because they have found, or they seek to find, more lucrative employment opportunities, others to escape situations of abuse and exploitation. And in the case of domestic workers, who are generally expected to reside with their employers, many abscond because they enter into common-law relationships with their partners. Unless they have committed crimes, foreign residents and migrants who have absconded from their kafeel can leave the country when the government declares an amnesty—periods when they can leave the country without penalty—but subsequently have limitations placed on their ability to return to Kuwait.[63]

Deportations rarely take place, but they are perceived to be a widespread occurrence. Rumors abound about them, creating the perception they occur at the whim of citizens. According to Kuwait's residency law of 1959, deportation is not subject to the discretion of employers; it can only take place as a result of a judicial or administrative decision taken by the authorities under three circumstances: the foreign resident or migrant has been convicted in a court of law, and the court has recommended she or he be deported; the migrant has contravened her or his work agreement and is unable to find a means of sustenance; the Ministry of Interior deems the migrant to be a "security or moral" threat to the country.[64] Regardless of whether it is in fact easy or difficult to deport noncitizens, the perceived threat of deportation looms large in discussions among migrants and foreign residents and their decision-making processes, leading many to become wary of, and comply with, the dictates of their employers.[65]

Similar to their sponsors, foreign residents and migrants bear significant costs in coming to Kuwait, usually in the form of the exorbitant fees they pay to labor recruitment agencies in their home countries. Most incur substantial debts or have to sell major assets such as bridal jewelry and landholdings in the hopes of finding employment and earning salaries that are significantly higher than what they can earn in their home communities (often at least triple the amount in the case of domestic work). In coming to Kuwait their first priority is often to recoup the costs they have incurred, then to begin accumulating further savings. Many domestic workers with whom I met, most notably well-educated Filipina and Indian women migrants (e.g., who had worked as nurses, teachers, etc., in their home countries), mentioned that they had initially migrated in the hopes of finding upwardly mobile employment opportunities in Kuwait, but once they arrived they realized that switching their kafeel and finding other jobs was logistically difficult if not impossible.[66] Consequently, most foreign residents and migrants remain with their initial kafeel, even under difficult, exploitative, or abusive conditions.

Cumulatively, these conditions systematically favor citizens, placing them in a position of privilege and authority in relation to noncitizens. Most foreign residents and migrants do, however, have recourse in situations of abuse and exploitation. Other forms of governance, arbitration, and adjudication have developed since the early 1960s, most notably the country's Labor Law of 1964, which protects foreign residents and migrants who hold visas to work in the public sector (visa number 17), or in the private sector (visa number 18). Adapted from Egyptian civil law, this law explicitly outlines workers' entitlements and rights, most notably the right to sue their employers if their work contracts are violated.[67] Workers who pursue such cases are often successful.

However, many foreign residents and migrants are unaware of or unable to access legal resources. In addition, this law does not mitigate the residency law of 1959, which stipulates that while a trial is pending, foreign residents and migrants are forbidden from working for any other employer in Kuwait.[68] Early in 2009, after a great deal of lobbying on the part of labor-sending countries, Kuwait passed an amended labor law focusing on improving the rights of foreign residents and migrants by making penalties for exploitative or abusive employers and kafeels harsher, by making it possible for foreign residents and migrants to form labor unions, and by expediting trial procedures and ensuring quicker court turnaround times.[69] However, as I discuss below, until very recently (summer 2015) domestic workers did not fall under Kuwait's 1964 Labor Law and its amendments.[70] However, like any other citizen and noncitizen legally residing in Kuwait, they did and continue to have recourse to other bases of legal protection, namely, through Kuwaiti civil law in situations of contract or property disputes, and Kuwaiti criminal law in situations of physical injury, harm, or abuse.

Migrant Domestic Workers' Precarious Positioning

The position of migrant domestic workers in Kuwait is similar to that of other noncitizens, yet also differs in significant ways. Like other foreign residents and migrants, domestic workers are subject to a set of interrelated processes that define and discipline them into a permanently temporary population in Kuwait. They are subject to Kuwaiti laws and policies that render their de jure citizenship and sponsorship of their family members a near impossibility. They enter into contractual arrangements that promote their regular visits, savings, remittances, and ultimately their return to their home communities—or further migration to another destination country. Their presence in Kuwait is contingent upon their obtaining work and sponsorship visas from their kafeel, citizens who are responsible for their everyday governance. Yet as I discuss in this section, domestic workers in Kuwait experience this temporariness in particularly acute form. These migrant women are part of a transnational domestic work sector that falls in and out of gendered focus by state policies and practices in ways producing conditions of precariousness, conditions that further compound these women's experiences of temporariness. Given the gendered understandings and practices that underpin state practices and legal systems, households and domestic work are often treated as though they constitute separate realms falling outside these systems. Situated at the confluence of gendered juridopolitical aporias, domestic workers occupy a precarious position that—in addition to an assemblage of policies, practices, and systems producing their noncitizenship—further disciplines them into conditions of temporariness in Kuwait.

Kuwait's transnational domestic work sector has expanded rapidly, particularly from the mid- to late twentieth century onward. Before the advent of oil, few families within Kuwait were able to engage what were then called "helpers" or "servants" to work within their households. Only the ruling elite and well-to-do merchant families had the resources necessary to retain wetnurses, concubines, and servants from indentured or slave populations or foster children from impoverished families.[71] Similarly, only the elite and well-to-do could afford, on a part-time basis, to employ socially and economically marginalized women and men to work within their homes.[72] To refer to these groups as domestic workers would be an anachronistic misnomer. The work they undertook was not understood solely in terms of waged labor relations, but included other valences of relationality including kinship and patron-client relations. The remuneration these groups received was not necessarily in the form of wages, but included other forms of economic exchange and distribution including gifting, apprenticing, fostering, financial pensions, and ongoing social support. These relations and forms of circulation were usually adjudicated at the household level. If difficulties arose, the women and men undertaking work within households often drew on immediate sources of sociopolitical support, including members of their family and religious leaders; in some cases, they would present their grievances to *diwaniyyat* or to the courts for arbitration and settlement. Those working part time within households could also leave and seek employment elsewhere.

With the country's oil-driven development, the number of Kuwaitis seeking to hire domestic workers grew exponentially from the mid- to late twentieth century and onward. In the late 1970s, 13 percent of households employed domestic workers, which increased to 62 percent by the late 1980s.[73] The number increased to 87 percent by the late 1990s, before stabilizing at 90–93 percent from the early 2000s onward. The size of Kuwait's domestic work population grew accordingly. In 1975 migrant domestic workers numbered just under 12,000 and comprised less than 1 percent of the total population. This number grew to 200,000 by the turn of the century, to 10.5 percent of Kuwait's total population. By the mid- to late 2000s, the number of migrant domestic workers increased to a staggering 500,000, or 16 percent of Kuwait's total population and 25 percent of its noncitizen population. Today, it is estimated that there is one domestic worker for every two Kuwaiti citizens.

While demand grew for domestic workers, few if any Kuwaitis were willing, or found it necessary to continue to undertake this work. They therefore began looking further afield for people to employ within their households. Initially, some sponsored male "houseboys" from Yemen.[74] Others hired the wives and daughters of less affluent foreign residents and migrants on a part-time basis.[75] From the late 1960s onward, Kuwaiti households increasingly began to hire women from South Asia, many of which were Christian women from Goa and the greater Bombay region.[76] Some of these women accompanied the Kuwaiti families for whom they had worked in India when they returned to Kuwait. Others, such as Mama Lulua's family, recruited domestic workers through their existing networks of relations in the subcontinent, or through intermediaries, including merchant families and church officials and, for the vast majority, through a growing legion of labor recruitment or "manpower" agents. During the 1970s, well over 90 percent of domestic workers came from South Asia, including Southern India, Bangladesh, Sri Lanka, and Pakistan.[77] This area expanded in the 1980s to women from other parts of the global South, including the Philippines, Indonesia, Thailand, and, starting in the late 1990s, from Nepal, Ethiopia, and Eritrea.[78]

South Asian domestic workers' migration to Kuwait is channeled by a transnational domestic work sector that has developed rapidly since the late twentieth century. Spanning the Indian subcontinent and the Gulf, this sector is a fluid realm whose actors, networks, and bureaucratic procedures operate in the shadowy interstices of a number of local and transnational juridopolitical systems, interstices sometimes shading into illegality. In particular during its early stages, this sector has developed largely outside the direct purview of state juridopolitical systems due to a concatenation of gendered factors, placing domestic workers in an ambiguous, frequently precarious sociopolitical position, one intensifying their experience of transnational temporariness.

In both the Gulf and South Asia, state institutions and officials initially envisioned their role in the transnational domestic work sector to be a circumscribed one, limited to regulating the cross-border movement of domestic workers. Both groups perceived the transnational domestic work sector to be a realm that falls outside the ambit of state adjudication and governance. Although their positions were similar, state officials from the Gulf and South Asia gave different (if complementary reasons) for their respective government's attenuated role in this sector: the labor-receiving countries of the Gulf were either unwilling or unable to intercede in household spaces, and the labor-sending countries of South Asia were either unwilling or unable to intercede in transnational spaces.

Officials in Kuwait not only attributed their state's minimal involvement in the transnational domestic work sector to the kafala system and the government's reluctance to become involved in the everyday governance of foreign residents and migrants—in this case migrant domestic workers. They also indicated that the Kuwaiti state is averse to interceding into households, a "family space" considered to be separate—and sacrosanct—from political affairs. Consonant with gendered discourses of households that have developed through processes of colonial modernity and of nation building throughout the Middle East and South Asia, this explanation not only naturalizes household spaces, and the division between the private and public, but it also elides the multiple ways households and states are closely interrelated.[79] Gendered discourses of households do not account for how Kuwaiti households—as the locus for reproduction and rearing of citizens—are mutually constitutive of the Kuwaiti nation-state. These gendered discourses also obfuscate how through its family policies (e.g., encouraging nuclear families, promoting fertility to encourage population growth), its welfare benefits (e.g., child bonuses that are unofficially known as "maid pay"), and its recognition and bolstering of the authority of male household members (e.g., many welfare allocations can only be distributed through male household members), the Kuwaiti state shapes and is integrally involved in the everyday functioning of the country's households.

The Kuwaiti state's minimal involvement in the transnational domestic work sector also relates to the gendered nature of the country's labor laws. Unlike other foreign residents and migrants, until only very recently (2015) domestic workers have not fallen under Kuwait's labor laws, and they remain outside the jurisdiction of the country's Ministry of Social Affairs and Labor. Due to gendered understandings of what constitutes labor—understandings that preclude socially reproductive work and gendered activities and relations centered on household spaces—domestic work has generally been excluded from the labor laws of most countries around the world, including of the United States and, until very recently, the United Kingdom and more recently, in the summer of 2015, Kuwait. Passed in 1964, Kuwait's labor laws were derived from Egyptian civil codes (in turn shaped by French civil codes), which also excluded domestic work. In addition, in the early 1960s when Kuwait's labor laws and Ministry of Social Affairs and Labor were being formed, there were few domestic workers in Kuwait—a group that was consequently overlooked by lawmakers and government officials.[80] As domestic workers became a larger presence in Kuwait, they were further excluded from these laws and institutions because, as one government official put it: "households and private citizens are not considered companies here." Otherwise put, labor laws and the Ministry of Labor and Social Affairs are focused on regulating the private sector, a realm comprising corporations and companies, from which household spaces continue to be precluded.

Part of a population (noncitizens) whose governance has been ceded to Kuwait's citizens, working in spaces (households) in which the Kuwaiti state is unwilling to directly intervene, and undertaking work (everyday affective and intimate labor) not recognized by Kuwaiti labor laws until very recently (2015), domestic workers are part of a transnational sector whose development and functioning has been largely disregarded by the Kuwaiti state. In the absence of the state's direct involvement, domestic workers' regulation has fallen to a mishmash of other groups, who function in a fluid, semiformal capacity. Most important are the kafeel, who sponsor, employ, and are responsible for domestic workers' everyday governance. Kuwait's kafala system is particularly significant to the domestic work sector given that migrant domestic workers not only interact on a daily basis with their kafeel, but that the vast majority also reside within their kafeel's homes. Domestic workers' experiences in Kuwait—most notably their everyday well-being and their earnings—are intensely dependent upon the types of relationships they establish with members of their kafeel's households, including members of their kafeel's family, fellow domestic workers, and drivers. Should problems with their employers or other members of their work household arise, South Asian domestic workers have several semiformal avenues of recourse. Many seek assistance from their home countries' consulates or embassies, where depending on the situation and the resources at their disposal, officials may help mediate disputes between domestic workers and their kafeel, provide short-term housing (often in shelters located on the embassy's or consulate's premises) and contact information for informal groups that offer aid, facilitate repatriation procedures, or assist domestic workers with filing civil or criminal cases in the Kuwaiti court system.

Domestic workers also seek support from the Kuwaiti labor or "manpower" agencies that recruited them to the country. The primary role of these labor recruitment agencies is to facilitate domestic workers' initial migration to the region, which, in partnership with labor brokers from domestic workers' home countries, they accomplish by triangulating contact between domestic workers, their kafeel, and state institutions.[81] In the absence of direct state involvement in the regulation of the transnational domestic work sector, particularly during the early stages of this sector's development, the role of labor recruitment agencies has been magnified. Although reports of labor recruitment agencies' exploitation and abuse of migration domestic workers are well documented,[82] perhaps less well known are some of these labor agencies' advocacy efforts and the assistance they provide migrant domestic workers. In Kuwait, help includes developing a union to regulate and monitor recruitment agencies, establishing procedures to ensure migrant domestic workers are paid fully and on time by their employers, developing a blacklist of exploitative and abusive employers, setting up temporary shelters, and providing legal assistance to domestic workers. Recruitment agencies' lobbying efforts have also contributed to the implementation of legally mandated insurance policies for migrant domestic workers (paid for by their employers) and the passing of laws making formal written contracts between migrant domestic workers and their kafeel mandatory and more recently, in the summer of 2015, the implementation of a new law giving domestic workers enforceable labor rights.

Another option available to migrant domestic workers, one often advocated to them by both embassy/consular officials and labor recruitment agents, is to seek recourse through the Kuwaiti court system. Although domestic workers have not until recently fallen under the purview of existing labor laws, like other citizens and noncitizens in Kuwait, they have had and continue to have legal recourse through Kuwaiti civil and criminal laws. When their contract stipulations are not being upheld, they can file civil cases, and in situations of physical harm and abuse, they can file criminal cases.[83] Few domestic workers, however, have sought redress through the courts. Many are wary of state institutions.[84] They may not trust Kuwait's police or judiciary or are unaware of or unable to access these resources. Those who do pursue civil or criminal legal cases have several options in addressing their situation: prosecuting their case, undertaking dispute resolution and arbitration, agreeing to out-of-court settlements, returning to their original employer, returning to the Kuwaiti labor agency that had recruited them, finding a new employer, or returning to their home country.[85]

In response to the systematic problems that have characterized the migrant domestic work sector—including abuse, exploitation and, most common, the nonpayment or withholding of domestic workers' wages—and to address pressure and lobbying efforts brought upon them by foreign embassies, local and international human rights groups, and local labor recruitment agencies, in recent years the Kuwaiti state has developed a somewhat more robust role in the transnational domestic work sector. It has passed a series of laws stipulating a minimum wage for domestic workers, mandatory trilingual contracts, the regulation of labor recruitment agencies, the expedition of legal cases, the establishment of shelters and very recently, in 2015, the passing of a law giving domestic workers enforceable labor rights.

South Asian labor-sending countries have also played an attenuated role in the transnational domestic work sector, particularly at the beginning of the sector's development. In interviews and reports, state officials and institutions attributed their limited involvement to their limited capacity, explaining that state institutions have historically been more concerned, and effective, in regulating the entry, rather than the exit, of populations from their territories. The wide-scale migration of South Asian domestic workers to the Gulf also coincided with the implementation of structural adjustment policies that led to the dismantling of South Asian labor-sending countries' state institutions— rendering these states less able to intervene. Although technically accurate, as Silvey has discussed with respect to the Indonesian case,[86] these explanations do not account for how South Asian states systematically deprioritize the needs and concerns of marginalized populations—most notably, working-class women—in their policies and practices. Otherwise put, South Asian states' lack of involvement in the migrant domestic work sector reflects gendered and classed priorities, not just their limited capacities.

As the scale and importance of migrant domestic workers' remittances became clear, and as news media and foreign embassies' reports of the workers' experiences of abuse and exploitation became more widespread, South Asian labor-sending countries increasingly began to develop policies and procedures to regulate the transnational migrant domestic work sector. The most widespread response of South Asian states has been to impose restrictions or outright bans on the migration of women who are seeking employment as domestic workers in Kuwait and the other GCC states.[87] These restrictions and bans may have assuaged public opinion, but have proved grossly ineffective in stemming the outmigration of domestic workers from South Asia. It is worth noting that although male migrants have also experienced harsh and exploitative conditions, they have not been similarly subject to such bans.[88] The restrictions placed on women's mobility are undergirded by gendered logics: women are often depicted as being weak and defenseless, the symbols of the nation's honor in need of protection, and the state is depicted as a benevolent patriarch seeking to protect women.[89] Contrary to their intended purposes, these restrictions have rendered South Asian migrant domestic workers vulnerable to *further* exploitation and abuse. Women from these countries have continued to migrate to Kuwait and other countries in the Gulf region, and have done so by traveling via other countries (e.g., Indian women traveled through Sri Lanka, Nepali and Bangladeshi women through India). Ironically, labor migration restrictions or bans have made the actions of these women "illegal" in relation to their home country governments and embassies abroad. Many domestic workers have thus found themselves in situations of being legal migrants in Kuwait (in relation to the Kuwaiti laws) but being *illegally present in relation to their home embas-*

sies and conationals in Kuwait. Rendered illegal in this way, domestic workers had no recourse to their embassies, which previously had constituted a significant if not primary line of assistance to redress problems they encountered in Kuwait.[90]

South Asian state institutions began to recognize that labor migration restrictions and bans were not only ineffective but also compounding the difficulties experienced by domestic workers. They also became increasingly aware of the importance of migrant domestic workers' remittances to their national economies.[91] These realizations led policy makers to begin to change their approach. State institutions and embassy officials became increasingly involved in regulating the industry, including monitoring and policing labor agencies (both in their own countries and the GCC), and passing laws that detail the contract stipulations for hiring domestic workers. In order to recruit domestic workers, Kuwaiti labor agencies need to submit job orders to the labor-sending country's embassy in Kuwait. This order is then processed by the embassy, and sent to the labor and/or foreign affairs ministries in the labor-sending country. If a Kuwaiti labor agency is found to be remiss (e.g., there are a lot of complaints and legal cases filed against it; it does not redress problems experienced by domestic workers), embassy officials will deny the agency's future job order requests. Labor-sending countries' embassies further stipulated that domestic workers and their employers should register and file their documents (i.e., contracts, copy of passport and visas) at the embassy. Embassies also began establishing and formalizing subdivisions and procedures to counsel and address problems experienced by migrant domestic workers abroad. The labor ministries and foreign affairs ministries of labor-sending countries were also instrumental in passing laws stipulating contract terms for migrant domestic workers.[92]

The resources allocated by South Asian labor-sending countries to safeguard their conationals and enforce these contract stipulations vary widely. While I was conducting research, the most effective was the Indian Consulate, which had statistical reports about the composition of its citizenry in Kuwait, and offered a range of services to its nationals, including in-country orientation sessions, legal support, and financial advice. At the other end of the spectrum was the Nepalese government, which did not have an embassy or consulate in Kuwait despite having a significant number of its nationals present in the country.[93] In the early to mid-2000s, the largest group of domestic workers migrating to Kuwait was Nepali women, who had no access to their state institutions while in the country. The administrative, bureaucratic, and governance problems that developed in relation to Nepali domestic workers became so widespread that in the absence of official state representation, the Kuwaiti government in what was then an unprecedented move banned Nepali women's in-migration to Kuwait from 2007 to 2008, until a consulate was finally established in the country.[94]

Although states from both the labor-sending states of South Asia and the labor-receiving countries of the Gulf have become more directly involved in regulating the transnational migrant domestic work sector in recent years, on the whole their involvement has been limited. These states have not simply ignored or overlooked the migrant domestic work sector. Rather, states' labor-migration bans; labor laws; priorities masquerading as capacities; and portrayal of the household as a purportedly private, "sacrosanct" space all point to the gendered ways states are engaged but disavow their involvement with the migrant domestic work sector. The gendered ways this sector comes in and out of focus by South Asian labor-sending states and Gulf labor-receiving states have made the transnational migrant domestic work sector a fluid sector in which informal and formal mechanisms of adjudication and governance are intertwined, and in which the groups who are often the source of difficulties encountered by domestic workers are the very groups who are tasked with the regulation and governance of these migrant women. These gendered aporias place domestic workers in an uncertain and a liminal position in relation to juridicopolitical systems—a precarious condition that further compounds their experiences of temporariness in Kuwait.

The Temporariness of Reproduction

To celebrate Geeti's thirtieth year of working for her family, Mama Lulua organized a gathering at her home. The affair, Geeti told me several years later, was "simple and classy." Tea was served, as were samosas, biscuits, and finely decorated miniature cakes from Geeti's favorite Lebanese bakery. Seeing her friends, distant relatives, and Mama Lulua's family members seated around the drawing room, sipping tea and exchanging pleasantries had been a peculiar if not surreal experience for Geeti:

Strange seeing everyone there like that . . .

I remember thinking . . .
I have been here [Kuwait] so long

I kept thinking . . . before I mean . . . many years before
I'll go back [to India] soon,

and then again I thought soon,
soon I'll go back . . .
But I did not. I never did.

I could have never thought
That this, this has been my life
I could have never thought . . .
[*shakes head and laughs quietly*] . . . still can't quite think of it

Seems strange . . .
Their lives [*gestures to the floor, indicating Mama Lulua's house*]
Their lives [*gestures outward, indicating relatives outside and away*] . . .
And then, this life here [*lightly slaps her thigh to indicate herself*]
I'm with them, but this [*lightly touches her leg to indicate herself*] is not the
same

To Geeti, the tea party celebrating her thirtieth year of working for Mama
Lulua's family in Kuwait was not simply an expression of her attachment to
Mama Lulua's family, her connection to Kuwait, or her longing to return to
India. It underlined something altogether more subtle, more unsettling, more
difficult to explain. Seeing the different people she was close to—friends,
distant relatives, her employers—mingling across ethnonational and occupational lines, a rarity in Kuwait, in a room that she ordinarily would be cleaning
or serving in, but was being celebrated in that day, gave her a sharp sense of
the strange, seemingly incongruous nature of her life. The gathering reminded
her of how years before she had expected to return to India, but instead, in
the continuous interim of being in Kuwait—where she has been a part of the
lives of both Mama Lulua's family and her own family in India—she has lived a
life that is "not the same," a life she "could have never thought," and "still can't
quite think."

Geeti's utterances index a broader set of sociohistorical processes characterizing migrant domestic workers' experiences, ones pointing to the interrelation
of temporariness and reproduction. With characteristic restraint and modesty,
her comments about being "with" Mama Lulua's household and her family's
household in India allude to how she has been vital to them both. Through her
work, relations, affect, personality, and earnings, Geeti has been essential to
the everyday functioning of Mama Lulua's household and the raising of Mama
Lulua's family and, at the same time, to the everyday provisioning of her family
members in India, and to supporting her sisters and brothers, and then nieces
and nephews through their school, college, and weddings. Dual agents of

reproduction, migrant domestic workers such as Geeti have been integral to the ongoing reproduction of citizens, households, and sociopolitical bodies in the countries they migrate to and migrate from.

Yet as dual agents of reproduction, domestic workers such as Geeti live lives that they, and others, find difficult to "think." A central reason their lives are difficult to acknowledge and appreciate is that these migrant women are assumed to be living in ways that are temporary. South Asian domestic workers are understood, and treated as though, they are working abroad in Kuwait for short durations of time, after which they will return back to the families and communities where they belong—to their "real" lives. This discourse not only elides the assemblage of practices, policies, groups, and institutions that produce South Asian domestic workers' temporariness. As detailed in this chapter, domestic workers are subject to an array of processes that produce them as a temporary population in Kuwait, including Kuwait's citizenship regime, kafala system, and these migrant women's precarious position as part of Kuwait's transnational domestic work sector. This discourse also obfuscates how rather than being a function of their dislocation, migrant domestic workers' temporariness is a necessary condition that produces their position as dual agents of reproduction. Domestic workers' temporariness does not simply reflect their being in a liminal position between their family households and work households, between South Asia and Kuwait. Their temporariness ensures their pivotal role in the dual production and reproduction of citizens, families, households, and ethnonational forms in both South Asia and the Gulf. It is only when we begin to account for how their temporariness is produced by broader sociopolitical factors such as the ones discussed in this chapter, and are not the natural outcome of their migration, that we can begin to discern, document, and describe their lives.

TWO

SUSPENSION

My house is there and I live here
Both places are sometimes my home
—Mary/Maryam

So much has happened to them [family in India],
they have done a great deal
while I am here, just working, just working,
day after day, same-same.
—Phoolan

Life, it cannot happen like that;
for us it is difficult,
for us it is not possible.
We help, we watch,
we stay in between.
—Geeti/Gertrude

A Part Yet Apart

Sleep-blinkered, Nadia rolled over in bed. The movie she fell asleep watching had long since ended, leaving a blank screen in its wake, one casting the room in a faint, flickering blue glow. In snatches of drowse and focus, Nadia slowly registered that something was amiss. The room was too still, too silent. She peered around looking for her sister. Hajira's bed was rumpled, but no toes peeked out from under the blankets, and no curls framed the edges of the sheets or trailed down the side of the bed—telltale signs her sister had wandered off during the night.

Muttering lightly under her breath, Nadia roused herself out of bed. After checking to see if Hajira had fallen out of her bed and fallen back asleep on the floor, she headed to the bathroom. Three years old, Hajira insisted she was old enough to go to the bathroom on her own, but in the wee hours of the morning she was prone to falling asleep there. Her sister was not in the bathroom, so Nadia quietly checked her parents' room. Hajira wasn't there either. Now joined by her mother, they checked Asad, their brother's room, the family room, the office—but found no sign of Hajira. Hearts racing and thoughts quickening with concern, they made their way down the stairs to the ground floor, where they noticed the kitchen door was ajar. Hajira was not there, nor was she in the adjoining laundry room, the hallway, or the small sitting room. The door to the room of their domestic worker, Phoolan, however, had been opened. Inside, on a bed stripped of its sheets, lay Hajira. Cheeks smudged with tears, she had fallen asleep there.

The next day, when they called Phoolan, they also found her in tears. "I was not expecting that," commented Dalal, Phoolan's employer and Hajira and Nadia's mother. Later in conversation Dalal elaborated:

DALAL: She [Phoolan] has not been to India for a visit in over 10 years. Her son is now finishing school, but Phoolan told me she wanted to come back [to Kuwait].
I said: you have not been home for so long, maybe you should wait.
I said: I will call back again tomorrow, and then tomorrow after that.
If you want us to, we will book you on an earlier flight back . . .
Then she spoke with Hajira on the phone for almost an hour.
AA: What did they talk about?
DALAL: Nothing really. Hajira, spoiled child (laughs) told her she has to come back. She asked her: when are you coming back home? She then told her about the movie she watched last night with Nadia. How she and Nadia had eaten their breakfast together this morning, but that her sister would not cut her apple in small pieces like she [Phoolan] does.

Perhaps more than any other story told to me, more than any other occasion that I witnessed, Hajira and Phoolan's temporary parting underscores a crucial feature of South Asian domestic workers' experiences in the Gulf. Despite the assemblage of historical processes, exclusionary discourses of national citizenship, citizen-devolved systems of sponsorship and governance, and transnational domestic work sector that define and discipline domestic workers into a temporary population, Hajira and Phoolan's story both belies yet looms with the expectation that domestic workers such as Phoolan constitute a temporary presence in Kuwait. Their story points to how migrant domestic workers have become an intimate and inextricable part of everyday life in Kuwait, and how many develop intimate connections in the face of deeply hierarchical relations with their employers.

The story of Phoolan and Hajira indexes the complex forms of relationships South Asian domestic workers develop in the Gulf, ones complicating our understanding of migrant domestic workers' transnational belongings. Their experiences contrast with Rhacel Parrenas's important and influential account of Filipina migrant domestic workers. Based on comparative research conducted in Los Angeles and Rome, Parrenas argues that the "dislocation of nonbelonging"[1] characterizes migrant domestic workers' transnational experiences. In her analysis, Parrenas discusses how multiple forms of gendered, raced, and classed oppression shape domestic workers' dislocation, which in turn produces their social exclusion or "nonbelonging."[2] Phoolan and other South Asian migrant domestic workers' experiences in the Gulf point to a different dynamic. Rather than the "dislocation of nonbelonging,"[3] these migrant women are subject to a number of everyday forms of interrelations, disciplining, and governance that produce their "suspended belongings" between South Asia and Kuwait, a position that produces and consolidates their role as dual agents of reproduction, and engenders forms of everyday conversion. South Asian migrant domestic workers are subject to intense, hierarchical gendered, raced (ethnonationalized), aged, and classed processes that shape how they both belong to, and are suspended between, their family and work households and between South Asia and the Gulf. Rather than marking their exclusion or "nonbelonging," the asymmetrical power relations that South Asian migrant domestic workers are subject to articulate the ways they are interrelated and integral to these transnational spaces. Here, belongings do not preclude hierarchical power relations, and are not premised on equality or egalitarianism. Reframing South Asian migrant domestic workers' experiences in this way provides a more capacious conceptual space to examine how in the face of (not despite) intensely asymmetrical gendered, raced and classed relations, migrant domestic workers develop complex, multilayered forms of affinities and belongings, everyday conversions not reducible to the binary logic of inclusion/exclusion, or to familial or ethnonational forms. Close examination reveals how the activities and relations that constitute migrant domestic workers' work do not just mark these women's exclusion, but how they are articulated into suspended forms of asymmetrical connections and belongings marked by everyday conversions.

Migrant domestic workers' presence suffuses everyday landscapes in Kuwait. When visiting a Kuwaiti or well-heeled foreign residents' home, domestic workers are usually the ones who answer the door and bring refreshments. Go to one of Kuwait's many bustling shopping malls and you will see domestic workers trailing behind their employers, laden with shopping bags or shepherding stray children. On walks in residential areas you will see domestic workers sweeping driveways, taking out the garbage, cleaning cars, or surreptitiously chatting or flirting with neighborhood domestic workers and drivers. Domestic workers often accompany their invalid employers to hospitals, tending to them and spending the night, sometimes even for weeks on end. During a charity walk-a-thon, I even spotted domestic workers alongside their employers, carrying water bottles.

For Hajira, the presence of domestic workers in Kuwait took on a specific and highly personalized cast—in the form of her relationship with Phoolan. Hired shortly after Hajira was born to look after her, Phoolan was the one who prepared breakfast for Hajira and her older brother and sister, who helped her get dressed, and, until she started playschool, whom Hajira spent her day with while the rest of the family was at school and work. Until Phoolan left to visit her family in India, she had been a fixed and constant presence in Hajira's life. Not being able to remember a time without Phoolan, and never having experienced her world without her, Hajira made her way to the one place in her home where she could both register and express her sense of loss at Phoolan's temporary absence.

Phoolan's own experience of their parting was also telling. Like many other domestic workers, she had migrated to Kuwait expecting to stay for one or two contract cycles. Initially she worked within the household of a prosperous Lebanese family. When her employer moved to Dubai, she decided to stay in Kuwait, where she found work in a beauty salon. There she met Dalal, a Kuwaiti woman with whom she developed a good rapport and who eventually hired her to look after her newborn daughter. What Phoolan had envisioned as a two, maybe four-year stay in Kuwait extended indefinitely, and her return "home" to her family members in India was postponed several times. In the weeks before her first visit back after ten years, Phoolan shared her excitement and trepidation about seeing her family again:

> "Varshan [her son], he has finished his high-schooling, and will start his college in the fall . . .

Madu, my sister who I told you about before, she has given birth three
times, three babies I haven't seen yet . . .

And my parents, they are old but they started cooking and selling
foods to shops in the neighborhood. . . .

So much has happened to them, they have done a great deal
while I am here, just working, just working, day after day, same-same.

When Phoolan returned to visit her family in India, the experience upset
and shocked her. Not only did she feel awkward and estranged from her family,
but she also missed Hajira and Dalal's family acutely, leading her (at least initially) to want to end her visit early. Rather than a return "home" and respite
from work, her visit to India confronted her with a messier reality, a scrambling
of deeply held assumptions about her most intimate relationships and expectations she had about her life trajectory.

Like other domestic workers, Phoolan often scripted her migration experiences in linear terms: she would come to the Gulf region for a short, delimited
period of time; work and save her earnings; and eventually return back to the
family and community to which she belonged. This script is one fostered and
actively produced by the region's migration system and domestic work sector.
It is also one shared by domestic workers and their families. Yet their experiences
of migration prove to be more complicated. As Nicole Constable argues, domestic workers develop ambivalent feelings and misgivings about returning
"home," becoming both "at home but not at home" in the places they migrate
to and from.[4] Based on ethnographic research conducted on Filipina domestic
workers in Hong Kong, Constable provides a comprehensive and nuanced discussion of different factors that account for this phenomenon.[5] She touches on
constraints and difficulties migrant domestic workers experience at "home";
the personal, social and economic possibilities entailed by their migration; and
changing tastes, sense of self, and preferred lifestyles that develop through their
migration experiences. South Asian migrant domestic workers' experiences in
Kuwait resonate strongly with Constable's discussion, and complement her
analysis by foregrounding the importance of domestic workers' everyday work,
interactions, and relationships with members of their employers' household as
sites in and through which their suspended belongings or being at home yet
not at home are produced. Although South Asian migrant domestic workers
are subject to deeply hierarchical relations with their employers, this did not
preclude them from developing affectionate and caring relations with them.
Many developed deeply wrought and fraught relationships with members of
their Kuwaiti, or "work," households. These relationships did not necessarily

lead them to shift their sense of connection and belonging from their "family" households in India to their "work" households in Kuwait. Rather, it engendered a different dynamic and temporality of connection and affinity, one in which their expectations and experiences of temporariness stretched into a related, yet different temporal horizon: one of unsettling suspension marked by everyday conversions.

Domestic workers' daily activities and relations are tethered to household and heteronormative family spaces of Gulf citizens and wealthy foreign residents, a sociospatial configuration that produces a particular set of diasporic experiences. Although all noncitizens are subject to processes that produce their conditions of temporariness in the region, different groups develop distinct forms of diasporic belonging in relation to how they are articulated into the sociospatial landscapes of the Gulf. Middle- and upper-middle class foreign residents, who are in a position to sponsor and support their family members, set up independent households. Many have established a multigenerational presence in the region, and in the absence of de jure citizenship, have carved out alternative de facto forms of citizenship articulated through their establishment of bustling neighborhoods and businesses, consumer practices, pageants and other large-scale community events, and informal networks of commerce and governance.[6] The forms of belonging these groups develop fall along ethnonational lines. Whether in Kuwait City, Dubai or Doha, they establish households that are "Pakistani," "Indian," or "Malayali" in nature—traditions of cuisines, dressing, and etiquette, and family and gender relations practiced in their households are understood and discussed in ethnonational terms. These groups tend to socialize with fellow ethnonationals, send their children to schools set up along ethnonational lines, and spend their annual summer holidays in their "home" countries, a designation given to countries in which they hold citizenship but do not reside permanently. Their reconstitution and consolidation of ethnonational forms in a transnational milieu are facilitated by state policies that encourage their remittances and investments in their "home" countries.

Working-class foreign residents—typically referred to as migrant workers, bachelor workers or lady workers—live in more marginalized circumstances. These groups have fewer options with respect to their living accommodations, which are usually arranged by their employers. The majority resides in dormitories, labor camps, or refurbished apartments that are located on the peripheries of residential areas and urban centers. Their living accommodations are organized along gendered lines, and although comprising noncitizens of a plurality of different backgrounds, clusters of ethnonational groups form in rooms and living spaces.[7] Separated from their families, these foreign residents develop transnational forms of communication (e.g., letters, telephone calls), cyclical travel, and patterns of sending remittances and goods, through which they maintain their relationships and belongings to their family members and communities at "home." Many anticipate returning home eventually or, with a move to more lucrative employment opportunities, being in a position to eventually sponsor their family members to join them in the region.

In different ways and transnational modalities, foreign residents' patterns of residence reproduce ethnonational forms, ones anchored by family networks and buttressed by state policies. Domestic workers' experiences are both similar and strikingly different from those of other foreign residents and migrants. Like middle- and upper-middle-class foreign residents, domestic workers reside within and reproduce conventional familial and household forms, yet they do so in the homes of Gulf nationals and foreign residents of different ethnonational backgrounds (in Kuwait and most other countries of the GCC, foreign residents cannot sponsor domestic workers of similar national backgrounds). Through their everyday work and sociospatially located as they are, domestic workers are integral to the everyday social reproduction of other ethnonational groups in the Gulf region. At the same time, they develop and are sites of everyday conversion through which alternative connections and affinities develop. As pointed to by Phoolan's experiences, Hajira's sense of being a Kuwaiti has developed in relation to her intimate connection with Phoolan. Phoolan's work is integral to Dalal's maintenance of a well-run Kuwaiti household, to the social reproduction of Dalal and her family, and to Dalal's family's sense of themselves as citizens in relation to the country's foreign migrant and resident population. Yet Phoolan's work with the family, as poignantly illustrated by Hajira's response when Phoolan left to visit her family in India, also fosters intimate connections and affinities across ethnonational lines. Through their work and sociospatial positions, domestic workers thus reproduce *and* also cut across familial and ethnonational divisions that are the cornerstone of the intensely hierarchical sociopolitical systems of governance in the Gulf region.

Domestic workers' migration experiences are profoundly liminal in nature, positioned as they are between their "family" and "work" households. Like other working-class foreign residents, they live apart from yet also sustain and provision their family members in their countries of origin. Their work is integral to the social reproduction and maintenance of both their family and work households, enabling those within these households to "do a great deal" and "live" as Phoolan and Geeti stated (see chapter 1). As the lives of their family and work household members unfold and develop—as they finish school, get married, have children—domestic workers often characterize their own lives in Kuwait in terms of a different type of life trajectory: what Phoolan and Geeti described as "just working, just working," and "helping and watching." Many perceive the type of life that is possible for others in their family and work households to be postponed for them. They instead describe their lives in terms of sacrifice and deferral: constituted by the work that is necessary so that others' lives may unfold and develop, and hopefully, eventually, their own lives as well. Similar to discourses and assemblages that discipline them into temporariness in the Gulf region, this understanding of their lives as suspended elides and glosses over a range of connections, intimacies and belongings they develop, ones constituting everyday forms of conversions, alternative trajectories of living that is not legible or considered legitimate where nuclear, heteronormative families that anchor ethnonational belongings are the hegemonic norm.

This chapter maps out different aspects of domestic workers' experiences of suspension and everyday conversions. My interlocutors consistently discussed their migration experiences through the everyday register of their shifting family and household relations. By recounting their migration stories, and tacking back and forth between their relations with members of their family and work households, I analyze the factors that produce their suspended belongings between, and the lives marked by forms of everyday conversions they have carved out in these spaces. Their stories weave together a dense tangle of issues—impoverishment, family tragedies and illnesses, new consumer tastes and class aspirations, social mobility and stymied opportunities in their home communities—that animate their move to Kuwait, and their suspended stay in the country. In Kuwait, many domestic workers developed unexpectedly close bonds with members of their work households, a dynamic of being a part of yet apart from their work households. Alongside their employers' policing of their activities, this dynamic effectively tethers domestic workers' social relations and intimacies to their family and to their work households, shaping the affinities, connections, and belongings they develop in and through these spaces.

Economic Routes

By far the most common reason domestic workers migrate to Kuwait is their families' straitened economic circumstances. Like others of the global South, their situations of impoverishment index histories of colonial resource extraction and exploitation, state-led development schemes that systematically exclude or worsen the socioeconomic situation of marginalized peoples and places of the subcontinent, inequitable global trade systems, structural adjustment programs, changes in economic systems including shifts from subsistence and redistributive systems to market-based ones, and gendered and classed educational and economic policies that deprioritize the concerns and needs of marginalized groups. These sociohistorical processes permeated the lives of domestic workers and their families in ways that made their everyday lives that much more of a struggle. These were often narrated to me in terms of cause and consequence: the rising cost of flour and lentils leading to slimmer meals, the loss of jobs leading to crushing debts and the move to cramped *bastis* (impoverished neighborhoods or slums), and higher school fees leading children to be taken out of school and put into trades earlier than hoped for. For many domestic workers, their economic precariousness was further compounded by personal tragedies, most notably, the deaths or illnesses of family members. Mary/Maryam's situation is illustrative.

Mary, or Maryam as she would insist on being called twenty-seven years after moving to Kuwait, a change coming about with her adoption to Islam, was the most punctilious of my interlocutors.[8] We first met in a *Salat wa Tah'ara* (prayer and purification) class at the Islamic Dawa movement's women's center. Sitting next to her in one of the chairs that ringed our classroom, I remember glancing at her notebook and being struck by her manner of taking notes. Each page was laid out in bands and blocks, columns and paragraphs so precise as to be geometric in their arrangement. Mary/Maryam opened up a similar notebook several weeks later when I visited her at her home. It was our first formal interview, which she had prepared for by writing out, in neat English, a chronology of important events in her life. For the next hour she recited them to me, and I—as she clearly expected me to do—duly recorded these in my own notebook.

They included the following:

September 14, 1949:	birth in N****
[name of the village]
January 8, 1950:	family moved to L****
[home community]
March 20, 1961:	Baba-ji accident in L****
[home community]
July 23, 1968:	leave Bombay
August 4, 1968:	arrive Kuwait
May 8, 1972:	marriage of Agnes [her sister]
June 23, 1974:	marriage of Sara [her sister]

Over the course of subsequent meetings, I asked Mary/Maryam to further describe these moments to me. Judging from her lengthy pause and quizzical expression, she was surprised at first—as surprised, no doubt, as I was by her chronology—but graciously accommodated my queries. Her responses were crisp and concise, focusing on recounting as accurately as she could important circumstances and activities related to these events. Rarely did she linger over details, or speak about—much less speculate over—what she and others felt and thought. There was a spare, elegant rhythm to her narration, a rhythm that was only occasionally disrupted or extended.

One such exception related to "July 23, 1968: leave Bombay," her first journey to Kuwait. The tales she told related to this event, and in the act of retelling, interwove details that were tantalizingly evocative. During our conversations Mary/Maryam repeatedly (amid sighs and pauses) mentioned how exhausted she had been that morning when she boarded the steamship. Bypassing the bustle of fellow passengers who were watching the port, then city, then harbor slip steadily and inexorably into the Indian Ocean, she made her way to the prow of the boat. Finding a nook where she could safely lay down her suitcase and sit for a while, she gazed out at the seemingly limitless expanse of glittering water. The respite was sorely needed. The weeks before had been busy and dizzying, drawing heavily on abilities and connections she had cultivated since "March 20, 1961: Baba-ji accident in L**** [home community]."

On that day, her father, a mason, was in the midst of unloading a truck full of building supplies when a large crate of bricks fell upon him, crushing both his legs. Upon his return to work six months later, the bones and muscles of his legs had ostensibly mended; however, Mary/Maryam's father found standing for extended periods of time excruciating and ultimately impossible. He was unable to sustain long-term work. With no steady source of income, the doctor's bills, the cost of medicines, the children's school fees, and the household's everyday expenses mounted and mounted. Mary/Maryam's family soon found themselves in spiraling debt.

Her parents were at a loss. Eleven years earlier, after converting to Catholicism, and finding their village no longer a hospitable place to live, Mary/Maryam's family moved to a village in the south, several hours outside of Bombay, with a thriving Christian community. In the face of her father's disability, their neighbors and church members proved sympathetic, and provided them with much needed support; however, long term the family had little recourse. Not having any familial or close enough relationships within the community, they had no access to ongoing means of support. As Mary/Maryam put it to me: "Our relationships there were not deep. A lot of care/concern was not possible."

To support her family, Mary/Maryam's mother began cleaning the homes of wealthy residents residing in their village and in the surrounding districts.

The amount she earned was a pittance—far too meager to even cover the family's everyday expenses. It thus fell to Mary/Maryam, the eldest of the three daughters, to help support the family. At the age of eleven she stopped attending school and through church contacts was placed with a well-to-do Christian household in Bombay. There she worked as a live-in servant, under the tutelage of a housekeeper and butler, stern taskmasters who brooked no insubordination. Mary/Maryam's life consisted of "shughl! kaam! work!"[9] These demands were interspersed with her mother's periodic visits on the weekend and, two or three times a year, short trips home when she could play with her sisters in the open fields.

Years passed, and although Mary/Maryam's wages were sufficient to cover the family's everyday expenses, with her sisters' school graduations and possible weddings looming, she and her mother began looking into alternate ways for her to earn additional money. Her uncle Bobby suggested she consider finding work in Kuwait. The only member of Mary/Maryam's extended family to maintain relations with her parents after they had converted to Catholicism, Uncle Bobby had experiences that both paralleled and starkly contrasted with that of her own parents. Like her father, Uncle Bobby learned masonry skills, and he too decided to move from their village in the North, a place where as part of a scheduled caste, he felt it would be impossible for him to prosper. Rather than moving to the village his sister and brother-in-law lived in, he decided to ply his trade in Bombay, and further afield in Bahrain and Kuwait from the mid-1960s onward. While abroad, he heard through other migrants that there were families in the Arab Gulf states seeking to hire maids from India, a fact he relayed to his sister and niece during his next visit home.

Mary/Maryam began to make inquiries and soon learned of a family residing in her employer's neighborhood with connections to Kuwait. The husband was from a Kuwaiti merchant family with long-standing ties to Bombay. Dubbed the "Bombay Kuwaiti-wallah" by Mary/Maryam, he kept a home in Bombay, where his second wife, a Hyderabadi woman, and their children lived. He himself only resided in Bombay during the summers, and when next he came, Mary/Maryam and her father went to see him and ask for his assistance. He told them of a respectable Kuwaiti family—a distributor with whom he worked, in need of a maid—and he helped Mary/Maryam establish correspondence with them in Arabic. After Mary/Maryam agreed to terms with the family, Mary/Maryam's mother came to town to help her prepare for her trip. They had a passport made, went to the Kuwaiti consulate to undergo screening and obtain a visa, and finally, dipping into the family's limited funds, Mary/Maryam and her mother went on several excursions to the bazaar, where they haggled down the prices for a small used suitcase, serviceable clothing, sturdy sandals, a brush, hairpins, and a glittering sari and delicate glass bangles for special occasions. Never before had Mary/Maryam purchased so much. Both before and during her ten-day voyage she kept a vigilant eye on her suitcase full of goods, and occasionally, when she thought no one was looking, she cracked it open long enough to peer at, or gently finger, the fabrics inside. Hard-earned through years of work and saving, they were the only tangible links she had of a home rapidly receding with every roll and sway of her ship. Her newly bought goods also carried with them refrains of her mother's counsel of how she should care for them, and how she should comport herself among the *Arab-lawg* (people), with whom she would now be living.

When I first met Mary/Maryam, she had been living and working with the same extended Kuwaiti family for almost forty years. Like other domestic workers and foreign residents, she initially thought her stay would be temporary; that at the most, she would be working in Kuwait for a few years. Yet every time she started to consider returning to India, there was always something necessitating her stay in Kuwait. The economic needs of her family—the ongoing need to support her parents, her sisters' dowries, fees for her father's back surgery, a bad harvest, repairs and renovations to their house, the death of one of her sister's husbands—stretched into a never-ending horizon of two-year contract cycles leading her to return again and again to Kuwait, and in the cycles of pay and remittances, of work and visits, to remain suspended between both places.

Other Connections and Affections

Mary/Maryam's decision to stay in Kuwait was also informed by her deepening connection with Fardous and other members of her "work" household. Although intensely hierarchical, her relations with her employers had become increasingly close, evident in her position in their household and in the care and consideration they showed toward her. In the mid-2000s, Mary/Maryam was effectively retired from work, yet she remained a fixture of Fardous's household. Mary/Maryam had suffered from numerous health ailments in the years prior, including liver and knee problems, all of which necessitated surgery and extensive physical rehabilitation that Fardous and her family had financed. Largely token in nature, her work consisted of occasionally assisting with the cooking, and coordinating the work of the other domestic workers in the household. When the family moved into their new home, they built Mary/Maryam a small wing—consisting of a bedroom, a small sitting room, and a bathroom—where she could live out the remainder of her days.

Although extremely close—certainly among the closest that I witnessed or heard of while I was conducting research—like those of other domestic workers, Mary/Maryam's relations were characterized by the dynamic of being a part of yet apart from Fardous's family. Mary/Maryam's life was interwoven into her employers' family history and ongoing functioning, yet her belonging was itself predicated on particular forms of hierarchical relations and exclusions. This dynamic of being a part of yet apart from, of hierarchy and connection, of both belonging and exclusion is produced through relations of sponsorship and governance discussed in the previous chapter. It also develops through everyday forms of othering and domestic workers' familial-like relations yet exclusion from kinship ties with their employers.

South Asian domestic workers are assumed to be and produced as "other" through their everyday activities and relations in their Kuwaiti work households.[10] Both domestic workers and their employers articulated the differences between themselves in two registers—culture and class-occupation. They highlighted how as South Asians and Kuwaitis, they differed in terms of their customs, ways of thinking, and traditions. They also pointed to their occupational and sociopolitical status differences—as domestic worker/chatelaine, employee/employer, migrant/sponsor, noncitizen/citizen. These bases of differentiation were often conflated and treated interchangeably, a feature of everyday discourse in Kuwait in which occupations were often pegged to ethnonational groups.[11] Some of my interlocutors described this as Kuwait's ethno-occupational totem pole, or a microcosm of the global division of wealth and labor. These differences—culture and class-occupation—were often discussed as fixed markers, in ways that glossed over the historical processes and everyday practices through which they have been and continue to be produced. Otherwise put, these bases of differentiation are relational and dynamic, produced and reproduced through everyday interactions, activities, and practices in the household. For example, domestic workers wore different styles of clothing,[12] rarely ate with their employers, often exhibited a discrete and cautious demeanor, and while they resided within the same household, their rooms were often at a remove from family members—everyday practices that did not simply express but also produced hierarchized differences between them.

Through their work, migrant domestic workers are not only involved in the social reproduction of Kuwaiti subjects and households, but they are also sites through which existing bases of hierarchical differences between citizens and noncitizens are produced and consolidated. Their activities, interactions, and interrelations with Kuwaitis do not simply reflect, but are the very sites through which they produce class-occupational and ethnonational differences on an everyday, intimate basis. Through domestic workers' work, Kuwaitis come to see, experience, and enact their positions of privilege—as sponsors, employers, and patrons and through the synecdochical linking of domestic workers to migrants and foreign residents as a whole, where they come to see noncitizens as their dependents and servants.

Geeti's experiences with Mama Lulua's extended family points to the stakes involved in "othering" South Asian domestic workers for some Kuwaiti families. Geeti's migration, like that of Mary/Maryam's, had been facilitated by her employers' long-term trading and kinship connections in India. In Geeti's case these connections were personal and immediate: her grandmother had worked as a cook for Mama Lulua's mother in India, and her uncle had worked as a driver for Mama Lulua's uncle in Kuwait. When I first learned about their families' transnational history of interrelations, I had assumed Geeti's hiring had been a relatively simple affair, smoothed by two generations of their families' connections, and by what I assumed would be commonalties and continuities stemming from their shared history. For Mama Lulua, however, this was precisely the problem. Geeti's coming had the potential to unsettle the work of "being properly Kuwaiti" she had begun since her family's resettlement back into Kuwait in the 1940s. Then a child, she found herself consistently at a disadvantage in a sociopolitical context in which being Kuwaiti was increasingly being articulated in Arabized and exclusionary terms. The burden of being properly Kuwaiti fell particularly hard on the women in her family. For her father, his connections to India and his ability to speak Hindi facilitated his development of a food and logistics business spanning the Middle East and South Asia (including the import-export of rice, which he would gift to people under his family's employment, including Geeti's uncle). For her mother, however, traces of her "Indianness" alienated and placed her at a "lower rung" vis-à-vis other branches of her extended family. For Mama Lulua, her association with India exposed her to her cousins' teasing and schoolyard taunts that she was "foreign." Subsequently married to a "properly" Arab Kuwaiti, a member of her extended family whose branch had previously resided in Basra, and the chatelaine of a burgeoning household requiring a domestic worker, Mama Lulua had initially hoped to hire a "houseboy" from Yemen and, in so doing, to continue to consolidate her household's Arab character. She found, however, that hiring a Yemeni houseboy was no longer a possibility, which led her to hire Geeti, albeit reluctantly. In the following decades, the two developed a lasting bond; however, early on during Geeti's hiring, Mama Lulua was at pains to ensure that Geeti's "cultural" difference did not influence the character and functioning of her household. Although members of her family were familiar with Hindi/

Urdu, she insisted that Geeti either speak Arabic or English at home, she encouraged Geeti to wear trousers and other Western-style clothing, and she instructed Geeti to cook foods suitable for Kuwaiti palates, by which she meant foods that were not heavily spiced. With strong connections to South Asia, ones she assiduously sought to dissociate herself from, Mama Lulua not only enacted being "properly" Kuwaiti through a myriad of practices that suffused her life and that of her family; she also enacted being properly Kuwaiti through her disciplining of Geeti's speech, dressing and comportment, while simultaneously depicting herself (and her family) in contradistinction to Geeti's "Indianness."

Mary/Maryam's relations with members of her work household differed significantly from those of Geeti. Her relations with Baba Ibrahim and Mama Alia were experienced in terms of "cultural" and "occupational" overlaps and disjunctures that were initially not easily reduced to stark, binary differences. Unlike Mama Lulua's family and the Bombay Kuwait-wallah, Baba Ibrahim and Mama Alia were from a family with little family or trade connections outside Kuwait City, and they were (at least in the 1960s) of more modest means. Mary/Maryam immediately registered this when she disembarked at Kuwait's port. As she recounted to me many years later, when she first met Baba Ibrahim and Mama Alia she was initially quite disappointed with them. Although kindly, Baba Ibrahim was different from what she was expecting. As Mary/Maryam explained:

> I don't know what I had been thinking, I thought . . . He wasn't big, he wasn't an emir [leader or royal figure] like the Bombay Kuwaiti-wallah. He wore a simple white dishdasha, [which was] a little dusty, and [he] was more simple. He spoke a little Hindi, but not well. The one [Kuwaiti merchant] in Bombay he spoke Hindi very well.

In contrast to her previous employers and the Kuwaitis she had met in Bombay, Mary/Maryam found Baba Ibrahim to be rather ordinary, a man who was not as cosmopolitan or sophisticated as her previous employers in India. Her work household also surprised her. Baba Ibrahim's house was a small and functional semidetached building, in which she found a large and bustling household consisting of his deaf and nearly blind mother, a frail woman who spent much of her time propped up on a daybed between the living and dining room areas; his three sons and two daughters, all of whom were in their teens or early twenties; and most important, his wife, Mama Alia, a tall stalwart woman with a quiet sense of humor.

Initially Mama Alia was a little uncertain about how to manage having Mary/Maryam working in her home. Unlike Mama Lulua's family, she had no prior experience employing domestic workers. Suggestions made by family members and neighbors were based on their experience of hiring local part-time "helpers," or Yemeni "houseboys." Mary/Maryam, however, did not speak Arabic, was not familiar with their customs and practices, and, moreover, she was residing with them in the household.[13] In particular, Mama Alia was concerned with how to manage Mary/Maryam's relationship with her sons, who were about her age. A devout Muslim, Mama Alia felt it was inappropriate for unmarried men and women to interact unless they were related or it was absolutely necessary. Mary/Maryam's position as a household helper made such interactions necessary and therefore permissible, but Mama Alia was at pains to ensure their interactions were kept to a minimum and remained decorous. The course Mama Alia decided upon was to divide the household work in such a way as to maximize Mary/Maryam's time with her daughters—whom she involved in the cooking and cleaning, alongside Mary/Maryam. She herself took care of her son's clothes, and other aspects of their daily care. She also kept a vigilant eye on Mary/Maryam's comportment, and those of her sons in relation to one another.[14] Her surveillance and policing of their interactions was one site and means through which hierarchical divisions between her family and Mary/Maryam were produced.[15]

For her part, the level of interaction she had with the family initially discomfited Mary/Maryam. Her own sense of her work and position within the household was informed by her experiences of working in wealthy Bombay households, contexts in which she rarely saw, much less spoke to "Sir-ji" or "Madam," and where she was managed by a housekeeper but undertook most tasks individually. In Mama Alia's household, Mary/Maryam ate with the family and worked alongside the women of the house. The intensity of the daily interactions initially overwhelmed her, particularly as the family spoke no Hindi. Communicating with them was a challenge necessitating ample gesturing in the short term, and her learning Arabic in the long term. She also found Kuwait to be "strong/severe hot [*sakht gharmi*]; not like Bombay, which is just hot [*sirif gharmi*]," and "empty"—with few amenities and little to do in comparison to Bombay, and a socially isolating place. Her sense of social isolation was partially mitigated by her weekly trips to the Catholic Church's compound in downtown Kuwait. Most of the other churchgoers were Goan, Palestinian, or *Angrez-lawg'* (i.e., North Americans and Europeans), with whom she worshipped and interacted politely (she spoke a little English, which also improved in Kuwait) but with whom she otherwise felt little connection, as she neatly summarized in her comment: "I went, then I came back. A few I was friendly with, but not close." Her social situation improved when her uncle came back to Kuwait—she visited with him and her cousin regularly.

Mary/Maryam's situation changed a few years later when Fardous, Mama Alia's eldest daughter, married. Unlike her parents, who had always lived in extended family households or who resided in clusters of homes in proximal distance to one another, Fardous set up her own household in a new subdevelopment located at a distance from both her parents and her in-laws. Realizing that her daughter was lonely and overwhelmed with housework, Mama Alia sent Mary/Maryam to Fardous's home, where she remained. Her work in Fardous's household was less integrated: Fardous cooked the household meals and did the work related to her husband's personal needs (e.g., ironing his clothes), and Mary/Maryam cleaned, did the laundry, and was in charge of cooking and serving when guests visited. As Fardous's children were born, Fardous focused on childcare and tasked Mary/Maryam with the cooking, and eventually she hired Ashu, another South Asian domestic worker, who became responsible for the cleaning. Mary/Maryam and Ashu were given their own room, and ate their meals separately from the rest of the family. Their work, activities, and interrelations became increasingly distanced and differentiated from the family members of their work household.

The differences between Mama Alia and Fardous's households index broader changes in Kuwaiti lifestyles that have taken place from the midtwentieth century onward, including the shift from extended to nuclear family households, residence in larger homes, and the increasing shift of household work to domestic workers, what one interlocutor once described as the "local out-outsourcing" of domestic work. The widespread presence of migrant domestic workers has been an integral part of broad sociopolitical transformations of Kuwaiti society. It has enabled Kuwaiti women and children, who were previously tasked with domestic work, to take up educational and work opportunities and to enjoy more leisure time. Similar to other regions of the world, the presence of migrant domestic workers has ensured the reproduction of existing systems of gendered labor division—where housework continues to be regarded as "women's work"—through the shifting of this work onto noncitizens. Positioned and tasked as they are, migrant domestic workers have not only become crucial to the social reproduction of Kuwaiti citizens and households, but also the production and reproduction of hierarchical differences between citizens and noncitizens in Kuwait. Mary/Maryam and other migrant domestic workers' experiences highlight how processes of othering have developed through—not in spite of or preceding—interrelations between domestic workers and their employers.

The dynamic of being a part yet apart animated Mary/Maryam's experiences within Fardous's household over the unfolding years. Her work changed and was reconfigured as the family grew with the birth of Fardous's five children. Her days passed with the rhythms of cooking, cleaning, caring, and, on her days off, attending church and visiting her uncle and his family. As the family grew, and hired other domestic helpers and drivers, she became the one to manage and coordinate their work. Mary/Maryam had become an integral part of family members' lives in intimate, ineffable ways. Her work, her care, her very selfhood were entwined with that of the family's. Their growth, their development, their stories involved Mary/Maryam, whether it be memories of her famed rice pudding during Ramadan, her gently scolding the children when they came home late, or her inconsolable tears at Mama Alia's funeral.

Mary/Maryam was never considered, and would never consider herself to be, a member of their family despite her intimate interrelation with the family, the familial cast to the ways in which she and other members of the household referred to one another, and her and the family's engagement in economic relations of gifting, reciprocity, and obligation that were associated with familial relations.[16] For domestic workers who stay with their work households for extended periods or time—or as in the case of Mary/Maryam, who stay with them indefinitely—their position as "nonkin" members does not change, and the hierarchical relations that exist between them may become less pronounced but are not leveled. As familiarity, intimacy, and care deepens between domestic workers and members of their work households, workers might come to be considered cherished household members who are "like family," but never family members. Numerous scholars focusing on migrant domestic workers have argued that the use of familial-like discourses is tactical—that they are deployed by employers to ensure their domestic workers' productivity, elicit unpaid favors, and temper their own anxieties and ambivalence about being an employer; or conversely, that they are deployed by domestic workers to make emotional and material claims on their employer, and to subvert their authority.[17] Mary/Maryam and other South Asian migrant domestic workers' experiences in Kuwait point to another dimension of the use of familial-like terms beyond a power/agency binary: their discursive possibilities. In the absence of other discourses that fully capture the nature of their relationships, familial-like discourses provide South Asian domestic workers and their Kuwaiti employer-sponsors with a ready-at-hand and shared means of expressing the complex, ambiguous, and often fraught nature of their relationship.[18] It is discursive terrain that acknowledges how domestic workers' presence in Kuwaiti households is predicated upon but not reducible to the category of waged labor, how their activities and relationships within Kuwaiti households entail much more. As

Mary/Maryam's and Phoolan's experiences underscore, their work necessarily involves and reshapes their personalities, comportment, affect, sense of self, and relationships—and those of their employers.[19] Their lives—not just domestic workers' livelihoods or their Kuwaiti employers' standard of living/lifestyles—become interrelated. Familial-like discourses provide a fluid discursive means through which migrant domestic workers and their employers acknowledge, make sense of, and calibrate their responses to the hierarchy and intimacy, othering and interdependence that constitute their everyday interrelations.

For Mary/Maryam, one such moment occurred during a visit to Mama Alia's home. The women from Mama Alia's extended family had gathered to plan out the trousseau for a cousin's upcoming wedding. Mary/Maryam was in the kitchen preparing Arabic coffee when Umar, the ten-year-old son of one of Fardous's cousins came into the kitchen. Here is Mary/Maryam's narration of the story:

> He was holding a cup and asking me to give him something more to drink.
> He was thirsty from playing outside and wanted more to drink.
> I told him to just wait a little.
> I am watching over the coffee right now, and it is about to boil.
> I will help you with the water jug in a moment . . .
>
> He got upset, and this time screamed: "I want water!"
> I told him to wait again.
>
> And then I felt something strike my back.
> He had thrown his cup at me!
> It had a little bit of water in it, and it splashed on my back . . .
> I was shocked.
>
> Mama Alia came into the kitchen a few moments later. I was still in shock.
> She saw Umar. His face was red. Now he looked scared.
> And she saw me still looking over the coffee. My back was wet.
> And she saw the cup on the floor . . .
>
> She didn't say anything; she just looked at me for what seemed a long while.
> And then she told Umar to come with her.
> I don't know what happened, but when I was coming to the room with the coffee tray, there were loud voices in one of the other rooms. One of the voices was Mama Alia's.

Later, Umar came to say he was sorry, he should not have been angry, he should not have thrown the cup at me. He was crying.
And later, his mother also came to say sorry.

Mama Alia didn't say anything to me until just before I left with Fardous.
She took me aside and asked me why I did not tell her?
Had this happened before?
I told her no, no . . .
She said: you tell me next time!

Roshni (domestic worker recently hired by Mama Alia) later told me she heard Mama Alia had been very angry, very angry.
She had argued with Umar's mother in a room away from the guests.
Umar was with them.

For Mary/Maryam, this event crystallized how she was both a part of yet apart from the family, "like family" but not family. Umar, she told me, would never have thrown a cup at Mama Alia or Fardous. Younger members of the family would never strike their elders. He might have gotten angry, even thrown a tantrum, but he would never have thrown the cup. Although she believed (based on what she knew) that Mama Alia had treated the situation in "the right way"—swiftly making it clear to Umar and his mother that his behavior was wrong, and having him apologize—for Mary/Maryam the way in which Mama Alia dealt with the situation was also telling:

AA: I don't understand . . . do you mean because you were not involved directly in talking to Umar and his mother?
M/M: Yes and no. Umar and his mother are family but not of the same house (branch). When they (families) argue they do not like outsiders to know. It would not have shown respect to Umar's mother for Mama Alia to argue with her with me present, you see? And also, I think she knew . . . that it would embarrass me. [pause]
AA: Embarrass you? [prompting]
M/M: Yes, embarrass me.
AA: I still . . . don't quite understand. [prompting]
M/M: I am in a weaker place than Umar's mother you see. It would not have been right for me to get angry with her, to go to her and say "your son did this and this." It would have brought problems for Mama Alia. It would make problems . . . Mama Alia, she had to be the one to talk to Umar's mother, that is what had to be done there . . . [also] she knew I am weak here, but did not want to make this a big thing you

see, a thing everyone is talking about, it would embarrass me . . . That is why Umar's mother came to me. I could not go to her. It was right for her to come and say her *sorries* to me.[20]

In her comments, Maryam points to how the matter was dealt with in ways underscoring the relational hierarchies between herself and members of Mama Alia's extended family, ones highlighting her fraught position within the family. Although Mary/Maryam might have directly addressed the matter had the child involved been one of Mama Alia's or Fardous's children—she was close enough to them to do so—as an outsider to the family who moreover worked for and was dependent upon the family for her job and ability to stay in Kuwait, an idea encapsulated by her term *weaker place*, she did not have the same prerogative with extended family members. According to Mary/Maryam, Mama Alia was well aware of her weak position and showed sensitivity to Mary/Maryam by not highlighting this point. Doing so might have caused further embarrassment to Mary/Maryam. It would have emphasized her position as a hired domestic worker, something she both was and acknowledged herself to be, but which did not entirely define her relationship and position within the family. This story reinforced the great trust, admiration and love Mary/Maryam had for Mama Alia, while simultaneously reinforcing the limits and hierarchies—tacit and largely unspoken—that characterized their interrelationship.

Eerie Doublings

Like Mary/Maryam and Geeti, both Chandani and Phoolan migrated to Kuwait because of their family's economic situation. The nature of their families' circumstances, however, differed in significant ways from those of Mary/Maryam and Geeti, ones that highlight other economic dimensions of migrant domestic workers' experiences of suspension between their work and family households. By the 1980s and 1990s when Chandani and Phoolan migrated to Kuwait, finding work as a domestic worker in the Gulf region had become a more expensive undertaking. In contrast to Mary/Maryam and Geeti, who had both found employers through informal channels and their own networks, both Chandani and Phoolan required the services of labor recruitment agencies. These businesses, which charged would-be migrants hefty fees, had come to play a more prominent role in the transnational domestic work sector.[21] Reflecting the increasing cost of migration, during this period the socioeconomic backgrounds of South Asian migrant domestic workers began shifting from predominately working class to lower-middle and struggling middle class.

Chandani and Phoolan had grown up struggling middle class, and it was their attempt to maintain their family's hard-won socioeconomic footing that precipitated their migration. Chandani had recently divorced from her husband. Without any formal education and work experience, her chances of finding what she called "respectable" employment in India were at best slim. She was also loath to return back to and become dependent upon her parents and brother, who themselves were struggling with her brother's stagnating wages and the increased cost of living in their community. Phoolan's decision to migrate was prompted by her husband's death and the need to support her teenage son, whose school fees were quickly outstripping her savings, her gold wedding jewelry, and both her in-laws' and parents' assistance. Leaving her son in her sister's care, she undertook the procedures necessary to migrate.

Saving their wages and financial planning were of utmost concern to Chandani and Phoolan in Kuwait. To achieve economic security and independence in the long term, they lived what Chandani described as "frozen lives" in the short term. Phoolan rarely spent any of her wages, and eschewed activities tempting her to do so. In particular she avoided going to the downtown core on her days off as many other domestic workers tended to do. Instead, she pocketed the money Dalal gave her to go the city, and stayed in her room penning letters to her son. In addition, both she and Chandani opted not to travel back to India during their summers.[22] Instead they collected their extra wages, as well as the money that would otherwise have been spent on their airline tickets. Phoolan's earnings went toward paying for her son's school fees, tutors, books, school uniforms, and the living expenses she paid her sister to look after him. With her brother's assistance, Chandani used her income to purchase a small tract of land in the village she was from, upon which she eventually constructed a house and established a small agricultural business. Both Phoolan's and Chandani's earnings were invested in a planned-for future. Life in the present was meaningful in relation to what it would bring in the dreamed-of distance—for Chandani as a flourishing proprietor and entrepreneur, and for Phoolan, as the mother of a well-educated and prosperous man, her son, who would look after her.

Their ventures were supported by their employers, not just in terms of the wages the women earned, but in other ways, through other means. Gul Nar, the chatelaine of the house in which Chandani lived, and her eldest daughter, Ilham Bibi, kept tabs on events in their domestic workers' lives, and the lives of their close family members, such as births, marriages, and deaths. To mark these events, Gul Nar and Ilham Bibi gave gifts or small amounts of money, which the women they employed would either keep or pass on as gifts to their relatives. Chandani's business was of special interest to—and admired by—Gul Nar, who assisted Chandani during a particularly tricky set of negotiations when her brother asked to have his name put down as co-owner. When Chandani prepared to return to India, Ilham Bibi gave her a lump sum amount to build a mosque in her village. Phoolan's employers were of more modest means; however, they too periodically gifted her and her son, for example, giving her a watch when her own broke and her son a large cash gift, and a cell phone model he had long been coveting when he graduated from high school. The family also donated part of their *sadaqa*, or voluntary charitable contributions, to support members of her extended family.

Both Chandani's and Phoolan's situations underscore how economic relations between domestic workers and their work households are often not reducible to wage labor—where their work is converted into a salary, their time into money. Their economic interrelations also entail patron-client type distributions, gifting, and charitable contributions.[23] In addition, whether in the form of sweets and a toy rickshaw Phoolan brought back after her visit to India, or other domestic workers who bring back jewelry or cloth for their "Mamas" after their holidays, or Chandani naming the mosque she built after Gul Nar, these relations also entail regifting and flows of goods, and actions back to the families/households with whom they work, even if these are undertaken from positions of asymmetrical ability, need, and a different sense of obligation (in conversations, one of my interlocutors and I used to term *debt in obligation* to articulate this sense). Rather than the linear conversion of labor into wages, these relations point to more complex configurations of economic exchange and distribution involving circuits of time, work, affect, goods, and money between asymmetrically positioned subjects, ones producing and reinforcing domestic workers' sense of belonging, intimacy, and obligation toward their work household.

If the economic relations between domestic workers and members of their "work households" exceed those of waged labor, taking on forms often associated with familial relations (e.g., allowances, gifting, obligation), they also experienced mirrored forms with respect to their "family households." Phoolan experienced this dynamic almost immediately during her first visit back to India. After over ten years of being away—years of work, years of saving her earnings, years marked by little leisure or any types of indulgence—she was upset to find herself confronted with her family's complaints. Her sister insisted that she should share more of her earnings with the rest of her family as the monthly amount Phoolan remitted to her was barely enough to cover the work that looking after her son entailed. Like other domestic workers,

Phoolan was finding that through her migration, her family's consumer needs spiraled as they became more entangled and disciplined into market relations, exchanges, and calculations. For his part, her son appeared more interested in the gifts—the bottles of cologne, the branded running shoes and electronics—she had brought with her than he did to see her. Coupled with acutely missing Hajira, her young charge, the situation prompted her to want to return early to her work household. Though she ended up staying in India to try to work through these difficulties with her family, the experience took a deeply emotional and affective toll on Phoolan: "So many years [of work in Kuwait] and all they did was fuss and grumble . . . and want more. I didn't know what to think or feel. [I felt] like my only place was to be here [Kuwait]; that that was what they really wanted. So I thought fine, I'll come back. But then I cried and cried, and then I said to myself: stop. Stop this crying. I should at least try."

Physically absent from the everyday worlds of their children, siblings, parents and husbands, migrant domestic workers' relations with members of their family households are increasingly mediated through the currency and consumer goods they provide.[24] This often led to recalibrations in their authority among their family members, in particular their increasing influence in decision-making processes, something Chandani was keenly cognizant of and did not shy from in her relations with her brother.[25] In some cases, as we see with Phoolan, this process led to the emergence of a calculative, self-interested cast to their family members' relations with them, ones my interlocutors often bemoaned.[26] The overall effect was of a blurring and eerie doubling between familial and economic relations—relations with their "family" households were becoming increasingly calculative or "economic" and mediated by commodity-based relations,[27] and relations with their "work" households were characterized by gifting and other economic forms associated with the familial.[28] This doubling effect was further compounded by many domestic workers' acute awareness that in their family households they were often expected to undertake gendered work similar to that which they performed in their work households, but in their family households, their work was not remunerated or recognized in the same way, an experience that not only points to a transnational gendered double-burden, but of the eerie doubling of the burden itself. Some transnational domestic workers hired other women to do the household work of their family households in their stead, hired women who became their proxies and doubles, and as Parrenas and Hochschild have written,[29] a further link in global chains of commodified caretaking. Animated by their family's economic circumstances and aspirations for a better life and socioeconomic mobility, domestic workers' migration to Kuwait led to a reconfiguration of relations with their family and work households that were articulated in and through capital and material goods, and inextricably related to their changing economic circumstances. The overlapping and complex circuits of wages, gifts and charitable contributions—within which migrant domestic workers were positioned as nodal points—both produced and consolidated their role as dual agents of reproduction and, as the eerie doublings and recalibrations in relations they experience also point to, also engendered forms of everyday conversion.

Household Protection

The circumscribing of domestic workers' activities to household spaces further produces their experiences of suspension. To a great extent, domestic workers' lives are confined to household spaces in Kuwait. They not only work within households, but the overwhelming majority of domestic workers also reside in the households in which they work. The scope of their social interactions and activities are often limited to their work households—to their employers and fellow domestic workers in their households, as well as to neighboring domestic workers and those employed by their employers' family members and friends.[30] On their days off work, many domestic workers go to the city center or the shopping areas of neighborhoods with a concentration of noncitizens. A significant number, however, spend their rest days in their households. Women such as Phoolan remained at home in order to avoid spending their wages and to earn additional income. In her case she pocketed the spending money given to her by Dalal. Others spent their days preparing and selling foodstuffs or craft items in their neighborhoods, or watching satellite television and entertaining family members or friends in their quarters. In discussing why they rarely went out, many domestic workers indicated that there were few public spaces that they could access on their own. Restaurants and shopping malls were too expensive, or they were concerned they would be barred from entering these spaces as "bachelor" workers often experienced. Outdoor spaces such as beaches and public parks were oppressively hot for long stretches of the year.

Concerns about their personal safety also limit domestic workers' mobility beyond household spaces. Unlike Dubai and other parts of the Gulf region, there is a palpable sense of gendered intimidation and threat in the streets and public areas of Kuwait. Particularly in residential areas, where most domestic workers reside, few people are seen in the streets, and those that do venture out, especially women and foreign residents, are often harassed with solicitation and honks by male passers-by and passing cars. This feeling of threat is further compounded by widely circulating stories and everyday newspaper accounts of women being abducted from the street, driven to empty sandlots or into the desert, beaten, sexually assaulted, and left there. The majority of women who have been targeted are foreign resident and migrant women, especially women from throughout Asia and East Africa who are assumed to be domestic workers. These women are marked as vulnerable and preyed upon because they are assumed to not have any family protection or wasta.[31] They are also assumed not to have connections that provide them with social protection and juridicopolitical recourse.[32] As a result of these obstacles, few domestic workers that I met were allowed to or wanted to go to public areas unaccompanied. If they were allowed to do so, they often perceived this as neglect or carelessness on the part of their employers.[33]

Venturing outside domestic spaces, especially alone, was understood to be a form of exposure, fraught with potential physical danger, as well as moral peril. Space in Kuwait was not conceived as abstract or morally neutral, but as eminently social. Households were spaces domesticated and cultivated through the establishment of propriety and moral order (although the form of this order may vary from family/household to family/household). Areas outside the household were potentially volatile spaces; there, the upholding of propriety and moral codes was more uncertain. Public spaces were not necessarily seen as moral vacuums, but as morally unpredictable spaces. Within such contexts—public parks or the city center on Friday or Sunday afternoons—domestic workers might not only be subject to what one interlocutor called "romantic hustlers," but to where they might also lapse morally (what the same interlocutor called "our own worst ro/man/tinstincts"). Here there is a mutually reinforcing relationship between the production of moral spaces and of subjectivities—subjects acting with propriety carve out and domesticate properly moral spaces, and such spaces are necessary to the formation of subjects that act with propriety.

These were views about the sociospatiality of Kuwait that many South Asian domestic workers and their employers both shared. Mary/Maryam alluded to this issue in discussing the reasons she had not married. Despite her parents' and her uncles' attempts to find her a potential husband, and even discrete inquiries made on her behalf by her employer Mama Alia, they had been unable to find her a suitable match. When I asked her if she had any opportunities to meet anyone in Kuwait, her response was quite revealing:

M/M: No, of course not! I met people at the church—saying "hi" and "bye," polite talk—but no, no. I know some go out in the street, especially now, and make eyes. It is very wrong. Not a good thing to do; very improper.

AA: Did you feel this way before coming to Kuwait . . . in India? Or was this something you have come to think here?

M/M: No, my parents they raised me like this too; they raised my sisters and I like this. They [her sisters] had proper marriages, not like now.

In her comments, Mary/Maryam emphasizes her disapproval at attempts to develop or engage in intimate relations, what she describes as "making eyes," on her own, a moral view and sensibility that she developed through her family in India, one coinciding with the moral sensibilities of her employers. For Fardous and others, they often viewed it as morally incumbent upon themselves to safeguard their domestic workers from what they deemed to be improper relations. As she explained to me: "They [domestic workers] come to us without their families, without protection. It is our duty, our duty to their parents, to them, to make sure there is no funny business. Not all Kuwaitis, *astaghfirallah* [I seek God's forgiveness], behave right here. We read about this in the papers. Not all these maids behave this way, astaghfirallah, you hear about this, about boyfriends, sneaking, and astaghfirallah, other things too. But it is our duty. Maybe I will never meet them, but how could I look their parents in the eye? They [domestic workers] are under our protection."

Fardous and other sponsor-employers felt it to be their duty to "protect" domestic workers from romantic liaisons and to ensure that members of their own households, in particular family members, also not engage in improper relations with their domestic workers. They viewed domestic workers as particularly vulnerable or potentially threatening of moral order due to their dislocation and isolation from their families. While their attempts were not always successful, Fardous and other employers believed it was their moral responsibility to both domestic workers and their families to ensure these women did not engage in "funny business." Couched in moral terms, employers' paternalistic practice of "protection" or policing domestic workers' social relations and sexuality, serves to reinscribe the familial and ethnonational boundaries between themselves and their domestic workers, and to ensure domestic workers' attachments to their preexisting families and ethnonational communities.

Household Policing

While domestic workers such as Mar/Maryam, Phoolan, and Chandani shared their employers' views about the impropriety of developing romantic and sexual relationships that are not supervised or sanctioned by their family or work households, others bridled against but were nevertheless subject to their employers' policing activities. For Hema and Ritu, their employers' control over their social interactions and mobility conflicted with one of their primary motivations for migrating to Kuwait. Unlike the majority of domestic workers, Hema did not migrate because of her or her family's pressing economic needs. She and her upper-caste family—consisting of her father, a prosperous farmer, her mother, the daughter of an equally prosperous shopkeeper with no sons, an elder brother serving in the Indian Army, and a younger brother in high school—did not want for anything. Her migration to Kuwait was prompted by a different set of considerations. When she entered into adulthood, Hema began realizing she was uninterested in men and did not want to marry. Initially, her mother tried to convince her to reconsider her position, but eventually came around and became supportive of her daughter's position. Wanting to secure her daughter's financial independence, she arranged for Hema to migrate to "Saudi."[34] Her wages would be saved and then invested, providing her with an independent income to do with as she wished when she returned to the family farm. In our conversations, Hema indicated that there were few educational or work opportunities for women of her social standing in her village and the surrounding areas. The region's school for girls had closed, and her mother was concerned that should she work for her grandfather's or, worse yet, someone else's shop—versus starting or running her own—their family's reputation and social standing would suffer. Migrating to "Saudi' would not only provide her with capital, but it would also enable her to work unencumbered by immediate social considerations. Being abroad would also place Hema out of her extended family and local community's "sight and mind" during a period in her life when she was expected to fulfill but refused the hegemonic expectation that she should marry. For her part, although initially apprehensive and hesitant to leave her family and home, Hema began to relish the opportunities migration would provide: the opportunity to travel, meet new people, and see more of the world outside her village and surrounding area.

In Kuwait, she worked in a household she described to me as a "ladies-only affair" consisting of a divorced Kuwaiti woman in her early forties—whom she referred to as Siham Mama, and her two daughters, Sadia and Farah, both of whom went to college and were about Hema's age. The family lived on the top floor of a villa that was adjacent to another villa shared by Siham Mama's parents, Youbba Ali and Youmma Fatima (grandfather and grandmother), her eldest brother, and his family. Although Siham Mama ran her household independently, Youmma Fatima (grandmother) was an influential presence. With her daughter working long hours at the bank, Youmma Fatima considered herself her granddaughters' watcher, and—as Hema was soon to discover—Hema's watcher as well. From her window, and with cell phone in hand, Youmma Fatima kept a vigilant eye on the activities next door, monitoring and directing the movements of members of her daughter's household. For her granddaughters, Youmma Fatima exercised this (self-imposed) duty by vetting their friends, and unless they were able to get rides with their mother or (previously vetted) friends, arrange for her driver and de facto chaperone to take them to school, shopping malls, or their friends' homes. Youmma's vigilant eye was a source of constant negotiation and periodic arguments among Youmma, Mama Siham, and her two daughters.

Youmma's policing of Hema was also thorough. Hema was not permitted to go outside on her own. If she wanted to walk to the *bakala* (corner store), another domestic worker from Youmma's household accompanied her, or she would be driven there. If she had to go shopping, visit the health clinic, or do any other activities outside the household, either Mama Siham, her daughters, or Youmma Fatima's driver would take her. While Mama Siham allowed her to entertain friends on her day off, Youmma discouraged these visits, which effectively restricted Hema from having her friends over when Youmma was at home. Youmma Fatima did, however, encourage Hema to befriend other domestic workers who were working in the households of friends and family members. Youmma Fatima knew these women, as well as the families with whom they worked. Their status and respectability were established, whereas those of the others were more uncertain, and relationships with them were not to be risked. In order to keep in touch with her "other" friends, as well as her family members in Nepal and India, Hema kept a cell phone, one she took care not to use or be seen with when Youmma Fatima was around.

Hema was ambivalent about Youmma Fatima's vigilant eye. In discussions she likened Youmma Fatima's actions to those of her parents in Nepal. If she went out in public in her village and the surrounding areas, a family member typically accompanied her. They did so not only out of concern for her personal safety (she resided in a region of significant Maoist insurgent activity), but also for their family's social standing. In her village, young women of her background, from a well-to-do upper-caste family, did not "go roaming about outside very much, and certainly not on our own, unless it could not be helped." Hema also likened her situation in Kuwait to those of Siham's daughters but underscored an important difference. Unlike both Sadia and Farah, she could not discuss or negotiate the matter with Youmma Fatima, and without a network of family and friends to call upon, she had little room to maneuver around Youmma Fatima's measures. Hema emphasized that she could not upset or "create hard feelings" with Youmma Fatima as upsetting a senior member of the family would make it difficult for Siham Mama to continue to employ her. Overall she saw restrictions on her social activities and mobility as a function of gendered and aged considerations, as well as ones related to her marital status, ideas of middle-class respectability, and resonant sets of moral sensibilities. These understandings and practices functioned in overlapping forms in both Nepal and Kuwait—ensuring that her experiences of travel and developing of relationships were largely tethered to her family and work household spaces.

Hema's social networks were largely women-centric, consisting of Siham Mama, her daughters and other domestic workers, a gendered configuration in line with her own desires and preferences. For other domestic workers, in particular younger ones, restrictions placed on their sociospatial mobility directly conflicted with a rarely spoken about but keenly felt hope that motivated their migration: the possibility of romance and meeting a potential boyfriend or husband. For Ritu, this was a much-longed-for outcome, one that would address the major source of anxiety plaguing her and her family in the wake of her father's death several years earlier. Ritu's father was an upper-caste Nepali man who—later in life, his children from his first marriage having reached adulthood—decided to marry again, this time to a woman from a scheduled caste: Ritu's mother. During his lifetime, Ritu's family lived in the shadow of her father's first family, but her father ensured that they were well taken care of. When he died, the inheritance he provided was sufficient (at least initially) to look after their economic needs; however, the family's already liminal social position became increasingly precarious. The eldest son from their father's first family—an influential man in the community—let it be known that he disapproved of their family, and rumors started to circulate that Ritu's mother had used magic and sorcery to "ensnare" her husband. Fewer and fewer people in their community interacted with them. When it came time to finding potential spouses for Ritu and her elder brother and sister, few families were willing to enter into marriage alliances with them, and those that were willing to do so were deemed unacceptable by her mother.

In Kuwait, where increasing numbers of male Nepalis had been migrating in the years prior, Ritu hoped to meet a potential husband. As she explained, the Nepali men in Kuwait were likely to be good catches: they were already relatively well off as they had the sufficient funds to finance their migration, and they were likely to earn more money and thus be in a position to marry. Also, she thought the experience of travel or, as she so incisively put it, "being away from home where things are strange and unexpected," would make many of the men more "broad-minded" about her mixed-caste background. Ritu's attempts to find a husband were, however, dashed at every turn. Her work kept her in her employer's home much of the time. When she accompanied her employers to shopping malls or parks, she was typically preoccupied with taking care of her employers' children, or she found few if any eligible men due to the restrictions placed on "bachelor workers" in "family" public areas. Her weekly rest day was Sunday, not Friday, when most male migrant and foreign residents have their rest days. And when Ritu went to the city, her Mama insisted that the family's driver—a humorless and grumpy older man from Southern India—accompany her.

Romance was not to be found until she received a fateful phone call one day. It was late in the evening, and her workday long since ended, Ritu was in her room listlessly reading magazines. As she narrated to me, Hema, and Heba:[35] "I was reading, and feeling bored with the magazines. My cell phone rang and though I did not know the number, I was *so* bored, so I answered anyways. The person calling, he was so nice. He spoke Nepali! He told me he had called accidentally. I see your face, Hema! He was nice, nothing silly or *haram* [forbidden]. His name is Hari. He is very nice to talk to!"

In the absence of other opportunities to meet, some foreign residents and migrants randomly dialed phone numbers in the hopes of finding someone with whom they can chat or potentially develop a romantic or sexual relationship. As Hema's expression indicates, she was skeptical about whether Hari's call was an accident as both he and Ritu claimed. Whether an accidental or a randomly dialed phone call, the two took to one another almost instantly. Their phone conversations continued for weeks. When Hari broached the idea of the two of them meeting, Ritu was uncertain about what to do and brought up the topic discreetly with the three of us in the hopes we might be able to assist her:

RITU: He wants to meet.
HEBA: Oh, Ritu, what is this? You don't know him, not really. He may say sweet words on the phone, but you don't know what he is really like.
RITU: Silly! [We would] not [meet] at his home or at Mama's house! That is the problem: where [should we meet]?
HEBA: . . . your Mama [employer] will not like this [i.e., meeting him]! I don't think this is a good thing to do.

Having solicited their opinion, Ritu mulled over the matter. Over the following weeks, prompted by continuing phone calls from Hari and her own cherished hopes, she decided on a course of action, one involving me. To get around the restrictions placed on her mobility, Ritu asked me to act as her go-between, delivering letters between the two of them. She recounted what happened when the four of us met a few weeks later:

HEMA: So, Rose, what's going on?[36]

RITU: . . . it was too hard to meet. . . . and I am still double-minded [uncertain], so Hari asked me to send him a photograph; and he told me he will send me one . . .

HEMA: Oh . . . [37] But you can't mail [it] here can you? Can he mail [it] to you?"

RITU: No, no. It would need to be dropped and picked up . . . so I gave the letter to Attiya, and the picture, and she took it.

AA: Yes, I took the letter to him.

HEMA: What was he like? Where did you go (to drop and pick up the letters)?

HEMA: Yes, what was he like? What did our *Roooomeo* . . . [*stops because of a warning look from Ritu*]

AA: Yes, he works at a hotel.[38] It was in a shopping center, towards the back. I went early in the day; the hotel was just opening. The security barrier . . . the barrier at the entrance of the door . . . had come up halfway, so I waited. There was no one inside that I could see, so I waited. Then I saw someone and called him over. I told him I was looking for Hari . . . um . . . Ritu asked me to speak to him in English.

My last comment elicited a pointed look from both Heba and Hema. When she handed me the letter, Ritu had specifically instructed me to speak to Hari in English rather than Urdu/Hindi or Arabic. As I was to learn, she had talked to Hari about me, her Canadian-Pakistani friend. In their estimation, my Canadian citizenship conferred upon me a relatively high status, something Ritu was keenly aware of and wished to impress upon Hari as Ritu's comments indicate:

HEMA: Yes, yes, you (looking at Ritu) are a big-person with friends from "big-places," huh?

RITU: Quiet! [*swats Ritu and looks at me*] Go on.

AA: He seemed surprised. I don't know that he quite understood me. But anyways, I gave him the letter and he told me to wait. He headed to the kitchen, where a group of other men had gathered.[39] They asked him questions, and I could hear some joking [*I turn to Ritu*] did he tell you about that? I could see him writing . . . then he gave it to me . . . and I brought the letter to Ritu when I next visited her.

HEBA: That's all?

AA: Yes. It was pretty quick.

HEBA: Ritu, so what now? What are you going to do now?

RITU: I am still double minded . . . but I do want to see him, see his hotel maybe, but Mama will not like it.

HEBA: No, she won't. . . .

HEMA: Yes, be careful, your mama, she will send you to the *bayt-shurta* to keep Hari and other boys safe from you![40] Or, she will keep you in *bayt-detention* to keep you safe from Hari and other boys! . . . And if your Nepali mama hears of it: watch out! then you will really need protection. She will keep you in *ghar-detention*! No Kuwait, no Hari, no problems!

Hema's utterance consists of a series of brilliant plays on words, conceptual doublings, and a repetitive rhythm. Moreover, it entwines a number of issues related to the policing of domestic workers' activities and relations. Her use of the trilingual words *bayt-shurta, bayt-detention,* and *ghar-detention* points to the resonances between house and police stations, of being detained and having movements constantly monitored and policed; and of being a domestic worker mired (detained) in the household, and an absconder detained by the police (mired in jail). Hema also inverts the common assumption about why restrictions are placed on domestic workers' mobility in Kuwait by cleverly asking who and what is being protected—they or others?—thus gesturing to how their sexuality and the possibility of their developing relationships outside the household are implicitly considered to be threatening. Her twin use of the word *bayt-detention* and *ghar-detention* underscores the workers' paralleled experiences of being largely confined to the household, both in Kuwait and in Nepal and India. The twining of these terms and places points to a further dynamic: whether intended or not, the restrictions on mobility and curtailing of opportunities to forge further relationships keep domestic workers limited to their work households in Kuwait and their family households in the places they migrated from. Domestic workers' belonging to these spaces—*bayt*-detention and *ghar*-detention—are not automatic or already assumed, but produced and reproduced everyday by the constant monitoring and policing of their movements and interactions.

Living in Suspension

South Asian migrant domestic workers' migration experiences are characterized by a double displacement: of being situated and suspended between the lives of their "work" and "family" household members in South Asia and the

Gulf, or, as Mary/Maryam put it: "both places that are sometimes my home." Their experience of suspension develops through a number of overlapping processes—the economic situation and crises within their families, their own and their family members' spiraling consumer needs and class aspirations, intensifying ties in the face of deeply entrenched hierarchical relations with members of their work households, and the policing of their everyday activities and movements in Kuwait—all producing a situation in which they are a part of yet apart from their family and work households.

In a context where migrant domestic workers are disciplined into thinking of themselves as temporary, many describe their time in Kuwait as one of deferral, where they have put their lives on hold, working in the present to save for a longed-for future. Ensuring their constant sociopolitical liminality, a position producing and consolidating their position as dual agents of reproduction, this dynamic of suspension also engenders another dynamic. At the same time that domestic workers are the nodal points reproducing their family and work households—as indexed by Phoolan and Hajira's responses upon their temporary parting, the eerie doubling of economic and familial-like relations between their work and family households, and Mary/Maryam and Geeti's connections with Fardous and Mama Lulua's families—South Asian migrant domestic workers' everyday experiences also cut across familial and ethnonational affinities, engendering fluid, often ambiguous and incipient affinities, belongings, and forms of living, everyday forms of conversion that are difficult to articulate and account for when heteronormative nuclear families and ethnonational belongings are the hegemonic norm.

THREE

NARAM

Naram! Naram! Naram!
We go there and we are there,
and we come here and we are here.
Men, no.
—Ritu

An Unexpected Gathering: "We Don't Show"

Sitting on her front porch, Ritu mused how far away Kuwait felt. It was a languorous afternoon. The monsoon rains had quickly come and gone but lingered in the heavied trees that shaded Ritu's mother's home. Set amid rice paddies and fields fallow or lush with subsistence crops, her home was a modest affair comprising two windowless rooms, a porch, and a small kitchen. Behind the house, a dirt path led to the outhouse and an enclosure where the family's cow was kept. The house had recently been painted mint green with a bright purple trim, a change Ritu financed through her work in Kuwait. Inside were other signs of the time she spent in the Gulf: the kitchen stores brimmed with rice, pulses, and neatly stacked canned goods. A sleek new television and DVD player were carefully placed on a trunk in the large room. A prayer mat and poster of Mecca hung on the walls.

We had just finished a meal that Ritu's mother had served in all-too generous portions. Bellies full, eyes drooping, we made our way to the front porch where we sat watching passersby heading to and from the main road. I had traveled down that same path a few days earlier, the beginning of my visit with Ritu and her mother. Journeying there to Nepal's Southeast—a lush agricultural region of tea plantations, swaying corn, and checkered rice paddies—had been difficult. A day-and-a-half bus ride from Katmandu, the region was only accessible by a series of narrow roads that ribboned their way through mountain passes and were precariously perched along swollen riverbeds. At this time of the year, many were rendered slick—or washed away—by monsoon rains. Add to that a general strike (*bandh*) that had been called in the region by the (then) Maoist insurgents, and indeed Kuwait felt very far away.

Hema, who was also visiting her family in Nepal, joined us later that evening. She and Ritu had developed a close friendship in Kuwait, one paved by their discovery that they were from the same region of Nepal, and the cascading realization that their families not only resided in the same district, but had homes located a mere hour-and-a-half drive from one another. Through their conversations I had learned much about their home district: its proximity to the border bazaars of India, the new hotels/restaurants opened up in town by returning migrants from the Middle East and Southeast Asia, and the scenic hilltop picnic areas overrun by the children of Nepal's elite, who attended an exclusive boarding school located nearby.

One thing I had not realized through their conversations was how unlikely their friendship would have been in Nepal. Hema—the daughter of a well-to-do, upper-caste family—rarely crossed paths with the likes of Ritu, a woman whose family was of far more modest means and status. It was only with my arrival—which Hema had carefully described to her parents as "the Canadian student girl doing her school project," a description that maximized my noteworthy qualities and mitigated any potential concerns they might have had about me—that Hema's parents had finally permitted her to visit Ritu.

Our impromptu gathering soon grew larger as word spread that "Saudi" returnees were visiting Ritu. Starting with Ritu's cousin who had worked in Qatar for six years, a steady stream of women who had either lived in the Arabian Peninsula or who sought to migrate to the region—women with transnational experiences or expectations—came calling the next day. The air thrummed with overlapping conversations. Seated on the benches that ringed the front porch, fanning themselves with folded papers, and sipping tea Hema had made in the "Arab style" to mark the occasion, the women reminisced and reflected upon the time they spent in the Arabian Peninsula, discussing a host of issues I scrambled to jot down: They compared their experiences with their employers and labor recruitment agents. They discussed changes they had made to their homes, or the properties they had purchased. They talked longingly of foods and luxuries missed. While expressing relief or ambivalence about being back in Nepal, they debated whether they should or how to return to the Gulf given recent migration bans.

Hours after the other women left, Hema, Ritu, and I continued discussing threads of the conversation. I had been particularly struck—and perplexed— by one woman's mention of the contrasts between how she and her brother demonstrated that they resided in the Gulf:

AA: She said he was not able to show it [that he had been in the Gulf] . . . but that she should not. I didn't understand. Do they mean the families do not like to acknowledge that women have been away? [Is this the case for] Men too?

HEMA: No, everybody knows she was away—two years; they know. And him too, they know he was away.

RITU: Some people, maybe, because they think you do this and that [something illicit] when you are away; they think you do not want to talk about being away. But no, in our house and with our people [relatives and close family friends], it means we are not being proper; you aren't doing it correctly.

AA: Umm . . . I don't understand. Doing what correctly? Being proper . . . how?

RITU: You aren't trying or behaving right. With men it is different.

HEMA: Yes different because we learn [when we are abroad], but we should not show it, where they don't learn, really. They [men] are really the same [as when they left] where we can change, but should not show it.

AA: You mean they, the men, they stay Nepali? But girls should stay Nepali?

HEMA: No, no. You know this Attiya! When I was in Kuwait I wore hijab, I wore abaya, I spoke softly and in Arabic. This is ok.

RITU: This is ok. But men they don't do this. They stay [the same] there and they stay [the same] here.

AA: But you said they [men] can't show. Does this mean they don't or can't change?

HEMA: We learn and we change; men no. They show [that they were in the Gulf] in ways that are not really different. They aren't naram.

RITU: Yes: Naram! Naram! Naram! We go there and we are there, and we come here and we are here. Men, no.

Hema's and Ritu's comments point to a gendered discourse of malleability that by its nature is difficult to discern. In part this has to do with the covert and seemingly contradictory nature of this discourse. As Hema and Ritu explained: women can learn and change through their migration experiences in a way that men are incapable of doing, yet at the same time, proper women "should not show" that they have been abroad, whereas for men it is acceptable to do so. Their comments not only highlight gendered differences in the experience and effects of migration, but they also highlight the gendered differences in how these experiences and effects are demonstrated and performed among members of their families and communities. Both issues point to an underlying discourse of South Asian women's subjectivity, the idea that proper South Asian women are *naram*, a Hindi/Urdu word denoting softness and pliability. In this chapter I trace the contours of this discourse and discuss how it suffuses and shapes South Asian domestic workers' experiences of migration and everyday conversion. I begin by disentangling this discourse from other processes that downplay or disregard South Asian domestic workers' transnational presence. I then examine the diffuse and relational quality of this discourse as it unfolds in transnational contexts of everyday conversion.

By virtue of their being naram, many domestic workers perceived themselves to be ideal transnational subjects, able to learn and accommodate themselves to unfamiliar circumstances, to adjust to the temporariness and suspension that characterize their migration experiences, and to have the underlying capacity to develop the skills that are necessary for the work they undertake in Kuwaiti households. My interlocutors often enacted and invoked this discourse in juxtaposition to their female Kuwaiti employers and domestic workers of other ethnonational backgrounds, as well as to their male compatriots. This discourse of gendered malleability thus functions in a dual sense: it provides South Asian domestic workers with a basis to assess and respond to shifting transnational landscapes, while simultaneously providing them with a means to account for the particularity of their gendered, aged, and raced positions across these spaces. Being naram enables these migrant women to be involved in the reproduction of households and ethnonational formations in both South Asia and the Gulf, and to simultaneously develop alternative forms of subjectivity and belongings that mark their everyday conversions.

Being naram is the lynchpin of South Asian migrant domestic workers' experiences in Kuwait. It brings into the foreground gendered dimensions of their transnational experiences that might otherwise go unremarked and disregarded. It points to a particular gendered modality—underlying logic and form—through which they accommodate themselves to their changing circumstances. It is an underlying normative expectation they are subject to and become subjects of: that they should accommodate themselves unobtrusively to new social milieus. They perform their skillfulness at being naram by seamlessly moving across different sociopolitical contexts, a gendered capacity and capability making possible their transnational circulation and mobility. Naramness is an underlying gendered discourse of subjectivity that is key to a range of affective relations, aptitudes, relations and skills they can develop, ones necessary to their undertaking of domestic work and their development of novel forms of religious sensibilities and dispositions.

We Don't Show: Gendered Legibility and Legality

Initially I associated Hema's comments about how women "should not show" that they have been overseas with a series of debates that were playing out among actors involved in the South Asian–Gulf transnational domestic work sector. At the crux of these debates were questions about the legibility and legality of South Asian, and in particular Nepali, domestic workers' transnational status. In the mid-2000s, labor agents, government officials, and activists in Kuwait were unanimous in their assessment that the country was experiencing a vast influx of Nepali women. Most believed Nepali women constituted the largest group of women migrating to Kuwait, with some estimating that as many as 1,500 were entering the country every month.[1] Yet when I traveled to Nepal during the summer of 2007, I was stunned to learn that few if any activists, academics, and policy makers seemed to recognize the magnitude of this trajectory of migration to the Gulf. Based on international news media accounts and human rights reports, many were aware of the abuse domestic workers were subject to in the Gulf, but most thought Nepali migration to the region was negligible.[2] One scholar who was in the midst of conducting household surveys in the same part of the region where Hema and Ritu resided went so far as to flatly state: "Nepali women don't migrate." When I told him of my own research findings in both Kuwait and Nepal, and moments such as the impromptu gathering of migrant women at Ritu's mother's home, he remained firmly dismissive.

What accounts for the marked discrepancy between Nepali women's migration to the Gulf and the recognition thereof in Nepal? Among women's rights and migration activists in Katmandu, the reasons were painfully clear. A group largely comprising former migrants to India and Southeast Asia who were linked to, if not funded by, the international women's movement and linked to Nepal's robust NGO sector, the activists told me of the widespread social stigma migrant women experience when they return as it is largely assumed they have been involved in sex work. Put more pointedly, a generalized under-standing equating women's migration with sex trafficking or sex work existed—something Hema alluded to in her comment that "some people . . . because they think you do this and that when you are away, they think you do not want to talk about it," a comment that recognizes the association of illicit activity with migration.

The activists also pointed to another issue, one resonant with a long-standing and pervasive discourse that posits women as symbols of the family, household, and nation who are both a bulwark against and vulnerable to foreign forces.[3] Within this context, women's migration was seen to index Nepali families and the Nepali nation-state's failure to provide for and protect their women, and given the synecdochical link between women and the nation, to ensure the well-being of their sociopolitical body as a whole. Underscoring how reluctant Nepalis were to broach the topic of women's migration and how returning migrants often felt shunned by members of their communities, the activists had developed a series of programs that sought to provide space for migrant women to "give voice" to their experiences. These programs included a public awareness–raising campaign, lobbying efforts, establishing workshops ranging from counseling to skills training for returning migrants, and establishing a database of actors involved in the transnational migration sector. One group published a magazine for migrant women that featured their writings and a "day in the life" section debunking common stereotypes and misconceptions about migrant women's experiences. The magazine covered the range of the women's experiences across the world, as well as their contributions to the economies of Nepal and the countries they migrate to.

Before arriving in Nepal, I had already begun tracing signs of another ex-planation for why women's migration to the Gulf often went unacknowledged. During our interviews all of my Nepali interlocutors, without exception, men-tioned having spent several weeks in India prior to coming to Kuwait (of which I will discuss more below). When I interviewed employers as well as labor re-cruitment agency officials, I learned that neither of these groups had to file doc-uments with Nepali embassies or state institutions as they did when sponsoring domestic workers from other countries. On my flights between Nepal and the Gulf, the airport lounges and plane aisles teemed with Nepali men. Women, however, were conspicuously absent. These seeming anomalies are connected by an event that transpired in March 1998: the passing of a law by the Nepali government making it illegal for Nepali women to migrate to the Gulf Cooper-ation Council states.[4] This labor migration ban was imposed after Rani Sherpa, a Nepali domestic worker in Kuwait, died under mysterious circumstances.

Ruled a suicide by the Kuwaiti police, Sherpa's family disputed their findings, insisting she had been murdered by her employers, who they further allege, had subjected her to constant physical and sexual abuse. Widely reported in the Nepali press, the Sherpa case led to a groundswell of public demand that the Nepali government take action to protect their citizens abroad. Under intense pressure and scrutiny, the cabinet convened a series of special meetings during which the migration ban was drafted.

Similar to other such laws, including ones passed by the Indian government that have led to similar such experiences among Indian domestic workers from the mid-1970s onward, this ban has proved overwhelmingly ineffective.[5] Over the course of my research, it was telling that most of my Nepali interlocutors were either unaware of the ban or were largely unconcerned about it. Rather than stymying their migration, they felt its effects in other ways. Barred from traveling to the Gulf from Nepal, they circumvented this restriction by traveling via India, a country they could enter with ease. Once across the border, they journeyed to New Delhi or Mumbai, where they had to learn to navigate new sociopolitical contexts, most notably dealing with labor recruitment agencies without recourse to their familial or community networks or governmental support as they might at home. In the Gulf, they were either unable or reluctant to seek assistance from Nepali consulates or embassies.[6] Domestic workers and other labor migrants in the region, in contrast, often sought their consulates or embassies as the first avenue of recourse in the face of difficulties they encountered (see chapter 1). Perhaps not surprising, given the labor migration ban's ineffectiveness and mounting evidence it was exacerbating the difficulties of Nepali migrant women, by the summer of 2007 government officials and policy makers in Nepal were considering repealing of the ban and in 2008 they repealed it.

We Don't Show: Being Naram

The position of Nepali and Indian women who migrate to the Gulf region is quite precarious.[7] Stigmatized at home, rendered illegal transnational subjects by their home countries' periodic passing of labor migration bans, South Asian women are unsurprisingly often unwilling to talk about their migration experiences. When the women gathered at Ritu's impromptu gathering mentioned that it was inappropriate for women "to show" that they have been in the Arabian Peninsula, however, they were pointing to another issue, one that has long been examined by works on marriage and changes in women's life cycles in South Asia, but that has yet to be addressed by scholarship focusing on the feminization of South Asian transnational labor migration. Ritu's comment "we go there [Gulf] and we are there [Gulf], and we come here [Nepal] we are here" references a gendered capacity of being naram that undergirds South Asian domestic workers' experiences of migration. Considered an intrinsic capacity and learned capability of young unmarried women to be shaped by their surroundings, this gendered discourse of South Asian women's malleability accounts for my interlocutors' firm conviction that they, rather than their male compatriots or domestic workers of other ethnonational backgrounds, are particularly well suited to engage the transnational spaces of the Inter-Asian region. Women demonstrate their skillfulness at being naram by their seamless integration into different social landscapes, making this gendered capability one that is often difficult to observe, one that can only be glimpsed at the corners and edges of encounters and exchanges, or one that appears in flashes of seeming failure and crisis.

The issue of being naram suffused numerous interactions among my interlocutors in Kuwait. One such interaction, a decidedly mundane conversation, took place late one morning in October. The summer's oppressive heat had started to wane, allowing Ritu and me to linger outside after she finished sweeping the yard. Priya, a domestic worker who lived with her employers in the villa next door, joined us. Picking idly at the leaves of a shrub, Priya updated us about Amita, the domestic worker her employer had recently hired.

> PRIYA: She is sad; crying, crying, crying all night. She misses her home.
> RITU: Does your mama [employer] know?
> PRIYA: A little. When she arrived mama talked to her: said it was normal to be sad, but this chance [opportunity to work] is good . . . that she will work hard, but she will be fine.
> RITU: Let's hope so. Let's hope she is not too *sakht* [hard and unyielding] and foolish.
> PRIYA: Yes. Inshallah.

Ritu and Priya both empathized with Amita's situation. They too had experienced intense feelings of alienation when they first moved to Kuwait. Priya told me she cried for weeks before she finally steeled herself to stop. Ritu's story was more involved. With a fake passport purchased on the Nepali black market, she managed to first migrate to Kuwait at the age of fifteen.[8] Overwhelmed, unable to cope, and desperate, she implored her employers to send her home. Upon her return, she felt an acute sense of shame and spent the next several years saving up in order to return. For Ritu and my other interlocutors, migration was an expensive undertaking, one requiring a great deal of financial organizing and planning. They considered migration to be a necessary invest-ment to attain a longed-for, more prosperous future. Economic considerations were of paramount importance when they explained the reasons for their mi-gration, but economic motivations alone do not account for *how* they deal with the intense dislocation they experienced once they had migrated. To conflate the two would elide a crucial dimension of my interlocutors' transnational ex-periences. When Priya discussed why her tears stemmed, when Ritu broached the shame she felt when she returned to Nepal, and when Ritu and Priya ex-pressed hope that Amita would not be foolish, it was not simply because of the financial costs they could, and in Ritu's case, did incur if they were unable to deal with being in Kuwait. They were referencing another dimension of their migration experiences, one that is very easy to overlook when the motivations for, or end results of migration, rather than the process of migration itself, are emphasized. Expressed in an affective register, my interlocutors were refer-ring to their ability to adjust to their newfound circumstances, an adjustment hinging upon a gendered characteristic they associated with proper woman-hood. Women, they repeatedly indicated, are naram. Women act qua women by demonstrating their facility and proficiency of being naram, of being pliable and adaptable in relation to their social circumstances.

Being naram is resonant with broader discourses of South Asian personhood and femininity. Ethnographies of everyday South Asian social worlds have long documented the fluid nature of South Asian discourses of subjectivity; in them, subjects are understood to be composites shaped by a dynamic configuration or assemblage of words, bodily interactions, social connections, foods, and en-vironmental factors.[9] These discourses take on a distinctly gendered cast as women are considered to be especially fluid and pliable. Women are described as being "like water, which, having no shape of its own, can take the shape of the vessel into which it is poured, or that she should be like soft and malleable clay, which has no form until it is worked into shape by the potter."[10] Studies have highlighted how women's malleability is channeled toward, and consid-ered essential to, their marriageability and ability to adjust to married life.[11] Marriage involves significant transformation, most notably, the remaking of women's subjectivities and social belongings such that they accommodate themselves to, and come to be identified with, their husband's household. As described by Lamb: "a woman would fare better if she were malleable like clay, to be cast into a shape of his choice by her husband, discarding earlier loyalties, attributes, and ties to become absorbed into her husband's family."[12] Enabling women to fit into new social environments, women's malleability is essential to marriage exchanges and their circulation between households.

In Kuwait, South Asian domestic workers' ability to be naram is not chan-neled toward or associated with marriage. Their household experiences are, however, understood in homologous terms. When domestic workers such as Ritu, Priya, and Amita migrate to Kuwait they encounter situations that are overwhelmingly different from those they have previously experienced. They must learn to negotiate a panoply of relationships with employers, fellow domestic workers, drivers, and government and agency officials, all of whom, more often than not, speak a multitude of languages they are not familiar with, such as Arabic, English, Tagalog, or Sinhala. Domestic workers must also learn to discern and come to grips with family traditions, cultural practices and un-derstandings, and traditions of religious practice that are largely inchoate and taken for granted. These traditions, practices, and understandings pervade the most mundane and intimate details of their work and everyday lives, including their dressing, comportment, and modes of communicating and interacting with others.

Affective Labor: "It Is Different"

The work Ritu, Priya, Amita, and other domestic workers undertake entails more than the (purportedly) simple household tasks of cooking, cleaning, or caring for children and the elderly. It is a realm of activity that necessarily im-plicates and shapes their dispositions, sense of self, and subjecthood. The na-ture of this work is challenging, as is the depth and breadth of what it demands of workers, involving difficulties that can be easily eclipsed or disregarded in analyses that are solely focused on the hierarchical relations that exist be-tween domestic workers and their employers, or on incidents of abuse and exploitation. Hema's experiences with her employers point to the challenges domestic workers encounter in their everyday work. Mama Siham and her two daughters, Sadia and Farah, were examples of "good" employers who, from a position of privilege,[13] and a nagging but rarely acknowledged sense of guilt and obligation, treated Hema and the other domestic workers working within their extended family with kindness and generosity. Yet in the face of—not in spite of—their kindness, Hema encountered the same set of challenges as other transnational domestic workers in the Gulf region.

The nature of these challenges was rendered visible through the triangulated yet starkly differentiated nature of my relationship with Hema and her employ-ers. Hema and I first met outside her "work household" at the Islamic da'wa movement's women's center, where she had been taking classes for over a year. When I arrived at the center, she was both curious and highly amused at my fumbling attempts to explain my research to the other women. Cutting through my long-winded and rather ineffectual explanation, she provided a more concise if not wholly accurate description of what I was about, telling the women present I was working on a school report that might eventually be published by a newspaper or magazine if the stories they told me were juicy enough. Thanks in large part to her easygoing and quietly confident manner, we became fast friends and she helped me immeasurably as I began to meet other women at the center. Extremely intelligent, quick witted and playful, Hema juggled words from four languages—Nepali, Hindi and Arabic, which she spoke fluently, and English, which she insisted I help her to learn—on the tip of her tongue, deploying them in different configurations for humor, and effect, as well as more prosaic, direct communication. I was extremely grateful for her skills and proficiency. As a translator, she facilitated and made possible numerous multilingual conversations I had with women at the da'wa center. Often in small groups, these discussions helped me to learn different aspects of domestic workers' understandings and experiences than did my individual conversations with them.

Several weeks after we first met, I was thrilled when Hema approached me with an invitation to meet her employers—Siham Mama and her two daughters—at their home. Hema's reports about my research had piqued their interest, as had my description, during one of our classes, of the old city of Jerusalem. The tea at their home was initially pained and quite awkward. After greeting me at the gate with a quick hug and smile, and then ushering me to the drawing room, Hema disappeared. I was left in the company of her employers as well as Youmma Fatima, their formidable grandmother, with whom I duly shared stories and pictures of Jerusalem's holy sites. Hema later reappeared with a tea cart and proceeded to serve us. Her hand was steady and practiced, but she looked discomfited. After pouring her own tea, she made her way to a chair at the outskirts of the seating area, where she sat quietly, listening and watching our conversation. Not accustomed to her reticence, but also unsure of her rapport with her employers and what was the appropriate thing to do in such a situation, I tried drawing Hema into the conversation a few times. Each attempt elicited a few perfunctory remarks from her. On my way home, I quickly wrote down my thoughts and apprehensions:

> Their [Hema, Siham Mama, her daughters and Youmma Fatima] rapport seemed respectful, fond even . . . when Hema left me with them in the drawing room, she had even joked with the daughters, who were about her age. Maybe it was something that had happened before I came, or

while I came, the switching between Hindi/Urdu, Arabic and English, or (more likely) maybe she isn't used to having her employers meet friends in this type of social setting.[14] Whatever it was, I really didn't know what to do. It felt as though my presence made more apparent, rather than less so, differences (hierarchy, power) between them, something we (?) all felt but didn't say.

A few weeks later, I broached the subject of my visit with Hema. It was during a break in one of our classes. She was in the midst of adjusting her hijab, and her hand stilled. Her eyes dropping to the desk, she considered the matter. She didn't appear surprised, and I suspected she had been thinking about it, knowing I would eventually question her about it:

Wallah, Attiya, I did not know what to do. It was nice, they were nice to have you come and meet you like that. And Mama had bought some cake before coming home [from work] just for our tea. They are nice.

But when you and I talk, it is one thing. When I talk with them, with Mama, it is different. With Sadia and Farah [daughters], it is also different. We are friendly, but it is different. Strange it was you people meeting.

The issue of "it is different" influenced my subsequent visits. Until the family's frequent trips overseas—and the preparation surrounding the wedding of Sadia, their eldest daughter—kept them too busy to meet, I visited Hema's household numerous times. During these occasions my time with both Hema and Siham Mama and her daughters rarely overlapped. I would spend my time with either Hema, in the kitchen or in her room, or with Siham Mama and her daughters, in the dining or family rooms. Both Hema and Mama and her daughters would occasionally ask me about what I had discussed with the other, and they certainly spoke to one another about conversations I had with them (something they would unself-consciously reference during our conversations). However, we all experienced this dense, overlapping, interconnected realm of dialogue in discrete segments—different times and spaces of interaction, each characterized by different registers through which Hema-myself, Siham Mama/her daughters-myself, and Hema–Siham Mama/her daughters related and conversed with one another.

Sitting on Ritu's front porch in Nepal many months and miles later, I again raised the issue of "it is different." Hema and I had been discussing whether she planned on returning to Kuwait, and this issue figured prominently in her decision making. By then I had developed a pretty clear sense of her routine in Kuwait, one I had come to learn in bits and pieces through my visits: Hema woke early in the morning, around dawn, when the family awoke to perform their morning prayers (*fajr*). She made breakfast for the family—eggs, toast, fruit, cereal—which she laid out in the kitchen, for them to come and eat when they were ready. In the morning, when the rest of the family was out of the house, she usually took care of laundry and/or cleaning. After taking a break late morning, she would then start preparing the main meal of the day, the afternoon meal, which would be ready by the time the family came home and was ready to eat around 3 PM. Hema would then clear and clean up, and take a late afternoon break. The last of her duties of the day came when she prepared the early evening tea, and sometimes ironed the clothes when members of the family headed out for the evening. Siham mama strictly enforced the rule that in the evenings, Hema was not to be bothered by anyone.

Breaks in this routine only occurred when the family was hosting or attending a large gathering (Hema would attend if they were attending an event at a close friend's or family members' home to help with the serving of food and to meet with the other maids/domestic workers), during Ramadan, when the family traveled (which they did frequently in the summers), and in the weeks leading up to their daughter's marriage, when Hema worked around the clock. During breaks, and her weekly day off, Hema would often speak to friends and family members on her mobile phone; attend her Islamic da'wa classes or do homework associated with them; continue her largely self-taught Arabic lessons; watch Nepali, Indian, and Arab programs on the satellite-linked television in her room; visit with the other domestic workers living in the extended family's home; and have friends over when Youmma was out of the house or abroad.

Siham Mama, Sadia, and Farah were conscientious and caring employers, who frequently told Hema (and me) that they regarded her as one of her own daughters or as a friend.[15] They were careful not to overwork her; they paid her wages regularly and on time; and in addition to her room, board, toiletries and clothes (as per contract stipulations) they also paid for her mobile phone and gave her pocket money when they went to the shops or traveled. On her journey back to Nepal, the family arranged for Hema to stay with friends of theirs during her long layover in Sharjah, and they gave her a lump sum gift of cash and/or reimbursement for her extra work shortly after Sadia's marriage, as well as gifts of clothes, watches, and perfume for her and her family.

Hema's employers were exemplary in their treatment of her, something few domestic workers I met experienced with their employers. In our conversations, Hema mentioned that she felt a deep appreciation for them, and was enormously grateful to have them as her *kafeel*, especially given the stories that circulated about the situation of other domestic workers in the Gulf region. In the same breath, however, she would also underline another dimension of her work, something she came closest to articulating during my visit with her in Nepal:

> When I am at their home, I feel as though it is my home for a while, but really it is their home . . . I try to remind myself that everyday there, whenever I have been out [of the house or away overseas] and feel good coming back I remind myself I am not really home . . . But this place [gestures to her front porch and lawn] feels strange now too, feels strange at least now.
>
> They [employers] are nice to me—but they are fond of me. They give things, they helped [gave gifts for her family] when I returned back. Although I don't ask, I didn't ask. I think they wouldn't like it if I asked . . . They are fond of me, and they *have* to be fond of me, I have to make sure of this, this is necessary, and to be fond of me I have to be close, but not too close, you know? Close enough for us to be friendly, for the house to be nice and easy, but not too close . . .
>
> You see, they have to like me. It can be hard [on me] because they have to like me . . . not like you, I can be frank with you . . . I can tease you and bother you . . . but I have to be nice with them even as I joke with them . . . I don't need to be nice with you unless I want, which I sometimes do [*laughs*]. It is different.

A thread running throughout our conversations, "it is different" underscores a dimension of domestic workers' experiences that is often elided. When Hema began working with "Mama," the training she underwent was not limited to learning how to operate appliances and cook foods unfamiliar to her. Her disciplining was not reducible to learning the routines and rhythms, and the particular preferences and tastes of the family. The work she undertook was intimate, but not just because it involved everyday interactions in the rooms and halls of the household. Hema's work also involved her very behavior and comportment, a continuous calibration of the way in which she engaged with Mama Siham and her family to ensure that they were fond of her, the constant awareness that a sharp remark, a sullen expression, uneasy rapport, or overstepped familiarity diminish her standing and situation with them. In her own words, this dimension of her work "was hard," one intensified by the constant interactions her living with the family in their home entailed.

Hema's experience points to how domestic work involves not just physical labor (e.g., cleaning) or the making of specific objects (e.g., meals), but also involves the performance of subjectivities that produce particular sets of affective experiences with their employers—in particular of their feeling at ease in their home, or other interlocutors described as "making *them* happy" and "making sure they are not bothered."[16] In contrast to gendered assumptions that domestic work is an unskilled occupation undertaken by subjects uniquely suited to this type of work (i.e., women), it is in fact a realm of activity that not only requires the development of skills, language abilities, and sets of cross-cultural and religious knowledge, but also necessitates the cultivation of dispositions and ongoing self-disciplining with respect to interpersonal interactions. Their work subsumes and blurs the boundaries between different categories of laboring, including socially reproductive labor that produces and sustains populations of workers and citizens,[17] emotional labor that requires the enactment of particular feelings and dispositions in the workplace,[18] and affective labor[19] that produces or manipulates affects. As Nicole Constable explains: "Domestic workers' labour extend[s] into her most private domain; her body, her personality, her voice, and her emotions."[20] An affective form of labor, domestic work is a realm requiring too much of the self rather than too little; workers' very personhood is a necessary part of and is produced through their work.[21]

The contrast—the "it is different" between my interlocutors' relationships with their employers and our own—helped them to articulate, and for me to identify this otherwise unspoken, intangible, and often overlooked dimension of their work. Although not all domestic workers experience this immaterial and affective dimension of their work in terms of their employers needing to be fond of them, as part of their work they do need to negotiate, and come to adopt particular sets of dispositions and modes of interacting that are suitable for their particular households. For some this includes being an unobtrusive and discrete presence in their work households, whereas for others, the adoption of an encouraging and soothing manner with their employers. Visiting my interlocutors in Nepal, I was struck by the differences in how they comported themselves in their family households. Hema, who was generally outgoing and talkative with her employers and myself (though not necessarily when we were all together), was a quiet presence in her parents' home. Ritu, who generally went about her work and engaging with her employers in a subdued, serene manner, was an assertive and vocal presence in her mother's and her sister's homes.

These differences in domestic workers' demeanor reflect what Hema and Ritu referred to as the "not showing" they had been overseas, the imperative of which took on several valences of meaning. Despite their transnational travel and the wages they had earned, as younger women they were expected to behave in ways that did not upset existing gendered and aged status differences in their families. They also had to be cognizant and careful in their speech and actions—assessing potential changes that might be acceptable to their family and community members, and those that would be frowned upon. My interlocutors were expected to not unsettle or change the existing dynamics of their work households, as well as their family households. There existed a tacit, unspoken expectation that they should adapt to these spaces rather than expect these spaces to adapt to their presence. Coalescing with other factors discussed in the previous two chapters, this dynamic intensified domestic workers' experiences of temporariness and suspension between their family households and work households, and ensured South Asian migrant domestic workers' position as dual agents of reproduction. Although they expressed apprehensiveness and found the process difficult—as Hema stated, "it is hard"; Priya's and Amita's tears upon first arriving in Kuwait are also poignant illustrations—as South Asian women they considered themselves to have the capacity, and based on their gendered training and disciplining, the capability to undertake this affective dimension of their transnational work, and to adjust to their changed circumstances. Their ability to do so both presupposed and further produced their being naram.

Prerogatives of Age and Authority

South Asian domestic workers' ability to be naram informed how they understood and assessed their own ability to engage and maneuver their transnational experiences. It also provided an implicit basis from which they assessed others they encountered on their transnational journeys. Ritu for example, was reluctant to discuss her first migration experience to Kuwait not just because of the illegality of her actions according to both Nepali and Kuwaiti law, or because of the money she lost when she returned home early, but because of the shame she felt for not having adjusted. She perceived her inability to accommodate herself to her new circumstances in Kuwait as a failing that she linked to a discourse of age: she had been too young to be able to fully enact being naram, and her inability to enact being naram, indicated a lack of discipline she associated with maturity and proper womanhood.

The experience of older South Asian domestic workers points to another dimension of the interrelation between being naram and age. Over time, South Asian women's ability to be naram is said to wane, a change that does not necessarily evidence the diminishment of their ability to adjust, but of the expectation that they should or need to adjust. When she explained why she wanted to remain in Kuwait after having effectively retired, Mary/Maryam, then in her mid-sixties, pointed to how she had lived and worked in Kuwait for over thirty years. She had become accustomed to the everyday rhythms and practices of her Kuwaiti household, had grown attached to the family, and had developed Islamic pieties that differed from the religious practices of her family and community in India. She underscored that she was unwilling, and not unable, to deal with the myriad adjustments her return to India would entail. Even if members of Fardous's household did not consider her to be kin, Mary/Maryam was considered to be an integral part of their family and household. To mark her retirement, the family had built a small wing for Mary/Maryam, a space of her own over which she held sway.

Geeti's situation was somewhat similar. Like Mary/Maryam she had also made the conscious decision not to return to India; however, every year she spent one or two months visiting her brother's family in India, a special arrangement she had come to with Mama Lulua. When she was in Kuwait she continued to work regularly, although her responsibilities had been considerably reduced. Her rooms—a bedroom, a small sitting room and an adjoining bathroom—were set apart from Mama Lulua's family as well as the other domestic workers of the house. Both Mary/Maryam and Geeti were responsible for coordinating and managing the work of the other domestic workers of their households. The expectation that both women should be naram eased as a prerogative of their age, and in relation to the relative autonomy and control they had over their everyday activities and living spaces.

In contrast to Ritu, Mary/Maryam and Geeti did not perceive their not having or wanting to accommodate themselves to their circumstances—their not performing being naram—as a lack or failing on their part. Rather, it indexed a shift in their position and authority within their family households and work households. Their situations were analogous to how South Asian domestic workers perceived a major axis of gendered differences between themselves and their "mamas" or female Kuwaiti employers. Based on their own experiences in Nepal or India—ones they generalized to the Arabian Peninsula, or based on common understandings if not Orientalist stereotypes that circulate in the Inter-Asian region, ones reinscribed and reflected by the training and "cross-cultural" orientation sessions some of my interlocutors participated in before migrating—many South Asian domestic workers expected family and household relations in the region to be patriarchal in nature, ones in which age-based status differences also existed. The realities they encountered tended to be messier and more complicated. Perhaps most surprising to many domestic workers, a surprise tinged either with their disapproval or admiration, was the authority wielded by Kuwaiti women. They perceived Kuwaiti women, both young and old, to be *sakht*, or tough and unyielding in their everyday inter-actions. Whether it was Kuwaiti cultural practices, or—as one interlocutor put it—the "character" of Kuwaiti society, or whether it was a function of Ku-waiti women's wealth and elevated position as citizens, women were not being taught or trained to be supple and accommodating to their family members' wishes. For many South Asian domestic workers, this explained the high inci-dence of divorce in Kuwaiti society, and why there were so many single-parent women-centric households. As Phoolan once described, being naram is like glue for women's families. In the absence of Kuwaiti women taking on this function, this responsibility has fallen to domestic workers, pointing to how their being naram not only helps them to accommodate themselves to their "work households" but their very presence is necessary to the production and reproduction of these spaces. Like their Kuwaiti employers—because of their seniority and the authority this conferred upon them—Mary/Maryam, Geeti, and other domestic workers no longer had to concern themselves with this matter and/or had devolved the responsibility to other domestic workers under their supervision.

Being Naram and the Particularities of South Asian Womanhood

Discourses of women being naram were also thrown into relief through con-trasts South Asian domestic workers drew between themselves and other for-eign residents and migrants. In particular, they often commented on Filipina women in ways that revealed their own understandings of what constitutes proper gendered behaviors and roles. During one gathering, a Friday afternoon when my interlocutors' employers were assembled for an extended family lunch, this issue was at the forefront of my interlocutors' minds. One of their employers had recently hired Alice, a domestic worker from the Philippines, to look after her children. It being her day off, Alice was not present, but the rest of the domestic workers employed by the extended family were gathered in the kitchen, preoccupied with last-minute food preparation. The seven women present—migrants from Nepal, India, and Sri Lanka—had lived and worked in Kuwait for periods ranging from two to fourteen years. They knew each other relatively well, the cumulative effect of having accompanied their em-ployers to numerous such social events. These meetings were important occa-sions when they updated each other about household news, shared advice and tips about living and working in Kuwait, and gossiped about all and sundry. Since her hiring four months earlier, Alice was a frequent topic of conversa-tion. The women present had met Filipina women, but none had worked with them on a close, sustained basis.[22] They were aware of general public discourse that portrayed Filipina women as the most accomplished of domestic workers.[23] It was this issue that framed their discussion about Alice:

LAKSHMI: Yes, she is good—with the children—she is really good. Very patient, very gentle. Good . . .

MEENA: But?

LAKSHMI: She is bold . . . loud . . .

NEELI: Does mama or baba [employers] mind?

LAKSHMI: They have not said anything.

AA: Have they asked you about this?

LAKSHMI: No. But I think they mind. Her clothes are not good, and I think they might mind this.

AA: How are they not good?

LAKSHMI: The clothes are good for the Philippines, for going to the city [on her day off], but in the house . . . I don't think so good for the house . . . not for this house. There are men present!

MEENA: Not suitable, huh? Have you said anything to her [Alice]?

LAKSHMI: Yes, but she will not listen . . . [and] says "no, no, I don't know what you are saying."

MEENA: Yes, they [Alice and unspecified others] can be hard [sakht]; it is difficult for them to understand about these things.

In part the women's critiques of Alice—that her clothes and demeanor were inappropriate—can be read as a wary and defensive response to Alice's presence in their midst given the widespread perception that Filipina women are the most skilled and valued domestic workers. As the labor representative at the Philippines Embassy once explained to me, an understanding echoed by many Kuwaitis, Filipina women were considered to be the "Cadillac" of domestic workers—an (objectifying) comment illustrating the quality of their work, and their being regarded as a luxury item and status symbol among households. Lakshmi and the other women's comments were also laced with an equally gendered and racialized discourse about Filipina women in the Gulf, one depicting them as immodest and flirtatious figures who are constantly trying to attract or "trap" men. Linking together their criticisms was their overall assessment that Alice was "hard," a characteristic making it difficult if not impossible for Alice to recognize how improper her behavior could be. As a case in point, Lakshmi focused her attention on Alice's clothes. Like the majority of my interlocutors, Lakshmi's dressing was markedly different from that of Alice and from most Filipina domestic workers. Rather than t-shirts, sweatshirts, khakis, and jeans, they often wore *panjabis*, maid's uniforms, *abayat*, or long, loosely draped housecoats.[24] Some of these outfits were similar to what they wore prior to their migration in their home communities, a sartorial similarity that indexes long-standing interregional connections between South Asia and the Arabian Peninsula. Others mentioned that they had received these clothes from their employers, or that they had developed a taste for them as a function of the time they had spent in the region. Many considered these clothes to be sophisticated and smart, bespeaking a form of modernity they associated with the Gulf. In discussing Alice's clothes and other comparable situations, my interlocutors indicated that it was not so much the selection of clothing they took issue with—as one put it: "we all have things that seem nice to us." What was of concern was how and when these clothes were worn. For Lakshmi, Alice's choice of clothes, which she felt were better suited to the Philippines, or to wear when going to the city center on her day off, demonstrated Alice's lack of attunement to accepted practice within their Kuwaiti household. Alice's lack of recognition or understanding was attributed to her being sakht, or hard. Here being "hard" was not associated with stubborn refusal as is common in English, but rather an inability to apprehend the acceptability or appropriateness of one's behavior and activities.

Being sakht was an attribute largely, though as we have seen not exclusively, associated with men. In addition to meaning being incapable of discerning the subtleties of sociocultural practices different from those of their home communities, the term *sakht* also carries with it the connotation of being inflexible and brittle in the face of these changed circumstances. The situation of Bipash, a driver working in the household of Chandani's employer's daughter, Ilham Bibi, provides a good illustration. Ilham Bibi had decided to hire a driver in coordination with her sister. She and her sister had daughters who were starting middle school in a neighborhood different from where both families lived, and far from where they and their husbands worked. The two decided the driver would live at Ilham Bibi's home, where the family had empty living quarters outdoors, adjacent to the family home. With the help of their father's driver, they were able to find Bipash, a driver who was already residing in Kuwait. Bipash had migrated from Sri Lanka three years earlier. For two years he worked as an agricultural laborer in the south of the country, close to the Saudi border. Through networks of fellow Tamils, he managed to find a job as an occasional driver at a warehouse on the outskirts of the city. Bipash shared a two-bedroom apartment with four other men, one of whom worked with Ilham Bibi's father.

When Bipash was hired, he was initially quite content. He continued to live in the city, his new quarters were luxurious in comparison to the dormitory and shared apartment where he had formerly resided, and most important, he was relieved to have a regular, relatively well-paying job. He had married a year before migrating, and in the intervening years, his wife had given birth to a daughter and was expecting another child. After several months of working in Ilham Bibi's household, however, it was clear that things were not going well. Chandani mentioned how stressed Bipash appeared and how short-tempered he had become, issues that came up during one of our conversations with Lakshmi.

AA: What is the matter? Is his family [in Sri Lanka] ok?

CHANDANI: Yes, they are fine, or so he says.

AA: Are there problems with his work here? Is he working too hard?

CHANDANI: No; he is working like all drivers . . . The girls [employers' daughters] can be difficult sometimes, but not too bad . . . But now he and they [employers] don't agree [get along] so well. I thought, maybe he is lonely [because] he is away from his friends [in the city]?

AA: Does he see them on his day off?

CHANDANI: Yes. And sometimes during the day while the girls are at school.

AA: Is he lonely here? Does he come into the house?

CHANDANI: Not so much; just to talk to Baba or help with things sometimes. But this is usual. He is [socializes] with the other men [drivers] in the neighborhood.

LAKSHMI: No, this is a problem men have. This work, this being away from their homes, this is hard.

CHANDANI: Yes, yes. You are right. They have these problems. It is hard for them.

AA: I don't understand. Harder for them than [for] you, than [for] women?

LAKSHMI: Different. It is different, you know? But we are better at this. They work, yes. But they are not good at . . . they are not used to this, here [extends her hand upward and moves it in a circular motion] like we are.

Bipash's conduct, most notably his anxiousness and short-temperedness with members of Ilham Bibi's household, was greatly affecting his work. Rather than only attributing Bipash's behavior to isolation, unhappiness, overwork, or as a response to their employers' actions, Lakshmi and Chandani understood his situation in different terms. They read his behavior as being symptomatic of male migrants' experiences in the Gulf. In describing the difficulties male migrants experience, Lakshmi indicated that they are not as skilled or accustomed to dealing with "this"—a gestured utterance referencing and blurring together households and Kuwait—as are she and other female South Asian migrant domestic workers. In anticipation of their circulation through marriage, women were taught to expect to move between households and to adjust to the changes entailed by their move. Men, however, did not have similar disciplining or embodied knowledge to draw upon, and consequently did not have the necessary training or sensibility to adapt to similar changes. Men were accustomed to being accommodated rather than accommodating themselves to new households, and by extension, to novel sociocultural circumstances that mark their migrations. As Hema and Ritu mentioned at the outset of this chapter, men remain the same or are "hard" in the face of these changes. Men were seen as having skills—for example, Bipash's ability to drive, maintain his vehicle and navigate Kuwait's often-treacherous traffic—which they were able to translate into and develop in the spaces to which they migrate. They were, however, unlikely to be attuned to, or transformed by, changes in the everyday practices and relations that characterize the places they migrate to. These gendered differences accounted for why Lakshmi and Chandani thought that drivers, gardeners, and other male migrants working for households often had their own quarters and were not integrated into household activities in the same way as were female migrants. As Bipash's situation highlights, men were likely to have difficulties and be disruptive in maneuvering these spaces in contrast to South Asian domestic workers' own seamlessness in these spaces.

Suffused Malleabilities

The discourse of South Asian women being naram—a gendered, learned capability of being malleable that indexes proper womanhood—helps us to understand why it is that South Asian migrant women consider themselves to be ideal transnational subjects, able to circulate and engage their surroundings in a way that distinguishes them from domestic workers and migrant women of other ethnonational backgrounds, and from male migrants. South Asian migrant domestic workers' ability to circulate transnationally is not predicated on intrinsic skills and temperament they possess, for example, that they are naturally more nurturing or caring,[25] or are already possessed of the ability to cook, clean, or care for children and the elderly of the Gulf region. Rather, they develop capabilities, dispositions, identifications, and belongings through the relations and activities that mark their transnational labor migration. This gendered discourse of subjectivity both accounts for and naturalizes their malleability, enabling them to circulate and have the necessary underlying ability to develop the skills and comportment necessary for them to function as dual agents of reproduction. At the same time, betwixt and between their work and family households—spaces they are suspended between—they develop aptitudes and dispositions that are both related to yet exceed these spaces, forms of excess or everyday conversions that by virtue of their being naram, they try not "to show."

This gendered discourse of South Asian women's malleabilities suffuses and shapes domestic workers' experiences of everyday conversions. It not only throws into relief the gendered and sociohistorical discursive locations of their care work and affective labor, but so too their attunement and adoption of Islamic precepts and practices, processes that I discuss in the following chapters. This discourse of women's malleability undergirds and works in tandem with contemporary processes of religious reform and Islamic ethical formation in reshaping South Asian migrant women's subjectivities, affinities, and belongings that mark their everyday conversions. Being naram resonates with the fluid, flexible student-centered pedagogies of Kuwait's Islamic da'wa movement, thus facilitating domestic workers' deepening learning of Islamic precepts and practices.

FOUR

HOUSETALK

This housetalk, what is its use; its importance?
—Chandani

A Question

Chandani and I were crossing the compound, making our way to the rooms in the servants' quarters she and her husband shared. She was carrying the cake I had brought. I was carrying the tea she had made. We were quieter than usual. The finality of this, our last meeting, loomed large. After decades of living in Kuwait, Chandani and her husband, whom she had recently married, had finalized their plans to return to her village in Southern India. My fieldwork drawing to a close, I was leaving Kuwait in a couple of days.

Years before, when I first crossed the compound's sprawl, it had struck me as a strange jumble. Consisting of several villas interconnected by a series of courtyards and gardens, the compound was an eclectic mishmash of architecture and decor. Passing through one caught glimpses of a blue-tiled and frescoed solarium that would not be out of place in Isfahan; a *diwaniyya* whose spare stucco walls contrasted with the room's intricately carved wood benches and gaily striped cushions; a sleek modernist building made of striations of stone and glass; a cavernous kitchen eminently functional in its design; and a colorfully tiled sitting area that could easily provide a backdrop for a Pedro Almodóvar film.

The compound was located in a neighborhood not far past Kuwait's first ring road, one roughly tracing the path of the city's historic defense wall. With the onset of Kuwait's petro-fueled development, the first ring road became less of a marker of enclosure and containment than of growth—of successive waves of urban development radiating outward from its path. Within this geography of growth, Ilham Bibi's family home was located close to the center. Over the tops of the trees, and through gaps between the villas on the horizon, I could see the city center's shimmering glass skyscrapers.

The compound's panoply of styles, and location in one of Kuwait's oldest and most exclusive neighborhoods were all visible, physical manifestations of what I had discovered through many visits: Chandani's employer, Ilham Bibi, was from a branch of a very influential family whose name was ubiquitous in Kuwaiti public life. Historically her family had maintained trade and familial ties with Basra and the coastal areas of present-day Iran. Since the 1940s, her branch of the family had shifted away from commercial activities and become an integral part of Kuwait's state-building efforts. No longer trading, the family continued to travel, mainly for educational purposes. Funded largely by state scholarships, both male and female members of the family were sent abroad in the mid- to late twentieth century to study at educational institutions throughout Egypt, Lebanon, Germany, England, and the United States. A part of Kuwait's then small but growing intelligentsia, members of Ilham Bibi's family had held ambassadorial posts abroad, deanships at local universities, and leadership positions in many of the country's social organizations.[1] Family members had held key positions within government as well.

The names and stories of Ilham Bibi's family members were now firmly interwoven into my understanding of the compound, helping me to recognize how the seemingly random parts of the layered whole expressed particular members' personal trajectories of travel and taste. Also interwoven into these spaces—a silent yet vital backdrop to the running of the compound and to the many accomplishments of Ilham Bibi's family—were the stories of another network of people, ones whose names would never appear in Kuwaiti history books or placards in public sites, but who had contributed to the family's ability to "serve their country" as Ilham Bibi's father once put it. This was a motley crew linked to one another not by blood or nationality, but by overlapping sets of work and migration experiences.

In one section of the largest house lived Umm Muhammad, Ilham Bibi's half-aunt, an elderly black woman, the daughter of a wet nurse and concubine who had been brought to Kuwait from East Africa by Ilham Bibi's grandfather. Every Friday just after the main congregational prayers, she along with Raquel, her

Filipina caregiver, and a revolving cast of her children and grandchildren who were not otherwise traveling or committed elsewhere, would join Ilham Bibi and others of their extended family for the weekly lunch gathering.

Hisham, a "houseboy" from Yemen whom Ilham Bibi's uncle had employed, had planted the hedges encircling the compound, and the rose trellis framing its side gateway. In addition to gardening, Hisham had been responsible for his employer's everyday care—tending to his clothes, shining his shoes, and chauffeuring him in a Mercedes sedan he both treated and drove like a tank. Hisham had long since retired to his village in Yemen, but his son and a grandson worked as drivers and bureaucratic fixers in a government ministry where Ilham Bibi's brother held a position.

Bilal, the family's Bangladeshi gardener, now tended the shrubberies and gardens Hisham had planted decades ago. Bilal had added jasmine bushes, and every year coaxed along flowers to withstand the devastating summer heat. Along with the extended family's three drivers, men from Sri Lanka and India, Bilal lived in a row of quarters located toward the back of the compound. Weather permitting, on the first Sunday of every month, they would assemble at an empty sandlot with the other South Asian drivers and gardeners of the neighborhood to play a few rounds of cricket—games they would bring up in winks and teasing comments when they crossed paths while going about their work.

Tucked away in various villas' maid quarters, ones located in basements or next to the kitchens, were the younger domestic workers, women from India, Sri Lanka, Nepal, Indonesia, and the Philippines. These women were tasked with the most demanding jobs. In the mornings, when their employers were away at work or attending to other affairs, they would fan out throughout the compound dusting, sweeping, mopping, scrubbing, attending to piles of laundry and dishes, or doing the preparation work for cooking. In the afternoons and evenings, these women assisted the senior domestic workers as they cooked, served the family and servants' meals, did the grocery shopping, looked after children or elderly family members, and tended to their employers' personal needs (e.g., ironing, dusting of shoes). Due to their status, one largely pegged to the length of time they had spent working for Ilham Bibi's family, the three senior domestic workers were given apartment-style quarters that were located above the multicar garage near the side gate. It was to these quarters that Chandani and I wended our way.

If my familiarity with Chandani and her work household was now expressed in companionable silence—my questions to her had long since become less scattershot or directed, easing into more relaxed conversation—for Chandani it proved the opposite. Of late she had begun asking me a fair number of questions about my research and even more personal questions about myself—questions that took me aback and moved me in equal measure. I felt as though at some point during our meetings I had begun taking on dimensions other than "the journalist" she would semiseriously refer to me as, that I had developed into less of an anomalous figure to her, becoming a category she sought to give more definition to. She had once told me that like her—I was "an independent working single-lady" going about my business without fuss—even if, she added, my business was a rather peculiar one. It was perhaps in this spirit of kindliness that she had become concerned that I complete my work successfully, what she referred to as my "passing your exams." Comfortably settled in her sitting room, it was this concern that spurred her to pose a question I suspected she had long been contemplating:

> Attiya, I still don't understand. This house-talk, what is its use; its importance? Those people who will see your report, what do they care about this? I am a practicing Muslim, yes, but my life is . . . well . . . pretty boring. Tell them about the life of the Prophet . . . that would be better.
> They'll like that better.

Chandani's comment prompts the central issue I address in this chapter. Over the course of conducting fieldwork, many of my interlocutors discussed their everyday Islamic conversions in terms of their daily activities and intimate relationships within their households—what Chandani referred to as "housetalk." When I first began meeting with my interlocutors, I often overlooked these matters. Chandani, Mary/Maryam, Phoolan, Ritu, Hema and others told me tales of seemingly simple mundane matters articulated in terms of temporariness, suspension or being *naram*: of work and gossip within Kuwaiti households, of financial and family matters back home, and of everyday Islamic practice. I waited for the unexpected, the underlying, the eventful, the dramatic related to their adoption of Islamic precepts and practices. I was watchful for any word, any gesture hinting of an employer who might practice Islam in an exemplary or coercive manner, or hinting of a life-changing encounter with a Muslim *da'iya* (those who call people to Islam), or to something more. Few such tales or hints were forthcoming. I was perplexed. I was also a little disbelieving. Domestic workers' articulations of their conversions contrasted with how others perceived and depicted them. Throughout the region domestic workers' Islamic conversions were either attributed to the direct outreach efforts of Kuwait's Islamic da'wa movement, or to domestic workers' precarious positioning within Kuwaiti households leading many to convert in the hopes of being treated better, or because of the pressure, whether implicit or explicit, brought to bear upon them by their employers.

Rather than focusing on reasons or explanations for why they were converting to Islam, a question others in Kuwait were preoccupied with, my interlocutors were more so intent on the question of what their becoming Muslim entailed, and how their conversions were developing through their everyday transnational experiences centered on household spaces. To my interlocutors, explanations for why they were adopting Islam were not the point. The significance of their conversions was intertwined with what Chandani referred to as housetalk. Domestic workers' housetalk, their discourse of becoming Muslim, differs from those who apprehend their experiences in terms of conventional discourses about "conversion"—where their adoption of Islam is seen as a radical break, departure, or rebirth in their lives, a radical change brought about and attributable to a clear reason, motivation, or explanation. Domestic workers' experiences are not legible in this discursive frame, leading many to misapprehend and question the sincerity of their conversions.

The Household as a Space of Confluence

In subtle and muted ways, domestic workers' "housetalk" points to their everyday relations and activities within households as generative of their adoption of Islamic precepts and practices, features I slowly became attuned to over the course of visiting with my interlocutors in their Kuwaiti households, meeting with their employers, and attending the classes some took at Kuwait's Islamic da'wa movement's women's center, and with respect to some of my Nepali interlocutors, visiting with them in Nepal. Through the gradual sedimenting and overlaying of these experiences I came to appreciate how both their family and work households were not just sites bookending their transnational migrations and journeys. Rather, their households were dense and vital sites of intimacy, laboring, affect, economic exchange, and asymmetrical gendered, aged, raced, and kinship relations that animated their transnational movements and experiences. Positioned and disciplined into becoming dual agents of reproduction, domestic workers often described their transnational experiences in the register of temporariness, suspension or being naram. Yet despite the assumption they live "frozen lives" of "just working, just working" (see chapters 1 and 2), domestic workers live lives marked by everyday conversions that they and others find difficult to conceive of in this way (or "can't quite think" as Geeti stated in chapter 1) when heteronormative nuclear families are the hegemonic norm, everyday conversions moreover that they tried not "to show" (see chapter 3). Domestic workers' adoption of Islam expresses and marks the culmination of one trajectory of everyday conversions. For domestic workers adopting Islamic precepts and practices, their households in Kuwait constituted spaces of everyday activity and interaction through which they gradually came to develop Islamic sensibilities—Islamic sensibilities through which they then came to reexperience their households. Far from experiencing their adoption of Islam as a radical change, stemming from a dramatic episode or sudden realization—and far from experiencing them as a rejection of their previous lives and practices—domestic workers' conversion to Islam entailed a gradual recasting and reworking of their lives, one rooted in the recursiveness of their everyday experiences within the household.

Their experiences underscore a facet of paid domestic work that recent scholarship on migrant domestic workers, and immaterial and affective labor has analyzed.[2] The work undertaken by domestic workers—such as tending to family members during trips and caring for the elderly or the infirm— necessarily involves the disciplining and training of their comportment, affect, and sense of self. What existing research has not accounted for, and what migrant domestic workers' housetalk in Kuwait points to, are the ways in which domestic work can be infused with religious ideas and practices and how households are spaces of confluence between Islamic ethical practice and the affective and immaterial labor entailed by domestic work.

Little focus has been given to migrant domestic workers' religious experiences. What research has been conducted focuses on how religion provides an important motivation for domestic workers' migration, for example, how religious imaginaries and aspirations provide the impetus for Filipina and Indonesian women's migration to Muslim or Christian Holy Lands (i.e., Saudi Arabia or Palestine/Israel). Or, existing research focuses on the support and sociality coreligionists (typically of the same ethnonational background) provide one another in diasporic contexts.[3] South Asian migrant domestic workers' housetalk and everyday Islamic conversions in Kuwait point to another dimension of migrant domestic workers' religious experiences: how religious sensibilities, affinities, and belongings develop in and through domestic workers' everyday embodied practice, work, and relations centered on household spaces. Domestic workers' housetalk and experiences of everyday Islamic conversion unsettle easy distinctions and point to the subtle imbrication of political-economic and religious processes, realms often assumed to be distinct and separate, or in Bruno Latour's parlance, treated as "purified categories."[4] Their stories point to the importance of examining the comingling and mutual constitution of the political-economic and religious without eliding or fetishizing the importance of each to the other. Housetalk pushes us to look at these processes in different ways.

To convey and illustrate housetalk requires us to dwell awhile with my interlocutors and for me to recount to you their stories, albeit in condensed and stylized forms, that address the major thematic threads crosscutting their stories of everyday conversion. This includes how becoming Muslim is part and parcel of processes that rework workers' subjectivities within Kuwaiti households, how their becoming Muslim develops through their relations with their Kuwaiti employers but does not eclipse existing bases of differences and hierarchies existing between them, and how their experiences of becoming Muslim are influenced by their previous traditions of religious or secular practice.

Reworking of Subjectivities: Affective Labor and Islamic Ethical Formation

CHANDANI

Chandani's story encapsulates several dimensions of domestic workers' experiences of everyday Islamic conversion, in particular how the process entails the reworking of their subjectivities. For Chandani the process was a long-term one involving a series of shifts in her role and relations with others in her employers' household. When she first met her employer, Ilham Bibi, Chandani was relieved. It was only when she met the other domestic workers of the compound that she became somewhat concerned. Telling me of her initial experiences two decades later, Chandani's recollections were in part colored by the intervening years she had spent in Kuwait. They were also inflected by a gritty bravado she had begun developing a few years before her migration.

Then in her early twenties, Chandani had come to a decision her family members and friends had vehemently opposed: she divorced her husband. When they first married, Chandani and her husband appeared to be well matched. Both were from families whose struggling middle-class aspirations defined their decision making in ways both big and small. Chandani's father had inherited a small plot of land in their village in Southern India, where he had started a chicken and egg farm, a business her two brothers had expanded. Both brothers had married well. In the hopes of further improving their fortunes, the family had pooled their resources together to provide Chandani a dowry that would also enable her to marry well.

Vinod, the man they set their sights on, was from a neighboring village and had been pursuing a college education both families hoped would qualify him for a government job. Chandani was initially thrilled with her family's choice. With his mustache and stylish jeans and shirts, Vinod cut a dashing Amitabh Bachchan–like figure, and Chandani relished the idea of moving with him to the city. Once in Mumbai, however, their hoped for future stagnated. Chandani's husband failed his exams and found a far less prestigious job as a clerk in a small shipping company. To compound their marital woes, the two were unable to have children, something Vinod and his family blamed Chandani for.

In the months before she left him, Vinod was "often away," a term Chandani used to hint at, and gloss over, a host of dissolute and illicit activities. Rather than returning to her family and to a life of polite ignominy in her village, Chandani sold off whatever was left of her wedding jewelry and dowry furniture to fund her migration to Kuwait (chapter 2). Her plan was to save up enough money to become what she called an independent single lady. Only then would she return to her family's village.

Initially resolute about her decision to migrate to Kuwait, Chandani became increasingly apprehensive as she waited for the manpower agent to process her paperwork. Life as a divorced woman for her in India of the early 1980s was proving quite difficult. She was constantly interpellated into a sense of womanly failure, and continually subject to suspicions of sexual impropriety. Would life in Kuwait prove much different—or, she worried—more difficult? What would it be like to work for another woman, a presumably successful wife and mother, one whose family and household were intact? Would she encounter problems working for Kuwaitis, a people who were starting to develop a reputation throughout the region for being arrogant in their newfound wealth?

Chandani's concerns were assuaged when she met her employer, Ilham Bibi. Only a few years older than Chandani, Ilham Bibi carried herself with a breezy confidence, had a kindly if sometimes condescending manner, and ran her home with businesslike efficiency—all of which met with Chandani's admiration. To her Ilham Bibi embodied the virtues of a modern woman: she was educated, had both a career and family, and always "looked smart." Far from being subject to the crushing judgments she experienced from her family and community members in India, Chandani found that Ilham Bibi "was too busy with her own life to meddle or make a fuss." Chandani attributed Ilham Bibi's attitude toward her to her being modern. Rather than seeing Ilham Bibi as irreducibly foreign—as Kuwaiti in juxtaposition to her own Indianness—Chandani read Ilham Bibi in relation to a set of aspirations—of being modern—that they both shared. Chandani saw Ilham Bibi as being able to emulate these aspirations by virtue of her position and wealth, aspirations Chandani strove to attain, ones prompting her migration and ongoing work in Kuwait.

If Chandani's concerns about her employer were assuaged, they quickly shifted onto another source, one she had not anticipated before coming to Kuwait. Working alongside her in the extended family's compound were several other domestic workers, women from throughout South and Southeast Asia. From the start, they did not get along with Chandani. Their accounts of what Ilham Bibi termed "the initial awkwardness" vary, but sifting through them, it is clear that the other domestic workers greeted Chandani with wariness if not aversion. Chandani fit awkwardly within their existing social schemas; she was neither an unmarried "girl," nor a married "woman," but rather a divorcee, a liminal and somewhat suspect figure.

In particular, Chandani found herself under the close watchful eye of Paromita, a senior domestic worker charged with overseeing the compound's cleaning. Chandani chafed under Paromita's treatment, and dismissed the other domestic workers as gossipy and silly. She disavowed what she considered to be their "backward" judgments, proof of their "traditional" outlook and aims. Despite their shared work and positioning, Chandani wanted little to do with her fellow domestic workers, women she felt herself to have little in common with.

For their part, Paromita and the other domestic workers felt it was normal for a newcomer to be subject to scrutiny—something they had all experienced to varying degrees when they first began working at Ilham Bibi's family compound. But rather than patiently bearing it, as they had done, Chandani's *sakht* rather than *naram* disposition toward other domestic workers, and her dismissiveness, alienated them. Many found her to be brusque and overproud, an attitude made worse by Chandani's more amenable attitude toward Ilham Bibi and other members of her employers' family. Their employers sensed the "awkwardness." To forestall any potential conflicts, Ilham Bibi moved Chandani to the kitchen, where she held sway for the next fifteen years. During that time she developed a reputation for being a skilled and efficient cook, and for having a demeanor that brooked no foolishness.

Given Chandani's somewhat daunting reputation, it therefore came as a great surprise to her—and others of the household—when Gul Nar, Ilham Bibi's mother requested that she be her caregiver when she developed cancer, an illness that kept her bedridden. Yet it was precisely Chandani's no-nonsense manner that her employer sought. As Chandani explains: "Gul Nar Bibi, she asked me to be the one to look after her because she knew that I am strong. She told me, may God look over her, that this illness is going to be difficult and I need someone who won't be too soft . . . I need someone who will make sure I am doing what I should."

For the next several years Chandani tended to Gul Nar, nursing her in the most mundane and intimate ways. Neither was fluent in each other's languages, so they cobbled together a patchwork of Arabic, Hindi/Urdu, and English through which they communicated. Much of the time they spent in a silence that soothed Gul Nar. Over the years they came to know one another's moods and responses almost instinctively. Their lives became meshed together through a routinized schedule in which Chandani washed Gul Nar, prepared special foods and fed her, wheeled her about the compound, sat with her as she read and napped, and accompanied her to doctors' appointments and treatments at the hospital. For Chandani, the period was one of cultivated evenness, where she learned to tamp down on the slow frustration she sometimes felt at the daily tedium and curb her occasional flashes of anger, as well as calm Gul Nar through particularly difficult moments. She became connected to Gul Nar in a way that defied description—a mixture of work, obligation, sympathy, and tenderness made more acute by the underlying, unrelenting sadness of the older woman's illness.

Gul Nar sought to face her illness with dignity and forbearance, dispositions she cultivated through her practice of Islam. In contrast to the other members of her family, ones her daughter once described to me as "culturally rather than religiously Muslims," Gul Nar had always been quietly devout. In coping with her illness, her religious practice redoubled. Rather than limiting her practice of Islam to religious holidays or ritual events as did the rest of her family, Gul Nar's prayers, fasts, engagement with the Qur'an, visits to mosques, and listening to sermons suffused the rhythms of her everyday life. Her religious practice became an aural, visual, and existential presence the other members of her household increasingly had to contend with.

Chandani initially dismissed Gul Nar's religiosity, what she called her "spiritual affairs." She admired and identified with the rest of the family (if not her fellow domestic workers) by virtue of their being modern, which for her necessarily precluded "religious superstition" and "nonsense." For her, Gul Nar's practice of Islam was a carryover from her having grown up in a "traditional" milieu, which she likened to her own mother's practice of Hinduism and to "village practice." In the face of her illness Gul Nar had turned to these spiritual affairs to find meaning and solace, which translated into a series of harmless, if sometimes baffling and irksome, set of practices that fell under Chandani's care work. After Gul Nar would tend to her "inner plumbing" (i.e., go to the bathroom), Chandani would assist her as she undertook her ablutions. In the beginning, this involved coming into the washroom to ensure the other woman did not fall or faint. Later, as Gul Nar became bedridden and infirm, it translated into a modified sponge bath. The older woman was also "stubborn" in the beginning, refusing to stop fasting even when her doctor prescribed against the practice, something Chandani tried to coax her out of. Chandani also traced the progress of Gul Nar's illness in the form of her changing prayer postures: at first she undertook the daily prayers standing up, then sitting on her chair, before finally reciting them with trembling lips as she lay on her bed.

In tending to Gul Nar, what Chandani remembered most was waking up early in the morning, going to Gul Nar's room, turning on a cassette recording of Qur'anic recitations, and sitting with her while the rest of the household busied themselves with the coming day. For almost five years they shared in this everyday practice and ritual. When Gul Nar succumbed to her illness, Chandani found herself continuing to listen to Qur'anic recitations. This was a practice and habit that soothed Chandani and helped her to cope with the loss of a person who had been such an integral part of her everyday world. Gradually Chandani began to supplement these recorded recitations with their Hindi translations, and with other readings about Islamic history and what she called "scientific" or "practical" Muslim books—books by authors such as Harun Yahya, an Islamic reformer from Turkey who used Islam to explain natural phenomena, and books outlining how to perform Muslim prayers and rituals.

HEMA

Chandani's everyday Islamic conversions developed through the interweaving of her care work, the pious tenor of her environment, the daily reminder of mortality, and listening to the refrains of the Qur'an. Both engendered what she referred to as a "mood" that surrounded her, a mood that gradually came to find resonance in her very self. Her conversion to Islam came about unexpectedly, something another interlocutor Hema also experienced, although in a different form. Hema's everyday Islamic conversion centered on her learning of Arabic, which itself was bundled into an underlying dream that precipitated her migration.

While Hema's mother was keen for financial reasons (see chapter 2), Hema's desire to migrate to the Gulf stemmed from a different set of motivations. In her own words, she was "hungry, but not for food or money, but for learning." A keenly intelligent and inquisitive woman, Hema's opportunities for education were limited in Nepal. When she was a teenager, the public girls school in her district closed due to government cutbacks and circumstances related to the Maoist insurgency. Although her parents were relatively prosperous, the only other local alternative, an elite boarding school, far outstripped their means. Not having any family members living in places where she might attend school, Hema had to content herself with piecing together an education based on whatever books and printed materials she could find, and her own quiet yet insatiable curiosity about the world.

Arriving in Kuwait, Hema was initially disappointed. "Kuwaitis," she confided, "are more interested in eating than reading." Rather than going to school part-time as her "manpower agent" averred would be possible, Hema ended up translating her skills of self-teaching to her new surroundings. Learning that her employer Siham Mama's two daughters both attended school (one in high school, the other in university), she asked if she could take a look at their school materials. The family was taken aback. As Farah, Mama Siham's daughter later explained: "Never had we received such a request. We never thought maids would be interested . . . Mama even looked into classes for her, but they don't have classes in Nepali here. So yes, we gave her whatever books we could find." Farah, an aspiring teacher, even began holding tutorial sessions with her. Hema's ability to engage with these materials was, however, limited by her inability to speak or read Arabic, something she sought to redress quickly. With Arabic lesson books written in Hindi (Nepali being unavailable) that Siham Mama purchased for her, Hema began teaching herself Arabic. Between her self-taught lessons and everyday immersion in an Arabic-speaking household, she learned the language at an astonishing rate, becoming fluent in spoken Arabic and functional in the written form in just under a year.

Learning Arabic had an unanticipated consequence. It helped Hema to "feel" Islam in new ways. Before migrating to Kuwait she had an amorphous sense of Islam. Hema grew up in a milieu where she encountered few if any Muslims. If the Nepali media had featured the odd press reports on Muslims and Islam, they had not left much of an impression on Hema. As she explained: "Before coming here [Kuwait] my only thoughts of Islam were pilgrims circling the *ka'ba* [a square stone building in the center of the Great Mosque] in Mecca . . . and ladies in their big abayas. It seemed strange to me. I didn't think much about it. It seemed odd, then I would just forget about it."

When Hema arrived in Kuwait, she had little sense of what to expect, but what she found surprised her. Rather than perceiving Islam as radically different from the Brahmanic Hinduism her family practiced, she was more so struck by the overt similarities between the two religious traditions. Siham Mama, like her own mother in Nepal, covered her hair with a scarf when she went out in public, practices both attributed to feminine modesty. Members of Siham Mama's family interwove religious expressions into their conversations and performed rituals of daily worship in their household in ways reminiscent of her family's everyday religiosity, a doubling furthered in Hema's mind by the fact their prayers both took place in alcoves off the main living area. Youmma, Siham Mama's mother, listened to tape-recorded Qur'anic recitations in ways similar to Hema's aunt, who played Hindu devotional songs while she was alone in her room or doing household tasks. During Ramadan, Siham Mama's family watched religiously themed television serials with the same fervor that her own family watched serialized versions of the Ramayana and Mahabharata. The parallels Hema initially drew between the two religious traditions helped her to make sense of Islam. They provided her with a conceptual grid on which to place Islamic practices, practices that then faded into the background of her attention.

As time passed, the conceptual grid she had developed became blurred. The analogies she drew between the two religious traditions became more slippery. She explained her changing understandings to me several months after she took *shahada* (the Islamic testament of faith). Although there were similarities in the "form" of religious practice between Brahmanic Hinduism and Islam, the "character" undergirding them was different. Citing pujas versus prayer mats, and devotional chanting versus silent *duʻa* as examples illustrating her point, Hema told me that Islam felt simpler to her. With its emphasis on inward rather than outward expression, Islam felt spare and streamlined to her.

Hema's changing understanding of Islam, and her differentiation of Islam from Hinduism, developed through her work environment. She often described Siham Mama's household as a "quiet space"—a place characterized by a solemnity that both instilled and insisted upon a sense of calm. Siham Mama carried herself with a quiet dignity, which she had trained her daughters to emulate. In unspoken ways, Hema was expected to follow suit. Hema had first assumed Siham Mama's household operated in this tenor because of her personal preferences, or because she treated her home as a space of refuge, one contrasting with the stress of her workplace, and the more boisterous environment of Youmma's household, filled as it was with her brother's young children.

As Hema began triangulating the tenor of her household, her newfound learning of Arabic, and her observations of Siham Mama and her daughters' practice of Islam, her understanding of all three began to change. She started to realize Siham Mama's bearing and the environment she fostered was a form of devotion she had been striving toward since setting up her household in the years following her divorce. Her pious demeanor bespoke her *sabr* (patience), *khawf* (fearfulness), and *salaam* (peace), virtues that she cultivated and were reinforced through her everyday religious practices. Learning Arabic anchored and made meaningful activities that suffused Hema's everyday work and experiences in Kuwait, helping her to "feel" differently about Islam. This feeling piqued her curiosity and quickened new registers of experience leading Hema to learn more about Islam.

Hema and Chandani's stories illustrate two key dimensions of domestic workers' experiences of Islamic conversion in Kuwait. Whether it be the "mood," as Chandani described it, or Hema's "quiet space," their experiences of conversion to Islam were marked not by the extraordinary, but by the everyday. Punctuated by few, if any, dramatic events, miracles or visions, domestic workers' experiences demonstrate the slow unexpected infusing of incipient protean Islamic sensibilities, affects, awareness, and practices into the folds of their day-to-day relations and activities concentrated within the household.

Domestic workers' experiences resonate with recent scholarship that problematizes the predominant understanding of religious conversion as an individual's radical shift in adherence from one religious tradition to another, a change brought about through divine intervention or guidance.[5] Works by religious studies scholars, historians, and anthropologists all point to this concept's underpinnings in Christian and Modern Western thought. In his examination of twelfth-century European understandings of conversion, Karl Morrison notes that the concept of conversion "had a profound, mystical sense in the West for which some great religions and languages of the world have no equivalent. Even in the history of the West, it has displayed different connotations at different moments."[6] His work points to how conversion as an eventful moment, marked by the supernatural or hand of the divine—including epiphanies, visions or dreams—is located within particular trajectories of Christian practice, ones that have become increasingly influential but that do not account for other historical contexts and religious traditions. Many accounts—whether they be of Pentecostals and charismatic Christians in present-day Sweden and Jamaica;[7] Bengalis, Javanese, or Inner Asian nomads who were becoming Muslim over centuries;[8] or Christians examining the story of Paul during the Middle ages[9]—point to religious conversion, both over individual lifetimes and the longer *duree* of history, as being gradual and processual rather than sudden and eventful.

By focusing our attention on their everyday activities and relations, domestic workers' experiences of Islamic conversion challenge another set of assumptions that undergird predominant understandings of conversion. In "Comments on Conversion" Talal Asad painstakingly excavates some of these assumptions.[10] He analyzes how the idea of a genuine or true conversion as being freely chosen by an individual by virtue of her faith, is itself predicated on particular understandings of religious experience and human subjectivity. Conventional understandings of conversion often equate religious experience with belief, which is set apart from and juxtaposed with embodied practice and regimes of discipline and power. Relatedly, by emphasizing individual choice and volition, this concept of conversion presupposes a particular form of subjectivity—the sovereign subject—rather than examining how religious conversion marks and is the site through which subjectivities are reshaped. Asad's work underscores how religious traditions are not simply a conceptual and ideational force, one that gives meaning to the world, but they are also regimes of knowledge/power that shape everyday practice, disciplining, and dispositions in the world in ways that are not simply reducible to individual choice or coercion.

As we see with the "mood" and "quiet space" Chandani and Hema experienced, domestic workers' subjectivities and belongings are reworked in relation to their everyday laboring and relations within Kuwaiti households, ones leading them to convert to Islam. Their experiences not only point to the importance of gendered relations and discourses, those centered on households, to processes of religious conversion and the spread of Islamic movements. They also point to how these religious movements are imbricated with political and economic processes, in particular the feminization of transnational labor migration. Recent scholarship has revealed the microdynamics of these macroprocesses. Both religious movements and transnational labor relations place emphasis on and rework individual subjectivities. In their examination of Islamic reform and da'wa movements, scholars have highlighted how these movements are animated by their members' ongoing ethical self-formation in relation to the Islamic discursive tradition.[11] Drawing on Marcel Mauss's concept of habitus,[12] and Foucault's writings on ethics and the care of the self,[13] their work painstakingly documents the everyday practices by which Muslim pieties are cultivated, whether this be through veiling; daily prayers; listening to homilies; or enacting patience, humility, and modesty. In a similar fashion, scholars analyzing labor in our late-stage capitalist world, most notably service-sector and care work, highlight the ways in which these forms of labor entail the disciplining and reshaping of workers' personalities and comportment.[14] Influenced by recent theorizations of affect, the autonomista movement, and a long history of socialist feminist writings, their work underscores the tensions and contradictions that develop as affective relations and the intimate work of social reproduction are increasingly mediated by market relations.

Domestic workers in the Gulf are positioned at the confluence of both the feminization of transnational labor migration and Islamic da'wa, religious and political-economic processes that come into confluence through the household. Unlike foreign residents who live within their own households, or other migrants who live in dormitory-type accommodations at the outskirts of Gulf cities, the overwhelming majority of domestic workers reside in their employers' households, spaces suffused with everyday religious practice and what some of my Kuwaiti interlocutors referred to as "culturally Muslim" practices. In these spaces domestic workers are tasked with the upkeep of their employer's households, as well as caring for children and the elderly, activities and relations that necessitate the development of new skills and dispositions. Domestic workers' transnational learning, and their ability to be trained and develop new forms of expertise, subjectivities, and religious knowledge, are further underpinned by a gendered discourse of South Asian women being naram, an intrinsic capacity and learned capability of these women to be shaped by and to adjust to their surroundings. The assemblage (confluence and interrelation) of these processes—the feminization of transnational labor migration, the increasing demand for care work and intimate labor, the development of Islamic movements, and everyday processes of Islamic ethical formation, as well as gendered discourses of malleability that facilitate transnational circulations and learnings—produce contexts in which domestic workers develop newfound subjectivities, social relations and networks, and belongings that are marked by their becoming Muslim.

Household Hierarchies and Muslim Belongings

MARY/MARYAM

Mary/Maryam's experiences of Islamic conversion also center on her everyday household experiences. They highlight another feature of housetalk: how domestic workers' conversions are intertwined with the relationships they develop with their Kuwaiti employers, but do not necessarily lead to corresponding changes in their position within their Kuwaiti households. When Mary/Maryam and I first met, I remember being struck by a rather ornate key strung with a blue satin ribbon that she had wound around her wrist. When she spoke, Mary/Maryam often gesticulated, and particularly pointed comments were accompanied by the swaying of the key from her wrist. During my first and subsequent visits to her home, Mary/Maryam would unwind the ribbon just enough to open the front door. Only two keys existed for the house, she told me, one held by Fardous, the head of the household, and the other that she held. Mary/Maryam's key indexed her position within the household: she had been living and working with Fardous's family for over forty years, and was considered to be the second mother of the house. Mary/Maryam had become

such an integral part of the family that when they decided to go on pilgrimage to Mecca together, Mary/Maryam accompanied them. Although Catholic,
and although she did not participate in the rituals, Mary/Maryam had asked to
go because of the significance of the trip to the family. Several months earlier,
Mama Alia—Fardous's mother, the matriarch of the family, and Mary/Maryam's
mentor since she had arrived in Kuwait in her late teens—had passed away. In
several months' time, Sayyid, the eldest son of the house, was going to marry.
Between their mourning and their hopes for the upcoming marriage, the family
had decided to go on pilgrimage, and Mary/Maryam accompanied them.[15]

During Mary/Maryam's stay in Mecca she spent most of her time in the
hotel room, where she could see the pilgrims and processions from her window. What she saw, struck her and spurred her "to think about Islam." Mary/
Maryam's trip to Mecca helped her "to really know something [she] already
knew." The "knowing" she referenced in our conversations—things she had experienced but never quite articulated, what she had felt but never quite fully
recognized—points to the simultaneity and porousness of her connection with
Fardous's family, and her increasing learning about Islam. In her then thirty
years of working with Fardous's family, Mary/Maryam had witnessed their religious practices, but she "did not note it." The family's practice of Islam was
interwoven into the everyday organization and functioning of their household
in a myriad of ways. The women of the house had designated parts of their bed-
rooms or sitting rooms as prayer areas, which they repaired to regularly for their
five daily prayers, while the men went to the neighborhood mosque to offer their
own prayers. During Ramadan, the family's religious strivings redoubled. They
not only fasted, but Qur'anic recitations and special television series created a
further layer of religious experience in the household. Fardous periodically organized halaqa, or religious study circles, during which the women assembled,
members of her family and close friends, would recite and discuss passages from
the Qur'an. Mary/Maryam had observed all of these activities, and to varying
degrees she had been involved in them through her work—for example, serving water to the women attending the halaqa, hearing refrains of the Qur'an
as she cooked, and ensuring the family dog did not sully the areas designated
for prayers. Mary/Maryam understood these practices to be part of an overall
constellation of Kuwaiti sociocultural practices that were unfamiliar to her—
activities that were meaningful for her employers, but not for her. They were
"part of the Kuwaiti background," practices that she was a participant-observer
of and that she compartmentalized as foreign.

Mary/Maryam's trip to Mecca marked a turning point. When she returned
to Kuwait, she continued going to church regularly, but she found herself be-

coming more attuned to Islamic precepts and practices. As she stated in one of our conversations, "I don't know really when or how, but I started thinking, seeing . . . not just with my head or eyes, but with my heart . . . differently." Mary/Maryam began reading a series of pamphlets in Hindi and primer books she had obtained from Kuwait's Islamic da'wa movement, and she began observing more closely the family's prayers, and their reading and recitation of the Qur'an. Two years later, still attending church, she began fasting during Ramadan, and attending classes at the da'wa movement's women's center. Mary/Maryam's adoption of Islam was a gradual process; precepts and practices she previously encountered but had disregarded developed a new significance and resonance in her life. She experienced becoming Muslim through the thickening of her relations with her employers, ones marked by her trip to Mecca. Her conversion, however, did not eclipse other bases of asymmetrical difference shaping her relationship with her employers, most notably differences based on kinship, ethnonationalism, and citizenship. By virtue of her becoming Muslim, Mary/Maryam was not considered to be part of the family or to be more Kuwaiti. Rather, her Islamic conversion constituted another set of connections, and another modality of belonging with Fardous's family, ones built upon and further sedimenting relations she had developed with them through her many years of work for them.

The circumstances surrounding Mary/Maryam's second trip to Mecca illustrate the duality of her intensified relations with Fardous's family, as well as the continuation of other bases of asymmetrical difference systematically privileging Fardous's family. I first learned about a potential second trip one afternoon at Kuwait's Islamic da'wa movement's women's center. Mary/Maryam and I had both arrived early. Classes had not yet begun, and we were both waiting in the large front room of the women's center. During my bus ride over, I had fallen asleep, and having missed the stop near the women's center, had to walk a good distance back in the crushing heat. Sweat stained, dusty, my head throbbing, I had taken refuge in the corner, trying to recover myself before heading to the bathroom to wash up. Mary/Maryam had joined me a short while later. Neither of us feeling particularly talkative, we both sat there.

As my clothes started to feel less sticky and uncomfortable, my thoughts turned to Mary/Maryam, who I realized did not usually come to the women's center on this day:

AA: Sister Hanan has convinced you to take [the] tafsir [class]?

MARY/MARYAM: No. . . . Wallah, I wish I could, but these days are usually busy for me. I came to drop [sic] these forms [taps her folder] for umra . . . But now, I am waiting for Sister Nasreen . . . to speak to her.

Sister Nasreen had not arrived with the other da'iya that afternoon. The da'iya usually arrived en masse at the center, dropped off by a bus hired by the center to take them to and from their apartment complex. Sister Nasreen had errands to do that afternoon, and was expected to arrive by taxi at any moment. Mary/Maryam waited patiently, but she appeared preoccupied. Her hands picked at her folder, her lips twitched, and her brow furrowed and unfurrowed in the way some people do so when they are quietly debating with themselves. When Sister Nasreen came, the reason for Mary/Maryam's preoccupation unfurled through their conversation:

ss: Salaam girls! What's going on here in the corner?
aa: Wa'alikum as-Salaam. Just catching my breath. I'll go and let you talk . . . [I get up to leave]
mary/maryam [to me as ss sits]: No, no need. Your face is still red. Sit. Sit. And anyways . . . this might be good for your report [my research] . . . Sister, I came to drop [off] my forms . . . but on the ride over Khaled [employer's son] called, and he told me, he said it is not good for me to go, it is too hot still, and we need you home for Ramadan.
ss: Oh ho! I thought everything was ok.
mary/maryam: I did too . . . I know I should be patient, but really, this is too much . . .

The reason "it was too much" went unspoken, but was very much understood by all present. In the weeks before, Mary/Maryam had been planning on going to Mecca with Sister Nasreen and a group of other women at the center. Organized periodically by the da'wa movement, trips such as these made it possible for migrant and foreign resident women who did not have mehram (male "guardians") in Kuwait to go to Mecca in order to perform hajj (major pilgrimage) and umra (small pilgrimage). The da'iya took care of visa-related bureaucratic procedures, made travel arrangements, and in some cases, dipped into the movement's budget and subsidized the costs of the women's travel. Mary/Maryam knew she did not have the physical stamina to undertake hajj.[16] She worried that if she put off doing umra, she would become physically unable to perform it as well.

Mary/Maryam had her heart set on going, something she had made quietly clear to all who knew her. In the months prior, she had been memorizing new suwar (passages from the Qur'an) and learning all the associated rites of umra. Aware of all this, I was appalled that Khaled, a boy she had helped to raise, had advised if not told her to reconsider going, and moreover, that he had done so over the phone in a rushed and insensitive manner. "I'll take your forms now and hold a spot for you," said Sister Nasreen. "Inshallah, be patient, go back home and Inshallah, talk to him and Fardous." A few weeks later, not having seen Mary/Maryam at the center, and my calls to her having gone unanswered, I asked Sister Nasreen if she had spoken with her. "Wallah, I have not heard from her, but it is usual. They [domestic workers] are often busy just before Ramadan starts . . . Inshallah, we will see or speak to her soon."

Although we were both eager to hear how Mary/Maryam had fared with her conversation with Khaled and his mother, neither of us wanted to be too intrusive. As Sister Nasreen pointed out, the situation was a "touchy, sensitive issue," one underscoring the hierarchies of and ambivalences about Mary/Maryam's position within the family. Mary/Maryam was a close and inextricable part of her employer, Fardous's family, yet as their domestic worker, their employee—even a respected one who had been with the family for years—she was also subject to the family's dictates. While I was not (then) aware of all the details of Mary/Maryam's relations with Fardous's family when she and Sister Nasreen discussed whether she should go on umra, I knew enough of the contours of her relationship with the family to be surprised—and quite indignant—that Khaled, of whom Mary/Maryam was especially fond, would ask her to reconsider or postpone going on her trip.

Several weeks later, after I had not seen or heard from her, Mary/Maryam finally called, and asked me to come over for *iftar* (meal at the end of the day of fasting). Assembled in her sitting room, a few days later, with her cousin, a few friends, and Sisters Nasreen and Zahida, she told us the story of what had ensued after she returned from the center that day:

> "I came home, still a little upset, you know, but alhumdullilah . . . Khaled, he wasn't home, and he came home late, too late . . . I had gone to sleep, upset you know. The next morning, before he went to work, he and 'Alia came to my room. They told me, alhumdullilah [her voice breaks and tears start to well up] that they don't want me to go with the group on umra. It will be too hard for me . . . the long bus ride, staying in a hostel . . . it will be too hard.
>
> They said [starts crying] you are like our mother . . . our second mother . . . we will take you. And so they did . . .
>
> They prepared everything, visa, everything. We went by plane and we did umra together, during the beginning of Ramadan, they took me, they went with me. Alhumdullilah.

In contrast to her (and our) initial assumptions that Khaled and Umm Ibrahim's family had asked her to postpone her trip to Mecca because it was inconveniently timed for them, Ramadan being a hectic time, Mary/Maryam learned that they had been concerned about her ability to undertake umra on her own, given her health. This concern led them, without her knowledge, to begin planning a trip of their own for her, one in which Khaled and 'Alia could accompany, help, and join Mary/Maryam while she undertook a journey and pilgrimage rites that meant so much to her. The fact that they undertook this trip during Ramadan, a time full of social engagements and obligations, further underlined their sense of commitment to Mary/Maryam. Whether they considered it to be a gift, benevolent gesture, or obligation, the trip to Mecca they had planned stemmed from a complex set of affects and motivations: a tangle of love, guilt, responsibility, and commitment to Mary/Maryam.

Mary/Maryam had been living and working with Khaled and 'Alia's family for over three generations, first in Mama Alia's, and then in Fardous's household. Having moved to Kuwait in her late teens, and now in her late fifties, she had become an integral part of family members' lives in intimate, ineffable ways. Her work, her care, her very selfhood were entwined with that of the family's. Their growth, their development, their stories involved Mary/Maryam in ways they mostly took for granted. Her trip to Mecca—a trip organized by Khaled and 'Alia, two children she had helped raised—instantiated how deeply wrought these relationships were. However, like the story of Umar and Mama Alia (see chapter 2), even though family members had acquitted themselves well in taking her on umra—respecting her feelings, and recognizing all that she had done for (and with) them—the initial assumptions she had made after Khaled's phone call to her, and her response "this is too much!," underscore how her relationship and belonging to the family are also characterized by hierarchies and ambivalences, ones that continued after she converted to Islam.

Domestic workers' inclusion and position within the household were not predicated on their being the same, or their being treated equally as other members (note: this is not synonymous with being treated with disrespect). In part this has to do with how relations among members of these households are themselves asymmetrical (i.e., no one is treated equally or as the same within households)—relations are animated, and influence and authority are differently weighted by age and gender (e.g., a mother may have authority over her son, but her son will have authority over his wife). Within this matrix of differential and hierarchical relations, domestic workers occupy a complicated, often fraught position. Their interactions and authority often differ and shift in relation to children, fellow domestic workers, elderly grandparents, and "Sir/ Madam" or "Baba/Mama." However, overall their situation in Kuwait remains shaped by their position as "temporary" migrants, subject to their *kefala* arrangements with their employers (see chapter 1 for a full discussion of this). As highlighted by the experiences of Mary/Maryam, although domestic workers may be close to, and an integral part of, their employers' family, they are not, and never will be considered kin or "Kuwaiti." Their everyday conversions do not undo or level these hierarchical bases of difference that structure their position within Kuwaiti households, but rather it constitutes another form, modality, and layer of connection that, as we shall see with Geeti, often has its own set of complications.

GEETI

If Geeti had a favorite among Mama Lulua's children, she tried to be subtle about it. Members of her work household, however, could not help but notice how she took just a little bit of extra care of Bilquis, the youngest of the family's daughters. Among her siblings, a strapping and confident crew, Bilquis was sweet and awkward, drawing Geeti's sympathy and affection that she expressed in encouraging smiles, extra portions of cake, and an almost preternatural ability to predict when to make the warm milk that helped the little girl to fall asleep when she was agitated. The two had an easy and quietly affectionate if asymmetrical rapport, one in which Geeti both worked for and nurtured Bilquis, and in which Bilquis both naturalized and appreciated the attention she received from Geeti.

When Bilquis divorced her husband and moved back into her parents' home, her family was therefore not surprised that Geeti hastened back from India, where she had been visiting with her family. "I had to come back," she explained. "I knew Biloo (nickname for Bilquis) would need me." In the following months as Bilquis battled depression, Geeti supplemented Mama Lulua's ministrations. She cooked Bilquis's favorite foods, and insisted the young woman leave her room so that the other domestic workers could clean up—a ploy designed to encourage Bilquis to visit her friends, go shopping, and "just be outside." Geeti empathized deeply with her young employer. Her own hopes of establishing a family and a household of her own had been dashed when her fiancé had called off their engagement many years ago in India. She too had to build her life anew.

Over the next few years Bilquis returned to work and began pursuing an advanced degree in business on a part-time basis. A feature of her new life that puzzled her family, and met with the vehement opposition of some, was her growing piety. Somewhere amidst the tumultuous changes in her life, Bilquis began listening to Islamic-themed television shows on Arab television channels, and attending Qur'anic study circles organized by one of her work colleagues. Her newfound religious learning carried over into other dimensions of her life. She began praying regularly, and after going on hajj, she started to wear a hijab and abaya. In discussing the shift from what she called her family's "cultural practice of Islam," and their "fairly staunch liberal-secular values," Bilquis explained that her conversion gave her a renewed sense of dignity and purpose.

Like others of her generation, Bilquis came of age during a period in which divorce rates among Kuwaitis were increasing at an exponential rate, particularly among newly married couples.[17] This issue was a frequent topic of discussion among my Kuwaiti interlocutors, who attributed the rise in divorce to changing gendered roles and expectations. They often depicted a situation of young Kuwaiti women overachieving and developing inflated expectations, whereas their male compatriots had little ambition or drive but a strong sense of gendered entitlement—a mismatching of life trajectories culminating in divorce. Women were outperforming their male peers in high school and university.[18] They were entering the workforce in higher relative percentages. They were also developing greater expectations with respect to marriage: gifts for prospective brides, wedding expenses, and the cost of maintaining what was deemed to be a normal or respectable household—which, I was told, included a domestic worker and at least one overseas holiday per year—were far outstripping young Kuwaiti men's ability to meet. Others argued that younger Kuwaiti men were opting to marry "more cheaply" (i.e., with lower wedding and marriage-related costs) to women who were mostly from other parts of the Arab world,[19] in particular Lebanon, Syria and Morocco. These women were considered to be more dependent and pliable than Kuwaiti women. As a consequence of this, Kuwaiti girls were growing up with the expectation that they should be self-reliant; or, in the case of women such as Bilquis, they were in the process of readjusting their expectations about marriage and family and were equipping themselves to become self-reliant.

In reorienting her life, Bilquis took inspiration from the life of Khadija, an important figure in early Islamic history. The first wife of Muhammad, Khadija was an independent businesswoman who had married the prophet later in her life—when she was a forty-year-old widow and he a much-younger, twenty-five-year-old man. Through her Islamic learning, Bilquis developed a more encompassing understanding of womanly respectability, one no longer defined in terms of being married and having a nuclear family, but defined in terms of piety, which included but was not reducible to marriage and which carried for her the broader connotation of doing good works in the world. In conversation, she emphasized how her practice of Islam animated and buttressed her attempts to carve out an independent and meaningful life.

An unexpected outcome of Bilquis's conversion, one causing some consternation among her family, was that Geeti became increasingly drawn toward Islam. After living in what she described as a "religiously neutral" household for over twenty years, Geeti had also been surprised by Bilquis's "turn to religion." Initially she was opposed. Bilquis's actions had created a schism within her family, one that Geeti, much like Mama Lulua, thought of in terms of an unnecessarily disruptive influence that set Bilquis apart from, and at odds with, her family. Yet as she saw the effect her deepening piety had on Bilquis, Geeti was gratified about the outcome. Bilquis—she would tell those around her with some measure of pride—had become a strong, independent woman. Whether it was initially to support a favorite child in her "work household," or her quickening curiosity about the gendered possibilities marked by Bilquis's piety, Geeti became interested in learning more about Islam. She began listening to Hindi translations of Qur'anic passages, and inquiring into classes at the da'wa movement's women's center.

Like Mary/Maryam, Geeti's interest in Islam quickened through her longstanding and intimate relationships with her employers. In Geeti's case, it emerged through her relations with Bilquis—the shared sense of sympathy, deep affection, and pride she felt for the young woman, affects that developed through her experiences of caring and working for her. Their stories also underscore how these conversions do not eclipse existing bases of kin-based and ethnonational differences that structure domestic workers' asymmetrical and hierarchical relations with their employers. Rather, domestic workers' becoming Muslim constitutes another layer of relatedness, one that entails its own set of questions, difficulties, and possibilities.

Geeti experienced this layer of complication in relation to Mama Lulua, who was vehemently opposed to Geeti's developing interest in Islam.[20] The situation intensified the anxiety Mama Lulua already felt toward changes in her daughter's life. Mama Lulua was concerned her daughter was becoming overly puritanical in her practice of Islam, something she associated with "traditional" and unsophisticated "Badu" Kuwaitis,[21] or with members of the Ikhwan.[22] Echoing a campaign spearheaded by the Ministry of Religious Affairs, Mama Lulua was a staunch advocate of the idea that Kuwaitis were defined by their practice of a "reasonable" or "moderate" form of Islam.[23] She felt that her daughter's practice marked external, "non-Kuwaiti" (i.e., Saudi and Egyptian), influences. Mama Lulua's response to Geeti's developing piety also had to do with her long-standing ambivalence about Geeti's presence in her home (see chapter 2). Mama Lulua had long sought to maintain a stark distinction between on the one hand herself and her family and on the other foreign residents in Kuwait, including the "helpers" of her household. Geeti's practice of Islam did not blur these lines, yet they added a further layer of complication to their already complex and deeply wrought relationship.

Of further concern to Mama Lulua was how those outside their household would respond to Geeti's newfound practice of Islam. How would Geeti's family in India react? The two families had been connected for generations (see chapters 1 and 2), based on carefully calibrated sets of relations of patronage, obligation, mutual respect, and trust. She worried about whether Geeti's adoption of Islam would mark the end of their families' relationship. Like other employers whose domestic workers were converting to Islam, she was also concerned about whether Geeti's family would disown her, leaving Mama Lulua and her family responsible for Geeti's future well-being. She and her family were also acutely aware of—and many shared—the view that domestic workers' conversions to Islam in Kuwait came about through their employer's coercion. Geeti's developing piety confronted them with circumstances and a series of questions they would have preferred to avoid altogether: Did the relationship between Geeti and Bilquis constitute a subtle form of coercion leading Geeti to convert? Is that how others—other family members, friends and neighbors—would perceive the situation?

Geeti and Mama Lulua's story illustrates an important feature of domestic workers' everyday Islamic conversions that I observed while conducting research in Kuwait. While many assumed employers, by virtue of their being Muslim, were invested in their domestic workers' Islamic conversions, this glosses over a more complex terrain of preference, choice, and religious practice. Like Mama Lulua and Ilham Bibi's families, many Kuwaiti families are "culturally Muslim" or committed to secular-liberal principles and are not necessarily concerned or interested in whether the domestic workers they employ are Muslim are not.[24] Those who are concerned about the religious background of their domestic workers—whether they are Muslim or Ahl al-Kitab (people of the book)—will typically hire Muslim or Christian migrant domestic workers to begin with. Many employers view the phenomenon of domestic workers' becoming Muslim as something implicitly or explicitly forced upon these women by their puritanical or fundamentalist employers, or they are cynical about domestic workers' motivations for becoming Muslim. Like Mama Lulua, their understandings of domestic workers' Islamic conversions are complicated as they experience this phenomenon firsthand within their own households. They also become concerned, and some hesitant or opposed, because of the potential implications or complications domestic workers' Islamic conversions pose for them: Will it result in these women being cut off from their family? What are their responsibilities and obligations to these women should this happen?

Mama Lulua's response was at one extreme of a spectrum of responses employers had when they learned of their domestic workers' developing Islamic practices. Mama Lulua reacted with intense anxiety and ambivalence, and initially, she was staunchly opposed to Geeti's Islamic conversion. Other employers' responses ranged from surprise and puzzlement to enthusiasm and encouragement. Rarely were they indifferent. For some employers, domestic workers' conversions led them to reflect upon their own religious practices, and the presence of domestic workers in their lives. One employer, Fatima, a woman of Shi'a background, had seen two domestic workers she employed become Muslim over a span of ten years. In our discussions, she mentioned how she had been taken aback the first time: "My practice was a'adi [normal, by habit] nothing exceptional. I prayed, but not always. I fasted, yes. I went to *Husseniyya*, or gatherings, but usually for mourning or some event, not regularly either. My husband, he asked me what happened and I told him, *wallah* I don't know." When another domestic worker converted to Islam while under her employment a few years later, it led Fatima to reflect upon and redouble her own religious practice: "People say they learned from me, but no, really, they humbled me. I thought they see something, something I don't. I've tried to be better [in her practice of Islam] after." Her experiences with her domestic workers led Fatima to reconsider her own practice of Islam, and to become what she called "more conscious and aware" of Islam rather than practice Islam by rote. Resonant with Islamic reform discourse, her experiences with her domestic workers led her to reexperience and rethink previously taken-for-granted Islamic precepts and practices that were interwoven into her everyday experiences. Other employers responded with enthusiasm and encouragement, for example, Hema's employer, Siham Mama, who redoubled her support of Hema's learning of Arabic in response.

Whether they were opposed, hesitant or encouraging, most employers insisted that their domestic workers should wait, carefully consider, and learn more about Islam before taking shahada. In some cases, like that of Mama Lulua, they did so out of concern about the implications for domestic workers' relations with their families. Others were concerned about whether domestic workers fully understood Islam, and the potential implications should these women take shahada and later change their minds about their practice of Islam.

In dealing with these questions and processes, most employers sought the advice of family members with religious learning, religious leaders with whom they had a preexisting relationship, and teachers and administrators from Kuwait's Islamic movements.

As the phenomenon of domestic workers' Islamic conversions became more widespread, a number of institutional and bureaucratic processes developed in its wake. Organized Islamic movements, in particular Kuwait's Islamic Da'wa movement's women's center (see chapter 5), began receiving increasing numbers of employers and domestic workers seeking counseling services as well as informational materials about Islam. These requests resulted in the Da'wa movement's expansion of their "New Muslim classes" and their production of multilingual literature (e.g., pamphlets and primer books) about Islam. Kuwait's Islamic Da'wa movement also took on an intermediary role with the Ministry of Religious Affairs. Within most traditions of Islamic practice, a would-be convert becomes Muslim by reciting the shahada, the Islamic testament of faith, in front of witnesses.[25] In Kuwait the act of conversion itself does not require religiojuridical approval; however, certain related activities require juridical recognition of the act of conversion. If a "New Muslim" or "revert" would like to go on hajj or umra, marry, or undertake any other activity that requires documentation attesting that she or he is Muslim, the person can apply for such documentation from the Ministry of Justice.[26] This process is similar for both citizens and noncitizens, with one important difference: Kuwait's Islamic da'wa movement mediates noncitizens' filing of their applications. In order for the movement to approve an application before it is submitted to the Ministry of Justice, the potential "New Muslim" or "revert" must pass a test (oral or written) establishing her or his familiarity with basic Islamic precepts and practices.[27] Alternatively, the prospective convert must have successfully completed the movement's New Muslim Class (see chapter 5).

Reworkings of Religious Difference

If Geeti and Mary/Maryam's experiences of everyday Islamic conversion push us to reconsider the widespread, implicit assumption that religious conversion leads to forms of Muslim belonging in Kuwaiti households that smooth or supersede other bases of hierarchical relations between domestic workers and their employers, Ritu's experiences of everyday Islamic conversion push us to consider how their adoption of Islamic precepts and practices develops in relation to their preexisting religious understandings and practices. Ritu's everyday conversions centered on a practice her employer, Yasmin Mama, had insisted upon when she first arrived in Kuwait. Like the other women of the household, family members and domestic workers alike, Ritu was expected to wear a hijab and abaya when she went outside the house and into public spaces. Early on, as we were getting to know one another, Ritu brought up the issue, but not in a way that I anticipated. I had gone over to visit her at Yasmin Mama's home. Greeting me at the door, she extended then quickly retracted her arm and paused awkwardly. Looking partly bemused, partly apologetic, she explained: "Every time you come over, I keep doing this [extending her arm]. I was about to ask you if you wanted me to take your abaya . . . I've gotten used to it; I do it [ask] when others come over . . . but I forgot: I don't need to ask you."

The hijab and abaya were interwoven into Ritu's everyday experiences in Kuwait. She wore it when she went out—whether to sweep the driveway or when she accompanied her employers to the jam'ayya [local cooperative grocery store and complex] or to the shopping mall. Ritu had also become accustomed to taking the abaya of her employers' guests when she greeted them at the door and to show them to the small, mirrored alcove where they could adjust, remove, or put on their abaya. It had become such a commonplace feature of her life that my not wearing the abaya literally gave her pause. As we made our way to the kitchen, where Ritu could keep an eye on the food she had spent all morning preparing, food now quietly simmering on the stovetop, she kept to the issue: "Actually, I've been wondering . . . why don't you wear the hijab or abaya?" Filling my glass at the water cooler, my hand stilled. A number of issues jumbled in my mind, rendering me mute. I thought of countless conversations I had growing up in Canada where I tried to complicate my friends, neighbors, teachers, fellow students, and work colleagues' largely Orientalist understandings about veiling—where it was popularly understood to be a practice that stymied women's sexuality and self-expression, and reinscribed their subordination to what was assumed to be an intrinsically patriarchal religious tradition. I thought of numerous friends I had grown up with, women who had started wearing the hijab, often against their families' wishes, as a means of enacting their piety, and/or as a way of affirming their Muslim identity in the face of the ever-present, if (at the time) often subtle racism and Islamophobia we faced. I thought of the times I had spent living and working in different parts of South Asia and the Middle East where the practice of veiling took on different forms, and had distinct yet overlapping traditions, histories, and meanings. All of these associations and experiences jumbled in my mind and turning to Ritu, I was uncertain how to respond: "I'm sorry, it's a good question, but wallah I really don't know where to begin. Maybe you can tell me a bit more about why you were thinking about it?"

As Ritu began her explanation, I was glad I had not been able to respond immediately to her question. It was clear she had been thinking about the hijab and abaya in a different register than I, one we otherwise might not have gotten to, or that I might not have recognized, if we had begun with my own explanation. When Ritu first arrived in Kuwait, and was shown her room, she noticed a small pile of neatly folded clothes on her bed. As part of her work (and remuneration), Yasmin Mama had purchased a green Panjabi for her to wear around the house, and a simple black hijab and abaya to wear when she went outside. A few days later, Yasmin Mama took her shopping, where Ritu chose clothes that were more to her liking and size. Among them were a couple of hijab trimmed with rhinestones and embroidered flowers, and another abaya. The family had established this routine based on their previous experience with domestic workers, women from Indonesia and the Philippines who had brought with them clothes that were not practical for housework (that ripped too easily, or were too heavy), or that the Yasmin Mama deemed unsuitable for her household, for example, jeans and t-shirts that were too form fitting or tunics that were too sheer.

When Ritu asked about the hijab and abaya, Yasmin Mama told her it was common practice for women to wear them in Kuwait and that doing so would separate and protect her from "the riffraff." Yasmin Mama's comments have a dual meaning. Unlike in Saudi Arabia or Iran, wearing the hijab and abaya is not mandated by law in many GCC states, but it is a ubiquitous practice in some countries, for example, Qatar and the United Arab Emirates, where it serves as a sartorial marker distinguishing citizen women from foreign residents and migrants. In Kuwait, the politics of who wears the hijab and abaya is more fluid and not tethered to ethnonational belongings: not all Kuwaiti women wear them, and the practice is not limited to Kuwaiti women. Many in Kuwait—both citizens and noncitizens—do, however, associate wearing the abaya and certain styles of the hijab with Gulf nationals and forms of Islam practiced in the Gulf. As Yasmin Mama indicated, it is a practice that separates or identifies people in particular ways—carrying with it connotation of the Gulf.

Whether because it is a practice associated with the citizenry or particular forms of Islamic piety, like Yasmin Mama, many in Kuwait believed that wearing the hijab and abaya protected women from harassment in public (see chapter 2). Although she had little opportunity to assess the veracity of this claim as she rarely went out in public alone (see chapter 2), Ritu shared the commonplace view that wearing the hijab mitigated unwanted public atten-tion. It therefore struck her as odd that as a person who often walked and took public transportation in Kuwait, a person who would clearly benefit from the practice, I did not wear the hijab or abaya, a fact prompting her question to me.

Not wearing the hijab and abaya also precluded me from a dimension of Ku-waiti life Ritu thoroughly relished: the changing hijab fashions. After initially finding the abaya and hijab an oddity she had to adjust to ("why wear a coat in such heat?"), a practice that necessitated and through which she enacted being naram, Ritu developed quite a liking for them. She considered them to be "smart" and elegant, and in conversations with myself and others, she often commented on the different ways in which women pinned and fastened their hijabs, and the different gaits with which they walked to ensure their abaya did not bunch together or gape open. She was also obsessed by the changing styles and kept tabs on the latest ways in which sleeves and bodices were cut, and the different trims that were used.[28]

Ritu's understanding of the hijab and abaya shifted as she learned more about their religious associations, and how they were considered by many to be a religious obligation, one that cultivated modesty and other Islamic virtues, and through which a subject enacted her devotion to God.[29] During one of our conversations, when we were discussing whether learning about the religious dimensions of veiling had changed her own views and experiences, I asked Ritu if she had considered or wanted to stop wearing the hijab and abaya: "No," she responded. "I don't want to stop, and I don't see how I can. It's a practice here they follow . . . or at least in this house." Ritu began by pointing out that even if she had wanted to stop wearing the hijab and abaya, she was not in a position to do so as it was a custom Yasmin Mama expected her to follow. It was part of what both Yasmin Mama and Ritu considered to be her uniform and her work. She then continued: "But this modesty . . . this I don't quite understand. I guess it can be so, but I also see many many ladies wearing hijab who still make eyes and Bluetooth[30] . . . [and] this idea of wearing hijab for God, this is something I don't see. I've been thinking about this . . . trying to make sense of it."

Based on her then many months of residing in Kuwait, Ritu had developed a nuanced understanding of the hijab and abaya. She was well aware that in ad-dition to its religious importance, the practice had other bases of significance (e.g., fashion, marker of identity) and that the practice did not necessarily en-sure the religious outcomes that some envisaged—that is, cultivation of mod-esty. She knew, for example, that wearing the hijab and abaya did not preclude women from acting immodestly—such as flirting or "making eyes." But her comment also pointed to something more: learning about the hijab and abaya's religious dimensions did not result in her wanting to dissociate herself from the practice; rather, it piqued her curiosity, raising questions about how it constituted a devotional practice. What could she not understand or see that made it so?

In many ways, Ritu's response—her interest and inquisitiveness about the hijab and abaya's religious valence, one prompting her to learn more about Islam and eventually take the shahada—bespoke her upbringing. The daughter of an upper-caste Brahmin father, and a mother from a scheduled tribe, Ritu grew up in a household with no single or fixed religious tradition. Ritu attributed the nature of the family household to her mother, who practiced what Ritu described as an open and syncretic form of religion, one she compared to the forms of Bon Buddhism practiced by several Nepali women we knew in Kuwait.[31] Growing up in this milieu, Ritu had developed a fluid understanding of religious traditions, which she considered to be a source of knowledge, moral teachings, and blessings that she was open to learning more about, ones pushing her to consider—to "understand" and "see"—new possibilities in the world. She did not conceive of religious practices such as wearing the hijab as a zero-sum game, one placing her in a clearly defined religious category or tradition at the expense of another. Rather, it was an embodied means through which she could experience parts of Kuwaiti life that were novel or initially not legible to her.

Ritu's experience illustrates another feature of "housetalk": how domestic workers apprehended, approached, and began actualizing their Islamic practice in relation to their preexisting traditions of religious or secular practice. The process of their conversion was not linear and unidirectional, marked by an abrupt shift, or a replacing of one tradition of religious or secular practice with Islam. Rather, it was a recursive process characterized by sticky entanglements and messy overlaps. Domestic workers apprehended Islamic precepts and practices in and through their preexisting understandings of religion, which they then came to reassess and reexperience through their developing practice of Islam. Their ideas of what constitutes religious practice, the differences between religious traditions, and the process by which they change their adherence from one religion to another were shaped by their preexisting religious understandings, ones that were then reconfigured through their adoption of Islamic precepts and practices. The form of this process varies significantly among domestic workers, related to differences in their preexisting understandings of religion and the Kuwaiti households within which they work. Ritu—who had grown up in a plural and fluid religious milieu in which her family practiced a number of overlapping religious traditions—did not initially conceive of her adoption of Islam as detracting from, but rather as a continuation of, her ongoing religious striving and learning. Chandani's and Geeti's experiences were inflected by their preexisting secular understandings and practices. Chandani's relationship with Ilham Bibi and Gul Nar was shaped by her aspiration of being modern, which echoing the secularization thesis, for her necessarily precluded religious practice. Chandani was initially impatient about Gul Nar's "spiritual affairs" and "religious superstitions," which she conceived in homologous terms, and as being commensurable to the Hinduism practiced in her home village. She considered both sets of religious understandings and activities to be anachronistic carryovers from "traditional" times. Her conversion to Islam was not only marked by her shift away from the (nominal) form of Hinduism she was born into. It also entailed her rethinking the role and place of religion in modern life. Before Bilquis's turn to reformist Islam, Geeti had lived in households she considered to be "religiously neutral," a "culturally Hindu" household in India, and a "culturally Muslim" household in Kuwait—ones with household members nominally part of a religious tradition but for the most part not religiously observant or devout. Like Chandani, Geeti's conversion to Islam not only entailed a shift from Hinduism to Islam, but it also involved her reassessment of the importance of religion in her life—an experience that paralleled and doubled that of Bilquis. From both their families' perspectives, their conversion constituted unexpected and unwanted developments that came about through external or foreign influences—in Geeti's case, in the form of Islam; in Bilquis's case, through forms of Islam they associated with Saudi Arabia or the Muslim Brotherhood. In Hema's case, her preexisting understanding of Hindu rituals and practices acted as a conceptual grid through which she initially identified and made sense of Islamic practices. She initially thought of Hinduism as similar in form if not content. Her learning more about Islam involved her coming to recognize different forms and dimensions of religious experiencing. Mary/Maryam's accounts of her becoming Muslim were also inflected by her preexisting religious understandings. She conceived of her trips to Mecca in terms similar to Paul's experience on the road to Damascus. They were journeys marking turning points in her religious understanding and practice. Cumulatively, the variations and striking resonances in the experiences of Ritu, Chandani, Geeti, Hema, and Mary/Maryam push us to consider how converts' preexisting traditions of religious or secular practice shape what they understand to be religious phenomena, what are the differences between different religious traditions, and what the process of conversion or religious transformation itself entails (i.e., what they understand and experience as changing). Rather than a linear shift between religious traditions, their experiences point to religious conversion as a process marked by the complex configuration and reconfiguration of religious and secular understandings, sensibilities, dispositions, and practices.

FIVE

FITRA

Because of their *fitra*, human beings are latently Muslim.
—Sister Aisha

Intertwining Stories

On a rare damp and cold afternoon, the women of Kuwait's Islamic *da'wa* movement's "Salat wa Tah'ara" (Prayer and Purification) class for Hindi-Urdu speakers were listening intently. Their teacher, Sister Zahida, was hitting her stride. Seated atop a desk, eyes aglow, hands outstretched, the ends of her *hijab* and *abaya* animated by her movements, she was telling a story, a recursive story, a spiraling story, a story steadily drawing her students into its narrative folds and repetitions, a story punctuated very occasionally by their comments:

> SISTER ZAHIDA: Saad Bin Abi Waqqas was a companion of Prophet
>   Muhammad, peace be upon him
> a companion is someone who was close to him
> who was next to him
> who accepted him as prophet when the Qur'an was revealed
> when he started to speak about the message—Islam
> when the message was revealed to him
> they are those who were becoming Muslim
> the Meccans, they tried to stop them
> they pressured

they coerced
to stop them from following the prophet
this should not happen, they said
the mother of the one of the companions, Saad bin Abi Waqqas
she said, she said she would no longer take food
his mother, she said:
I will not eat
I will not drink
so long as my son is part of this *dharam*,
this *madhhab*,
this religion,
this *din*
I will stop from eating
even if I die . . .
MARY/MARYAM: Oh . . .
PHOOLAN: Hai Hai!
SISTER ZAHIDA: the people, they heard her . . .
HEMA: What to do?
SISTER ZAHIDA (nods in acknowledgment and continues): . . . they
    heard her story
and they pressured Saad bin abi Waqqas
they pressured this companion
they pressured this Muslim
they said: go!
go!
go!
go to her!
she is your mother
go to her, listen to her, prepare food for her,
listen to her, make her food, eat with her
she is your mother
he came to her, and he said:
oh my mother, I found something so beautiful
I found Islam, and oh my mother
I accepted
and now, even though it would hurt me more than you can know
even if you should die in front of me one time
even if you should die in front of me a second time
a third time

a fourth time
even if you should die in front of me a hundred times
even though it would hurt me more than you could know
it will not make a difference
I will not leave Islam
RITU (interjecting): But this isn't a good word. This isn't right. Isn't it
   wrong to disregard what our mothers say? You said this before

[*Class murmurings.*]

SISTER ZAHIDA: Young ladies, listen . . . *listen:*
Ritu, you spoke correctly
I told you this story because if your mother asks you for something
   reasonable
for something just
then you must take heed
if your mother isn't Muslim,
if she is a Hindu, a Buddhist, a Christian, or if she worships [*puja karte*]
   something else,
and she asks you for money, to eat, to drink
then, you must give it to her
feed them, give them drink [*kilao, pilao*]
but if she pressures you to again become Hindu, Buddhist
or something else
you do not have to listen
you should not listen
I told you this because . . .
it is difficult,
it is a difficult matter
one of the most difficult
but this is what makes our din *mazbut*[1]
it is like reciting the *shahada*[2]
La Illah a illallah Mohammedan rasul-ullah
it makes our spirit, our bodies, our being *mazbut*
it makes us Muslim . . . and . . .

Intertwining themes of kinship bonds with religious commitment, loving attachments with torn loyalties, Sister Zahida's narrative of Saad bin Abi Waqqas's
experiences resonated deeply with the women of the class. Migrants and foreign residents from the Indian subcontinent and its diasporas, both "newly

practicing" and "already practicing" Muslims who had developed emergent Islamic pieties through their everyday experiences of living and working in Kuwait, these women's everyday conversions to Islam were reconfiguring their own familial relationships and sense of belonging.[3]

As Sister Zahida was nearing the end of her account and the class was about to break into discussion, another event occurred, one further intertwining edifying Islamic tales of the past with ethical strivings of the present. The classroom door opened, and as discreetly as she could, in walked an older Nepali woman, a student who had not been to class for many months. From the gleam in her eye and the way that her lips quirked, Sister Zahida was undoubtedly tempted to tease Sonia about her long absence. Most probably she would have used the (suspect) joke she reserved for Nepali students—"arré, what mountain have you been on?"—but she let Sonia pass by without comment.

The students' attention, though, was not easily regained. The murmuring that usually accompanied an interruption or lull in class did not abate; rather, it increased as Sonia made her way to the back of the class, and it peaked when she reached another student, a much younger and relatively new student, Karima, who had, in the interim, gotten up, bowed her head, and started to quietly weep. Kissing her, Sonia sat her down gently.

Perplexed, never having seen a similar display among her students, Sister Zahida turned to Ritu. "You didn't know?" said Ritu. "They haven't seen each other since they came to Kuwait together six months ago. Sonia is Karima's mother."

As the women of the class quietly took in Karima and Sonia's reunion, a feeling that had long since suffused the class became palpable. As foreign residents and migrants residing in a country where they will never become naturalized citizens and where they are disciplined into temporariness, as domestic workers living lives suspended between their family and work households—being both a part of yet apart from these households—the women of the class were acutely aware of being out of place, of being socially liminal. Through their migration experiences of everyday conversion, their sense of themselves and feelings of connections with others were being reconfigured. Many were grappling with the anxious recognition that they would be reencountering their families and places of home—as did Saad bin abi Waqqas, Sonia, and Karima—as newly practicing Muslims.

In analyzing the form of Muslim belonging and organizing promoted by the da'wa movement women's center, in this chapter I return repeatedly to the moment of Sister Zahida's recounting of the story of Saad bin Abi Waqqas and of Sonia and Karima's reunion. By discussing different dimensions that comprise this moment—the da'wa movement's development in relation to population shifts in Kuwait during the late twentieth century, the *naram* pedagogical approaches its teachers espouse, and how students' learning intertwines their everyday relations and experiences—I highlight the processual nature of members' Muslim belongings, and how they develop in relation, rather than in opposition to, their existing religious practices, familial relationships, and ethnonational belongings. The form of Muslim belonging cultivated through the da'wa movement's activities is not one that supersedes or subsumes members' existing relationships and belongings, but develops through them in a tension students are taught and disciplined into thinking as productive. It is a contingent form of cosmopolitanism based on resonance, not synthesis or dialectic; on repetition, not identity.[4] Commonalities are not abstractly conceived or assumed, but cultivated through shared practice, in particular moments of pedagogical and ethical strivings like the one described at the outset of this chapter.

Kuwait's Islamic Da'Wa Women's Center

The Prayer and Purification class for Hindi-Urdu speakers that Sister Zahida teaches is one of many courses offered at Kuwait's Islamic da'wa movement's women's center,[5] a large, nondescript villa located just off one of the country's ring roads.[6] The women's center brims with activity morning and night. Evenings are often the busiest. After the midday break, when many in Kuwait go home for their afternoon meal and siesta, masses of vehicles start converging on the center. Dropped off by their drivers, alighting from public buses or taxis, or making their way from nearby parking lots, hundreds upon hundreds of women stream through the center's front gates. Wearing maid's uniforms to Missoni silks, *shalwar kameez* to jalabiyya, and speaking Tagalog to Tigre, their occupational and ethnonational heterogeneity is readily apparent.[7] Once inside the center, they filter into a series of retrofitted classrooms, portables, prayer rooms and *diwaniyya*, where their classes are held.[8] Taught in the myriad of languages spoken by the women, according to varying traditions of learning and at different proficiency levels, these classes largely reconstitute the women's ethnonational backgrounds yet they are also crosscut by marked commonalities of purpose and practice. The complex configuration of difference and resonance that characterizes the da'wa movement's classes—where ethnonational and linguistic differences are reproduced in relation to shared Muslim practice—indexes the cosmopolitan form of belonging the movement cultivates through its activities.

This movement has developed dialogically in relation to Kuwait's shifting demographic history. Overweening nationalist discourses notwithstanding, it is well documented that the country is part of an area that has long been en-meshed in interregional relations, and whose citizenry comprises a dynamic mix of peoples from throughout the Middle East, the Indian subcontinent, and East Africa (see chapter 1).[9] With the development of Kuwait's oil industry and concomitant state formation, stark distinctions began emerging between the country's citizen and noncitizen populations. Citizenship became increasingly restricted, excluding the vast majority who have migrated from the early 1950s on, a population that has played a crucial role in the country's post-oil develop-ment (see chapter 1). Kuwait's first wave of migrants was predominately Arab, most coming from Egypt or Palestine in the wake of the *Nakba* and creation of Israel. These ties to the Arab world had a profound effect on religious practice and organizing in Kuwait. The precise nature of these effects was a source of great debate among many of my interlocutors, attesting to the varied nature of these effects. Some argued Kuwait became increasingly secular and liberal-Westernized through their interactions with Arabs whom they characterized as being more cosmopolitan, cultured, and "free" than themselves.[10] They cited discotheques, miniskirts, and alcohol, which they told me were widespread in Kuwait during the 1960s–1970s, as important indicators of these influences. Others argued that Kuwaitis—a population that I was told was already pious and socially conservative—did not necessarily become more religious, but began practicing Islam and developing forms of Islamic organizing consonant with those in other parts of the Arab world. An illustrative example here is the influ-ence of the Muslim Brotherhood in Kuwait. Fleeing increasingly hostile gov-ernments in Egypt and Syria, members of the Muslim Brotherhood migrated to Kuwait, where they became part of the country's judiciary, public university, and the Ministry of Religious Affairs. In tandem with Kuwaiti citizens who had studied or worked with sympathizers of the movement while abroad, mem-bers of the Muslim Brotherhood played a significant role in the development of Islamic reform and activist organizations in Kuwait. Another example are *salafi* networks that have become increasingly entrenched in Kuwait through the country's Bedouin population, one with dense transnational connections to groups in Saudi Arabia.[11]

Starting in the mid-1970s the demographic composition of Kuwait's foreign migrant and resident population began shifting. In the span of two decades it went from being predominately Arab to largely South and Southeast Asian. This shift further transformed the region's religious topography. Non-Muslim populations swelled, in particular Hindus and Christians of different sects and denominations. Existing transnational Islamic networks were reinvigorated, most notably enduring connections between Islamic reformers critical of established schools of jurisprudence, ones associated with *Jamaat-i-Islam* and *Ahl al-Hadith* in South Asia, and *muwahhidun* and salafi groups in the Arabian Peninsula. Locally or nationally based Islamic groups such as *Tablighi Jamaat* and Al-Huda from Pakistan began to spread into Kuwait and other countries of the Arabian Peninsula. Groups of Muslim migrants and foreign residents in the region became more pious or began to adopt new forms of religious understandings and traditions of Islamic practice—including what is often glossed as *Wahhabism* or *salafism*.

The growing presence of non-Arab foreign residents and migrants in Kuwait also led to the emergence of an Islamic da'wa movement focused on "presenting" Islam to non-Muslims and Muslims who, in the movement's estimation, were not pious in their practice. Kuwait's da'wa movement developed fluidly and became increasingly consolidated in the mid-1990s. It has influenced the development of other da'wa organizations in the Arabian Peninsula, and has become more closely integrated into networks of similar Islamic movements around the world. In discussing the processes through which their movement developed, several founding members emphasized its haphazard nature. They described a situation in which, from the late 1970s, increasing numbers of migrants and foreign residents began trickling into mosques and Islamic charitable centers wanting to learn Arabic. Initially most were Muslims who sought to improve their ability to engage the Qur'an. As word spread that Arabic lessons were being offered at no cost to students, other foreign residents started attending. With few exceptions, the teachers tended to be unfamiliar with the languages spoken by their students, prompting many to seek out the assistance of individuals who were fluent in these languages, individuals who were typically fellow ethnonationals of the students.[12] Language instruction began extending to Islamic classes, which I was told were largely at the request of students. These classes were informal and organized on an ad hoc basis— dependent on students' interest, teachers' abilities, and their joint schedules. For example, one of my interlocutors, a Filipina salon worker, mentioned how she and her classmates approached their Arabic teacher, a Palestinian woman, to teach them about Qur'anic exegesis. At first these classes were held in a neighborhood mosque, but were later moved to the home of one of the students. Another example is classes on hajj rituals that one instructor, a Kuwaiti-Indian woman, taught every year in her family's *diwaniyya*.

Da'wa members' depiction of their movement as initially naram and reactive to the interests and concerns of migrants and foreign residents—rather than actively seeking them out—points to how they positioned themselves in relation to Christian missionary work. Many da'wa movement members were critical of Christian proselytization activities, associating them with past and present Western imperial and colonial projects in the Indian Ocean region. They argued that the subjugation and impoverishment of peoples of the region created the conditions in which the activities of Christian missionaries, in particular their provisioning of goods and services, were not just successful but predatory of the subjects they sought to convert.[13] Members of Kuwait's Islamic da'wa movement juxtaposed their own approach to da'wa, believing it to be qualitatively different from proselytization. They acknowledged that although there are historical incidences of the spread of Islam through force and coercion, the most successful forms of da'wa occur through "peaceful" and "passive" means such as contacts with Muslims through trade networks and charismatic Sufi leaders.[14] Many expressed their fervent conviction that Islam's message is simple, elegant, and self-evidently true, and as one interlocutor stated, "it spreads naturally on its own." They also repeatedly cited a passage from the Qur'an, that "there is no compulsion in religion," to theologically explain and justify their approach to da'wa. Rather than "pushing" Islam onto others, they saw their work as "presenting" Islam to others, particularly to redress Orientalist and Islamophobic understandings of Islam.

In the late 1980s the classes that anchored the fledgling da'wa movement started to become more consolidated. A group of teachers, both citizens and noncitizens, and officials from a variety of Islamic organizations, began coordinating their activities with one another. They founded a network focused on teaching Arabic and Islam to Kuwait's foreign resident and migrant populations. As the network grew, the classes they offered became increasingly differentiated along gendered and ethnonational lines. The first women's center was established in the early 1990s. From thereon the women's section of Kuwait's Islamic da'wa movement began organizing its own activities and programming—with occasional coordination and overlap with the men's movement. Aside from the five pillars and the basics of 'aqida, members of the da'wa movement's women's section do not necessarily have identical understandings and practices of Islam, and the movement does not promulgate a univocal position in this regard.[15] The da'wa movement is linked to a broad range of Islamic groups such as the Muslim Brotherhood, Salafiyyun movements, and some Shi'a groups. The movement neither espouses nor eschews any *madhahib*, or Islamic school or jurisprudence. Rather, like Islamic reform and da'wa movements in other parts of the world, the movement is animated by a common objective: to promote Islamic learning and practice in Kuwait.[16] The movement knits together shared spaces of learning and deliberation in which members try to ascertain what is incumbent upon them to do as pious Muslims. Members' religious strivings are both spurred by and inform their migration experiences, which are marked by significant changes to their social, economic and political circumstances, and to their religious understandings and practices. Non-Muslims and newly practicing Muslims typically take classes because they are curious and seek to learn more about the Islamic precepts and practices they encounter in Kuwait. Already practicing Muslims come to the center to further their understanding of Islam, often because in Kuwait they encounter Muslims practicing different traditions of Islam from what they are familiar with, leading many to reassess their own understandings and practices of Islam. Kuwait's Islamic da'wa movement is a focal point of these processes—it has developed as a result of foreign residents' and migrants' desire to learn more about Islam in Kuwait, and the movement facilitates and promotes this learning.

When I began conducting fieldwork in the mid-2000s, the women's section had developed into a sprawling and fluid movement consisting of tens of thousands of newly practicing and already practicing Muslims of different linguistic, ethnonational and occupational backgrounds, and of different sects and madhahib. The movement was organized into three main groups: administrators who coordinated the women's section's activities; a handful of staff tasked with producing and distributing Islamic instructional materials; and an extensive multilingual, transnational group of teachers and students. Classes continued to be the mainstay of the movement, taught in the various languages spoken by the students, in traditions of learning and pedagogies familiar to them. Of generally the same ethnonational backgrounds as their students, the teachers were either recruited locally or overseas with the assistance of Islamic officials and organizations located in the countries Kuwait's foreign residents and migrants are from. Organized in this way, the da'wa movement's courses reconstituted the ethnonational belongings of students, while simultaneously fostering emergent cosmopolitan Muslim belongings.

Firmly rooted in localized histories that are inextricably interwoven with global processes, Kuwait's Islamic da'wa movement cultivates forms of Muslim belonging and practice that are cosmopolitan in form. Religious movements are rarely considered cosmopolitan, a term that traces its genealogy through Western Enlightenment thought and that is typically associated with global democracy, world citizenship, and elite mobility.[17] My analysis of Kuwait's Islamic da'wa movement draws from recent scholarship that extends cosmopolitanism beyond its initial formulation by the Stoics and Immanuel Kant. Here cosmopolitanism refers to sensibilities, practices, and projects involving a multiplicity of people whose differences are neither erased nor reinforced through their engagement with one another.[18] Cosmopolitan forms are necessarily emergent, contingent upon their historical conditions of possibility, whether this be elite travel under the aegis of imperialism; Christian and secular civilizing global designs developed through processes of colonial modernity; or contemporary movements emerging through uneven globalization, migration, nationalism, and multiculturalism.[19]

The cosmopolitan form of Muslim belonging engendered by Kuwait's Islamic da'wa movement is formed in relation to national and transnational processes. In Kuwait, foreign residents and migrants are subject to an assemblage of processes producing their temporariness and exclusion from Gulf citizenship, one predicated upon and further reproducing their existing ethnonational belongings. In contrast to the situation of migrants in North America and Europe, where there is an emphasis on integration, the Gulf states actively facilitate foreign residents and migrants' development and ongoing maintenance of transnational connections with their home countries, for example, by embedding yearly holidays and repatriation costs into labor contracts. Foreign residents and migrants' preexisting ethnonational belongings are further reinscribed by the de facto ethnoracialization of Kuwaiti neighborhoods, a school system organized along ethnonational lines, and a laboring system in which many occupations are tied to ethnonational backgrounds.

Although plural and diverse, Kuwait is not necessarily cosmopolitan. The Islamic da'wa movement both reproduces and goes beyond this sociopolitical organization of Kuwaiti life. The movement's classes are organized along linguistic lines, which effectively reproduce students' ethnonational belongings. Yet da'wa members articulate their classes, informational materials, and other work in relation to what is imagined as a more encompassing horizon of belonging: the Muslim *umma*, which predates and exceeds ethnonational belongings. Being Muslim is understood to constitute another horizon of belonging, one that does not flatten or overcome ethnonational differences in Kuwait, but produces other forms of interrelations that are knit together by members' shared concern and learning about the role Islam should play as they navigate their transnational spaces of life and work. Da'wa members describe their movement's cosmopolitanism in multiple, overlapping registers: that it is ongoing in terms of being a part of a broader history of Muslim belonging—the umma—that stretches over time and space; that it is aspirational in terms of being an ideal, just community that they strive toward but can never quite fully form; and that it is immanent to practice insofar as the form of Muslim belonging they produce develops through their ongoing activities—their classes, their everyday pious practice—which are produced in relation to contemporary transnational processes, in particular transnational migration.

The cosmopolitan form of belonging the movement cultivates does not develop through students' plural interactions in classrooms, nor conversely do they develop through the dissemination of identical classroom teachings. These belongings are cultivated through shared objectives and pedagogies that crosscut students' learning. The experiences of Sister Aisha, one of the da'wa movement's most active and influential teachers, illustrates these processes and how they are interrelated with da'wa members' transnational experiences. Sister Aisha's route to Kuwait and the da'wa movement was a circuitous one. Born and raised in Cairo, she and her husband moved to a large Canadian city in the mid-1960s. There, she studied and later practiced dentistry, and became an integral part of the city's nascent Muslim community. Her experiences in Canada were quite formative. In our conversations she mentioned how dealing with her neighbors' and patients' misconceptions about Islam, how meeting Muslims from all over the world, and how her transnational dislocation and reworkings, led her to redouble her efforts to learn and practice Islam. Her experiences mark the interrelation between several processes—being hailed or othered in relation to discourses of Orientalism, Islamophobia, and anti-immigrant discourses in North America; encountering a plurality of Muslims practicing different traditions of Islamic practice; both of which she experienced in a transnational milieu—that placed emphasis on and redoubled her identification as Muslim.

Late in the 1980s, after her husband received a lucrative job offer from a large Kuwaiti institution, they relocated to yet another plural milieu, Kuwait City, where she put her newfound learning about Islam to work. First, she began organizing informal *halaqa* meant to strengthen the *din* of already practicing Muslims and to address questions posed by people unfamiliar with Islam. Her halaqa became rare spaces in Kuwait where women of different nationalities, languages, and lives rubbed shoulders and found means of conversing. As Sister Aisha's reputation for charismatic teaching spread, these halaqa grew into lectures and classes drawing more and more people. Thereafter, her work snowballed. Women contemplating taking shahada approached her for counseling and guidance. She started to write what would become a series of manuals about how to undertake da'wa. When members of Kuwait's da'wa movement began to develop their women's section in the early 1990s, Sister Aisha played an instrumental role.

Generally advocating a naram, or fluid, approach to learning and teaching—what she called a student-centered pedagogy—Sister Aisha was stringent when it came to the introductory Salat wa Tah'ara classes she helped develop. She was adamant that these classes needed to be "practically oriented" and insisted students were interested in learning *how to be* Muslim,[20] rather than what it *means to be* Muslim and the intricacies of 'aqida.[21] In these classes, she focused on awakening and furthering her students' *fitra*. The discourse of fitra pervades the work of Kuwait's Islamic da'wa movement and Islamic reform movements throughout the world. It is a universalizing discourse of the human condition that is often presented as transcendent, but whose invocation and iteration by Sister Aisha and other da'wa members is animated by contemporary circumstances. Sister Aisha's understanding of the term was shaped by her transnational experiences—of grappling with and making sense of the diversity of Islamic practice among Muslims in both Canada and Kuwait, as well as her rethinking of the similarities and differences between Islam versus other religious traditions. A concept central to how she understood Muslim forms of belonging, Sister Aisha explained *fitra* as follows: "The prophet (PBUH) said that everyone is born with fitra. Every baby who comes from her mother's womb comes with this *fitra*. We are all already born with this guidance, this first guidance, this leading guidance, this ability to distinguish what is good from what is bad. Every baby is born Muslim."

Here fitra is understood to be a God-given blessing, an attribute intrinsic to humans, an innate capacity to distinguish right from wrong, a form of moral reasoning that guides people's actions. For Sister Aisha, as well as other women involved in the movement, because of their fitra every human being is latently Muslim. Being Muslim is a capability that everyone is endowed with, but it is one actualized through constant effort. This constant work is necessary because if people are born with fitra, people also have the propensity to be "forgetful": "We stray. That is something we tend to do: be forgetful and stray. So Allah sent us secondary guidance, through messengers and revelations, to remind us . . . that is why one of the names of the Qur'an is Al-Zhikr, the remembrance, that is why we must constantly recite the Qur'an, why we recite its passages, like Surat Al-Fatiha 17 times a day in prayer: to remember." To be Muslim people must constantly remember and strive to live in accordance with this guidance. People may take up practices not in keeping with this guidance, or they may not heed it, but this does not nullify their being Muslim. Their capability of being Muslim remains. It remains something that can be actualized through practice.

The da'wa movement's Salat wa Tah'ara classes were developed to encourage and facilitate students' return to their fitra. Sister Aisha and other teachers designed these classes to be spaces in which students would not just learn about Islam, but would actualize being Muslim by beginning to incorporate

Islamic precepts and practices into their lives. Held around the time of sunset, the time of day during which *maghrib*, the fourth of the five daily prayers, are performed, these classes centered on the instruction and performance of *salat*—prayer—and *tah'ara*—purification or ablutions associated with prayer. In cultivating their performance of these rituals, students not only learned the bodily postures they entailed, but also how to recite and commit to memory passages from the Qur'an. Through explications of these passages, the teachers would open up further realms of discussion, including the five pillars of Islam and the lives of the prophets, most especially the life of Prophet Muhammad and the *sahaba*, his companions. In these discussions, students learned Islamic precepts through an examination of how exemplary Muslims elaborated and strove to incorporate them into their lives. Sister Zahida's telling of the story of Saad bin abi Waqqas is an example of this. It opened up space for the women of the class, women such as Sonia and Karima, to discuss how their own learning and emergent practice of Islam were reconfiguring their relations with family members and fellow ethnonationals.

———————

Da'wa members' cosmopolitan belongings are developed through the interweaving of Islamic learning with their everyday experiences. The movement's Salat wa Tah'ara classes played a crucial role in facilitating this process. A challenging task requiring a range of pedagogical skills as well as an attunement to a naram sensibility that pervades the da'wa movement's women's center's activities, teachers longed for the opportunity to teach these courses. Sister Zahida, for one, waited three years before she finally had the chance to teach them. She had made no secret of her hopes to the other teachers, but they had advised against it, telling her that her oratory skills, which were prodigious, were best served elsewhere, in the women's da'wa movement's media activities, for instance. When prodded further, the other teachers admitted, reluctantly, that Sister Zahida was not quite ready to teach the class. Her manner was *tori sakht*: a little too forceful, a little too unyielding, not supple or fluid enough—not naram enough—to deal with the dynamics particular to this class. But when Sister Nasreen, one of the regular teachers, went on maternity leave, and Sister Kulsum had to return suddenly to India due to a family emergency, Sister Zahida was the only teacher remaining who could speak Hindi/Urdu. She found herself presented with the opportunity she had been longing for. Seizing her chance, she walked into class brimming with enthusiasm.

Sister Zahida's lecture about the five pillars of Islam was eloquent. The cadence of her speech and the questions she posed were perfectly timed. Her

exhortations were vigorous. But despite these and other rhetorical flourishes—
of which she had many—the students were strangely unmoved. Ten minutes
into what would become an hour and a half lecture, I sensed uncomfortable
shifting in the seats. Fifteen minutes later, students were listless and looked
bored. A few minutes after that, most had dropped all pretense of listening.
Surreptitious messages circulated. Under the guise of taking notes, one student
started to write a letter to her sister in Goa. Another student text-messaged on
a cell phone she hid behind her Hindi translation of the Qur'an. Sister Zahida
responded by redoubling her efforts. The situation spiraled: intensified effort
on her part resulted in intense restlessness on the students' part. Frustration
hung heavy in the air. Three weeks later the situation had not improved. I ran
into Sister Zahida in the halls after class: her red-rimmed eyes bespoke inner
turmoil.

The moment when Sonia and Karima were reunited several months later,
the situation was entirely different. Students were engrossed and at ease. What
had changed in the interim? An explanation begins with Sister Zahida's dawning realization that her speech (*baat*) was not quite right: what was needed was
not forcefulness or univocality of speech, but enfolding speech, speech that
would encompass and include students by words, by rhythm, and by resonat-
ing with their experiences and issues of concern to them. Like other teachers
at the da'wa center, Sister Zahida had to develop a pedagogical approach that
was naram, soft and malleable, in relation to her students' understandings and
concerns, an approach resonant with a gendered discourse of subjectivity that
pervades students' transnational experiences of migration and work (see chapter 3 for further discussion on this topic).

Sister Zahida had longed to teach the "class for newly practicing Muslims"
because she "very much felt with them [students]." Like many of the women
in the class, the trajectory leading her to Kuwait had been one of hard work
and sacrifice. She grew up in a modest neighborhood in Hyderabad. She was a
few years shy of finishing her high school education when her father abandoned
her, her mother, and her younger sister. A bright and capable student, Sister
Zahida supplemented her mother's meager wages as a seamstress by tutor-
ing middle-class students at a nearby grammar school. She then paid her way
through both undergraduate and master's degrees in English at a local college
by working as a secretary and a teacher, and later an administrator at an Islamic
organization. In addition to supporting her own education, Sister Zahida's
earnings also went to support her mother, whose failing eyesight had made it
difficult for her to continue working, and to pay for her younger sister's dowry
and wedding.

When Sister Zahida was in her late thirties, unlikely to marry, her mother and sister for the most part taken care of, one of her closest friends chanced upon an advertisement in a local newspaper. It told of an Islamic group based in Kuwait that sought to recruit an Islamic teacher who was fluent in Malayalam, Telugu, Hindi/Urdu, and English. Unbeknown to Sister Zahida, her friend forwarded her biodata to the organization.[22] Several months later, after her initial shock, a telephone interview, a videotaped interview sent to Kuwait, her mother's anxious and mounting excitement, the packing of her favorite lawn shalwar kameez ("because who knew if they had them there?"), and tearful promises to call as often as she could, Sister Zahida found herself on a plane to Kuwait. "If I wasn't going to get married in India, it was good to know my life wasn't over. *Alhumdullilah.*"[23]

Over the next few years Sister Zahida zealously applied herself to improving her knowledge about Islam and her repertoire of skills, gaining much admiration and accolades from her peers. She took courses in public speaking; Islamic jurisprudence (*fiqh*); the biography of Prophet Muhammad (*seera*); the traditions of Prophet Muhammad (*hadith*); the exegesis of the Qur'an (*tafsir*); and the recitation of the Qur'an (*tajwid*). When Sister Zahida began teaching the Salat wa Tah'ara class, she meticulously wove this newfound learning into her class lectures. She also took pains to draw parallels between her life and those of her students, and she underscored how important Islamic learning had been to her personal development and to her ability to achieve success in life.

Despite these efforts, solidarity and pedagogical success were not to be found. Frustrated, and a little bewildered, Sister Zahida sought Sister Aisha's help. Sister Aisha suggested Sister Zahida sit in on the other "Salat wa Tah'ara" classes, ones offered in languages she spoke and languages she did not speak, paying particular attention to the students' expressions and responses, and not just the content of the class or the teachers' techniques. Several months after having attended a smattering of classes in Tagalog, Bahasa Indonesian, Sinhala, Tamil, Telugu, Bengali, Marathi, Kannada, Malayalam, Amharic, Tigre and Chinese, and after having discussed her impressions with the students and the other teachers from the Philippines, Indonesia, Sri Lanka, India, Bangladesh, Eritrea and China, Sister Zahida gradually started to develop a different feel for things.

In conversation she mentioned a moment when she was making her way up the steps of the da'wa movement's building alongside students who were on their way to class. As these women filed into their respective classes, the diversity and repetition of what Sister Zahida saw struck her. It dawned on her that her initial understanding—that each class imparted the same information but in different languages—woefully failed to capture the dynamism and diversity of these spaces. Learning Islam was not simply a matter of translation, of translating similar principles into different vernaculars and cultures. Rather, each and every class marked a space in which students—and teachers—were struggling to understand what was incumbent upon them to do as Muslims and how to incorporate these Islamic precepts and practices into their lives. Moreover, they grappled with this in and through the existing understandings and practices that shaped their lives. Islam was not a set of principles to be mapped onto their lives, but rather principles understood and practiced in and through their lives.[24]

Sister Zahida's newfound approach to Islam, still incipient and inchoate, what she often described as "a feeling," wove its way into her subsequent thoughts and encounters. She sensed it while speaking to other teachers as they rode home on the da'wa movement's bus. It flitted through her mind while she gave a talk explaining the month of Ramadan to a group of nurses at a public hospital and while she met with a Kuwaiti woman who was organizing a gathering for domestic workers in her neighborhood. She felt it in informal chats she had with her students before class and during break, moments when she strove to learn, rather than assume she understood their experiences and how they were approaching Islam.

This "feeling" further unfurled into her class, expressing itself through speech, a recursive, repetitive speech through which she sought to enfold students into Islamic learning and living. Her retelling of the story of Saad bin abi Waqqas, with which I began this chapter, is illustrative. Prompted by a discussion Sister Zahida had with a student, Sara, who was shortly to return home to Goa and her devout Christian parents, her retelling of the story sought to be inclusive of students. It did so not simply by virtue of its topic or subject matter—which resonated deeply with students' experiences—nor by simply encouraging students to directly comment or pose questions—which they certainly did—but by subsuming them into its very telling.

The recursiveness of Sister Zahida's speech, every repetition, every fold, wove together words from different languages and dialects, and a range of affects meant to enfold students into the story's very telling.[25] Take, for instance, what I translated as the fourfold repetition of *go!* Here, Sister Zahida used the words *jao, chalo, yalla, go*—Urdu/Hindi, Arabic, and English words she uttered with ringing command—all of which conveyed the pressure Saad bin abi Waqqas came under to visit his mother, to encourage her to eat, and to stop practicing Islam. Another example are the words I transliterated directly from her lecture: *dharam, madhhab, religion,* and *din,* words Sister Zahida spoke with a hint of contempt meant to convey Saad bin abi Waqqas's mothers' dismissal of Islam. But Sister Zahida's use of these words was also meant to express another idea: that as a realm of belief and practice, Islam encompassed, but was not exhausted by, these terms and their span of meanings and associations. By speaking in the plural, by speaking in a proliferation of languages, and by evoking sadness, dread, joy, fear, love, and longing through her utterance and play with words, Sister Zahida's speech strove to resonate with and reverberate further into her students' subsequent thoughts, feelings, encounters, and experiences.

Rerouted Connections and Belongings

Karima had difficulty stemming her tears while Sister Zahida was telling the story of Saad bin abi Waqqas and his mother, but they overflowed as her own mother walked into class. In that moment, that tumult of speech and event, that entangling of stories and experiences, containing—as I was to learn—anxiety and hope, hunger and prosperity, newfound worlds and hard-fought homes, separation and reunion both juxtaposed and overlapped, Karima's tears flowed. It had been over six months since she had last seen her mother. Six months earlier, they had arrived together in Kuwait and were separated at the airport.

Karima and Sonia had been separated before, frequently in fact. When Karima was still a child and her family lived on their subsistence farm several hours outside the Kathmandu Valley, her mother and father realized that their means of livelihood were no longer adequate to meet the demands and pressures of a rapidly transforming Nepal. What they produced no longer sufficed to feed, much less clothe and educate, their children. Karima's father migrated to an Indian border town, where he became a *kaam-wallah banda,* a laborer who took whatever work he could find. Few and far between were his visits home and remittances. So few were they that it took Sonia several months to realize it when he disappeared. Frantic with worry, she mobilized her network of family and friends to find out what had happened. The news was grim. Her husband had remarried and started a new family in India, leaving his—now old—family in Nepal.

Dismayed but resilient, Sonia moved to Katmandu, leaving Karima and her two younger brothers under her family's care. In Katmandu she started to make and sell small handicrafts to tourists and supplemented her income by working as a laundress to foreign expatriates. Eventually, she saved enough to bring her children to Katmandu, where she hoped they would receive an education that would lead them to a prosperous future, especially Karima, who was unlikely to receive anything other than an indifferent education in their village and whose brilliance and industriousness was roundly praised by her teachers.

When Karima turned fourteen, disaster struck her family yet again. Her youngest brother developed a serious respiratory ailment, a chronic one requiring expensive treatment and medicines. Realizing her earnings would not cover his medical costs, Sonia began looking further afield for work, eventually finding an agency that would send her to Dubai and, she hoped, a lucrative job. After selling her farm to pay the agent fees, arranging with a half-brother to keep watch over her children in Katmandu, crossing the Indian border, taking a train ride lasting a day and a half, and waiting three weeks for her paperwork to be processed in Mumbai, Sonia finally boarded a plane several months later. It took her to Kuwait.

She did not see her children again for two years. In the interim she called regularly, and the system that she had set up to ensure her daughter received her remittances ran smoothly. When she returned home for a two-month stay, Karima surprised Sonia by asking to accompany her back to Kuwait. While Sonia had been away, Karima had developed a relationship with a classmate's older brother. The two were intent on marrying. What they lacked, however, was the means to marry. They devised a plan whereby Karima would earn money abroad while her boyfriend finished high school. Her mother vehemently opposed the idea but, after much wrangling, relented. Paying the necessary people, they procured a passport attesting to Karima being twenty years old—three years older than her actual age and two years older than the legal age required for a woman to work as a domestic in Kuwait. Karima then followed her mother on the well-worn circuitous route through which Nepali women overcome the ban imposed by their government on women traveling to the Arabian Gulf region. When they separated at the airport in Kuwait—Sonia picked up by her *kafeel*, Karima taken to the manpower agency that had recruited her—neither expected it would be over six months before they next met.[26]

Their experience of separation is partly a story about how space articulates the types of social encounters and relations possible in Kuwait, and about how these spaces are delimited for domestic workers. Like the vast majority of domestic workers in Kuwait, Sonia and Karima both lived "inside," residing where they worked, in rooms tucked away in their employers' homes. Unfortunately for them both, these homes were located on opposite ends of Kuwait City, a distance impassible by public transportation, and both risky and prohibitively expensive to maneuver by taxi. Further complicating matters, there were few, if any, public spaces where they could meet on their respective days off since restaurants are expensive, shopping centers intimidating, and parks intolerable in the oppressive Kuwaiti heat. But more important, perhaps, were the ways in which their communication and mobility were channeled—and in Karima's case curtailed—by their employers.

Unknown to Karima, she had been hired because her employers' former domestic worker, Nirmala, had "absconded," "running off with some man from the jam'ayya."[27] In a social context where premarital and extramarital affairs were frowned upon, or at least kept discreet, Umm and Abu Khalid, Karima's employers, had been greatly offended by Nirmala's actions. For Karima, the implications of her employers' experience with Nirmala were evident from the outset. From the moment they first met, Umm Khalid made her position very clear. Issuing an ultimatum, she told Karima she would only proceed to hire her if she agreed to a certain set of conditions:[28] (1) not to develop any immoral relations, (2) not to run away, and (3) to allow Umm Khalid to monitor Karima's calls and movements outside the home. Having only just arrived, feeling disoriented, and finding herself in an extraordinarily difficult position, Karima agreed, but she bridled against Umm and Abu Khalid's paternalistic treatment. Karima was further frustrated by what she felt was her mother's complicity, or at least complacency about her situation. When speaking to Karima over the phone, her mother told her that her situation was not unusual and perhaps it was best given the perils faced by young migrant women in Kuwait (see chapter 2).

Though their paternalistic and controlling behavior continued, Umm and Abu Khalid did encourage Karima to get to know domestic workers who were neighbors or working with the families with whom they visited. Karima also told me of the consideration and small kindnesses they showed her. It was, therefore, surprising to me that they would not allow her to visit with her mother. When I asked her about this, Karima evaded the issue. Pressing her further, she finally admitted several weeks later that she and her mother were reluctant to bring up the matter because they feared doing so would bring to light certain matters they hoped to keep concealed. They were worried that Umm and Abu Khalid (Sonia's kafeel being fairly flexible and relaxed in disposition) would not believe they were mother and daughter or, worse yet, that they would notice the discrepancy between Sonia and Karima's basic information since Karima's information was based on a passport that was "not exactly correct" (i.e., she was an underage migrant according to Kuwaiti laws). Consequently, for the first several months Sonia and Karima resorted to telephone calls in order to communicate with one another.

During one such call Sonia suggested her daughter check whether her employers might permit her to take classes at the da'wa movement, classes Sonia had recently started attending.[29] To her delight, Umm Khalid agreed and arranged to have the family driver take Karima. Although an extreme example, Sonia and Karima's story underscores an important dynamic of the da'wa movement's classes. Residing as they do with their employers, domestic workers usually have very few opportunities to meet with people outside the social networks and activities of the families with whom they work. There are few public spaces where they can meet, and their mobility is often curtailed by a confluence of factors, including the limited transportation available to them, a general sense of unease about their safety in public, and their employers' policing of their activities and movements. Within this context, the da'wa movement provided a unique space for domestic workers in Kuwait—one in which they not only have the chance to meet and interact with women who are of similar backgrounds and who speak the same language, but one in which their kafeel can be certain they are in a safe, supervised, and same-gendered space.

Although the da'wa movement's class provided Karima and Sonia with an opportunity to meet, their story of separation, sadly, did not end. When Karima arrived for the next class, her mother was not there. As she was introduced to the other students, given copies of the class books and handouts, and as she sat through her first of many classes, the circumstances leading to her mother's absence played through her mind incessantly. Karima's youngest brother had contracted a liver disease, one that had gone initially misdiagnosed, a complication leading to his hospitalization and a somber prognosis. Concerned and not trusting her half-brother to manage the situation, Sonia had returned home in haste. They feared the worst. For weeks Karima's expressions in class bespoke his fluctuating condition. During breaks and whispered conversations, she slowly began opening up to other students in class, including me, with whom she loved to practice her English. In the class, Karima found a space to speak Nepali; circulate magazines, pictures and stories from home; and share with others their shared grief, worries, longings, and hopes.

If the promise of seeing her mother initially drew Karima to the Salat wa Tah'ara class, and if much-needed camaraderie encouraged her to come again, Sister Zahida's speech cemented her commitment to coming regularly. It is hard to pinpoint when—perhaps after her brother's condition improved; perhaps after the fluid Hindi, English, and Arabic and hand gestures she used to communicate with Umm and Abu Khalid started to gel; perhaps after she started to feel more surefooted in Kuwait—but after several weeks of attending class, Karima started to become more engaged and animated. Her eyes glistened as she listened more and more intently to Sister Zahida. She posed questions with increasing deliberation, and soaked up other students' stories about their experiences in Kuwait and how they came to practice Islam.

After taking shahada, Karima's adoption of Islamic precepts and practice was rapid and assured. Within a few short weeks, she had learned how to perform salat, her body postures punctilious, her pronunciation precise. She had begun interweaving stories from the seera and early history of Islam into her conversation. Reveling in newfound scripts, sounds, and expressions, she was also learning how to read and write Arabic. Cementing Karima's reputation as a prodigy, when Sister Zahida was called away one day, much to her obvious delight Karima was called upon to lead the class.

Several months later Karima's mother finally walked into class. After being so long apart, after so much had happened to them both and to their family, the two were finally reunited. The moment was starkly moving. As Karima gently wept, a hush descended over the other women. Their separation and reunion—spanning and crossing local and transnational spaces, interweaving as it did exacting work, everyday tragedies, and longed-for futures—affected everyone. In a context of everyday lives spent in the homes of others, in intensely intimate yet liminal spaces, and with limited mobility, the space of the class gave these women a chance to meet as fellow Tamang, as fellow Nepali, as fellow Hindi-speakers, as fellow South Asians, and as fellow domestic workers. For Sonia and Karima, the class also provided them the chance to meet as mother and daughter. But in that moment, that moment of overflowing tears, tears of joy and anxiety, they were aware, as were the other women, that the multiple forms of belonging being reconstituted through the class were not just routed through the perils and promises of transnational migration and localized domestic work. Their reunion was also routed through their conversion to Islam, the broader implications of which—for their families, for their places of home, and for themselves—they were just beginning to grapple with. Sonia and Karima supported one another in their practice of Islam, were confident their extended family, which practiced "Bon Buddhism"—what they described to me as a syncretistic, inclusive religious tradition that incorporated elements of many religions—would not be opposed to their conversion to Islam. Unclear though was the implication of Karima's practice of Islam to her relationship with her fiancé, something she would not broach with him until her return to Nepal.

Women came to Kuwait's Islamic daʻwa movement's women's center to learn Arabic, to meet fellow migrants and foreign residents, and to learn about Islam. For South Asian domestic workers—Mary/Maryam, Hema, Ritu, Phoolan, and other women—the women's center was the space through which their further learning about Islam was channeled. The daʻwa movement is widespread and well known in Kuwait. Domestic workers seeking to further their understanding and practice about Islam learn of the movement's resources and activities through word of mouth—from fellow domestic workers, other foreign residents and migrants, or their employers. Most of my interlocutors obtained pamphlets, books, and cassettes produced by the movement. Many also attended classes offered by the women's movement—most notably their "Salat wa Taʻara" or "Classes for Newly Practicing Muslims." These classes were spaces in which the students could learn Islamic precepts and practices among women of similar backgrounds, and could address issues specific to their situation and circumstances—issues that more often than not revolved around their relations and responsibilities within their work and family households.

Like everyday life in the household, these classes were infused with repetition and rearticulation of everyday experience through Islamic stories, precepts, and practices. Simple in their design and execution, the classes focused on discussions about the five pillars of Islam, and on the performance of prayer, and purification or ablutions associated with prayer. Teachers would repeatedly and recursively cycle through these Islamic precepts and practices, elicit and interweave their students' questions and comments. In so doing, the instructors tried to establish connections and underscore the resonance between Islamic precepts and practices and students' everyday activities.

Mary/Maryam's experience of attending these classes illustrates how the teachers interwove the everyday into the classroom. Mary/Maryam initially began attending these classes in order to improve her recitation of the Qurʻan. She told me that her *zabaan*—her tongue/language—was different than that of members of her work household, and to her ears her tongue was unable to properly recite the passages of the Qurʻan. She hoped that being taught by and alongside women who had her same zabaan would address this problem. During the class in which Sister Zahida was telling her students about the story of Saad bin Abi Waqqas and his mother, Mary/Maryam found herself with an opportunity to ask about an issue she had been worrying about. She had recently spoken to her parents in India over the phone, a conversation during which she had broached with them her emergent interest in Islam. As she had feared, their response was overwhelmingly negative. Her parents told her—in no uncertain terms—that should she convert, they would cease to have anything to do with her. This worried Mary/Maryam because her parents were old and infirm, and her remittances were their only sources of income. Mary/Maryam concluded her account to the class by saying that though she had begun reading the Qur'an and fasting, and though she would probably live the rest of her life in Kuwait with Fardous's family, she dared not take shahada, the Islamic testament of faith, for fear of alienating her parents and because of her sense of duty toward them.

In the ensuing discussion, several suggestions were given. One woman proposed Mary/Maryam take shahada because her parents would eventually come around and accept her decision: "They would have to, wouldn't they?" Another woman suggested she take shahada but not tell her parents: "How would they know? . . . and that way Mary/Maryam, you can fulfill your duty to both them and Allah." Hema suggested she wait awhile, and gradually broach the topic again with her parents: "Allah will understand." In deference to Sister Zahida's greater knowledge of Islam, Mary/Maryam asked the teacher for her thoughts:

Maryam, I think you are right to wait.
Taking shahada as you might wish will not be good for your parents right
    now, and as we have learned in the Qur'an and hadith, we must treat
    our parents with kindness, gentleness, respect. . . .
Maybe they are in shock,
maybe they don't understand Islam,
I don't know.
But I think Hema's idea is good: wait awhile and then talk to them again.
And when do you next go back to India?
Maybe wait until you have a chance to visit with them, talk with them,
    tell them about Islam, and so maybe they will change their mind.
Have patience.
Being patient and honoring our parents are things Muslims should do.

For the next year, Mary/Maryam struggled with simultaneously trying to practice and reconcile two Islamic precepts and virtues—being dutiful to her parents, and using patience to deal with her parents' opposition to her becoming Muslim. Her attempts to cope with her situation, a source of ongoing discussion and sympathy among the women of her class, points to how these classes were not simply conceived as informational and instructional spaces of

Islamic learning. Rather, these classes constituted spaces of ethical formation and deliberation, in which students struggled to understand what was incumbent upon them to do as Muslims. In these classes, students learned Islam not as a set of rigid principles to be mapped onto their lives, but as discussed by Saba Mahmood,[30] Charles Hirschkind,[31] and Heiko Henkel[32] with respect to Islamic ethical practice in Egypt and Turkey—they learned Islam as principles understood, instantiated, practiced, and striven for in and through their day-to-day activities and experiences.

Phoolan's experiences resonate with those of Mary/Maryam and also underscore the often porous boundaries between different religious traditions as discussed by many of my interlocutors. Phoolan initially began to attend the da'wa movement's "New Muslim" classes because of her puzzlement and skepticism over Sakina, Dalal's mother's repeated assertions that "Christians are Muslims too." Bible in hand, she attended the classes periodically in order to address questions related to these and other issues: "I remember thinking Islam is simple, and Sister Kulsum understood Jesus simply . . . this was a problem for me, so I kept going [to the classes], I kept pushing. But this idea of asking God to lead us on the straight path . . . this is something I did before. I used to ask Jesus to show me the right path in what I do . . . I started to think maybe it [Islam] isn't so very different."

Here, Phoolan was referring to the concept of fitra. A term often invoked by women participating in Kuwait's Islamic da'wa movement, fitra was understood to be a form of moral reasoning that guides people's actions, an innate, God-given capacity to distinguish right from wrong and "stay on the right path." The da'iya often told me that because of their fitra, human beings are latently Muslim. They pointed to prophets and revelations, including Jesus and the new and old Testaments, as being forms of secondary guidance to shepherd people back to the straight path. People may take up practices not in keeping with this guidance, or they may not heed it, but this does not nullify their being Muslim. Their capacity remains. Within this context, the da'iya pointed to the inadequacy of the term *converting*. As one explained: "We never say that this person, that person was made a Muslim because they are already Muslim. That is why we don't say they convert, because they are *reverting*, they are coming back to their fitra. Just as we Muslims are trying to keep to our fitra."

In our discussions, the concept of fitra held deep resonance for Phoolan. She often puzzled over the term, and used it when discussing similarities between how she practiced her religion and how her Muslim friends practiced theirs. When Phoolan went to visit her household in India—consisting of her son, her sister, and her sister's husband and children—she used the term *fitra* to explain her interest in becoming Muslim: "I thought this might help them see some similarities, make them softer to Islam. I was wrong. At first my son thought I was interested in Islam because I had met a Muslim man, but after I explained this wasn't true, he said I had brought a devil spirit with me from Kuwait." Phoolan's sister and mother-in-law told her she was being selfish and that her actions were jeopardizing the family's cohesion. They urged Phoolan to reconsider her position and weigh the potential consequences of converting to Islam—likely estrangement from her son, and ostracism from her extended family.

Seeking counsel, Phoolan went to visit Sister Kulsum at the da'wa movement's women's center. She suggested that Phoolan be patient, wait awhile, and broach the topic again with her family, saying, "It will be better for you and them." Several months of back and forth telephoning later, Phoolan's family decided on a course of action: they assembled their financial resources, making it possible for her son to migrate to Kuwait. Her son hoped that by being in Kuwait with her, he would preempt her taking of shahada. Phoolan hoped that by living in Kuwait, her son would come to understand her interest in Islam. When I left Kuwait, their situation remained unresolved. Before I left, though, I had a chance to ask Sister Kulsum about Phoolan's predicament: "What to do? She has a son, her family, as well as herself to consider . . . Maybe her son will become Muslim or at least understand Islam? . . . Inshallah, she will take shahada and embrace Islam fully [later], but she is acting with *iman* [faith] and *sabr* [patience] now. She is learning and doing what we Muslims should do."

Sister Kulsum's response, emphasizing Phoolan's continued engagement with her household members in India *through* her practice of Islam, underscores an important dimension of domestic workers' experiences of their newfound practice of Islam. Domestic workers come to apprehend and approach Islamic precepts and practices in and through previous understandings and social relations that comprise their daily lived experiences. Greater understanding and proficiency in their practice of Islam is achieved through constant striving, a constant tacking back and forth between Islamic precepts and practices and the stuff of everyday life through which these precepts and practices are apprehended, approached, and actualized. For domestic workers who are developing newfound Islamic pieties, the stuff of everyday life necessarily includes their preexisting religious traditions and household relations. As Phoolan's situation illustrates, their becoming Muslim is thus not seen as a renouncing or rejection of their previous lives, their preexisting religious traditions and household relations, but as a reengagement and reworking of them. It is understood as a dynamic and encompassing process in which the boundaries between different religious traditions and other forms of belonging can be porous and fluid.

In addition to providing students with a space for grappling with the reconfigurations taking place in their familial relations, the da'wa movement's classes also provided them with an opportunity to discuss and solicit advice from one another about their situations at work, in particular their relationships with their employers. One such discussion took place during an evening class in March. The spring's balmy weather, an all too short respite between what had been an unusually cold winter and the summer's oppressive heat, had shifted the rhythm of the class somewhat. Rather than darting to the bathroom or to the small tuck shop for a snack during break, the students lingered in the center's courtyards, taking pleasure in the evening's gentle breezes, and the easygoing conversations engendered by such moments.

After twenty minutes or so, Sister Nasreen usually began ushering her students back into class, but that evening she was preoccupied with another matter. During her lesson, she along with a few other students had not failed to note that Jacintha, usually an active presence in class, had appeared visibly upset. Anxiety simmered in Jacintha's expressions, alternating between long stretches of her gazing unseeingly out the window and steeling her features into a masklike expressionlessness, and other moments of dropping her gaze to her notebook as she struggled to blink back the tears that kept welling in her eyes. Once the room cleared at break, Sister Nasreen and two other students approached Jacintha:

MADHU: Can I bring you some water? Something to eat?

JACINTHA: Oh, no, Thank you, that is kind of you. [*she starts crying softly*] But no.

SISTER NASREEN [*touches her shoulder*]: What is the matter Jacintha? What is going on?

JACINTHA: Oh, sister . . . [*pause*] it's madam. She is so difficult!

PUSHPA: What happened?

In the ensuing discussion, Jacintha discussed her ongoing frustration with her employer, a woman she described as loud, impatient, and overly demanding. Since moving to Kuwait over a year earlier, Jacintha had worked hard to learn the housekeeping methods preferred by her employer, including how to separate and fold the family's clothes in the way they were accustomed to, what cleaning duties to prioritize, and what tasks her employer preferred to do herself. Yet no matter how hard Jacintha worked, no matter how attuned she became to her household's daily rhythms and accommodated herself to the family's needs, her employer always found something to fault her for. "My days," Jacintha told us, "are filled with her complaints and criticisms. She is like a bell that keeps ringing, keeps ringing, ringing, ringing, ringing, no matter how hard I try to stop it."

That afternoon, things had come to a head when Jacintha's employer, finding her bathroom untidier than she would like—the towels her husband had dropped on the floor earlier that morning had not been placed in the laundry basket—began a long tirade, berating Jacintha for her supposed shortcomings:

> it was terrible.
> Her voice was raised so the whole house could hear.
> She kept telling me I was so sloppy, stupid and hopeless . . .
> that she should look for another maid, but didn't have the time.
> And as I was going, she said . . .
> [*sobbing*] in this very nasty way: "how smart do you need to be to do this?"

The women proceeded to commiserate, comfort and counsel Jacintha, their thoughts and advice further bolstered by the students who began trickling back into class from break. Facilitated by Sister Nasreen, the ensuing discussion continued until the end of the class. The majority of students being domestic workers, they had a lot of suggestions for Jacintha: Could she check with the other domestic workers in the family's household or who worked with her employers' relatives? If it were possible, could she approach a kinder older member of the family or "Baba," who might intercede on her behalf? Although she facilitated the discussion, Sister Nasreen said very little until the end of class:

> Kuwaitis; there is only one Emir, but many of them act like Emirs.
> They have a lot of money.
> They have a lot of power.
> It has made many of them arrogant and full of pride.
> Sisters, you are weaker than them, and that is how it is.
> Whether we expect it or not.
> Whether it is right or not.
> That is how it is here.
> Remember why you are here; what brought you here and focus on that.
> Your families, your futures
> Remember so you can be patient and bear the difficulties here.

Inshallah, they will see the wrongs of their ways in God's eyes.
And remember:
God will have justice;
Here, or in the afterlife.
And remember:
We are Muslims who set a good example.
And Inshallah, Allah subhanahu wa ta'ala knows best
They may one day see.

Sister Nasreen's comments illustrate the limits of Muslim cosmopolitan belongings in Kuwait, and yet why these belongings are important to her and other da'wa members. In her comments, she explicitly makes a connection between ethnonational belongings, occupation, and status in Kuwait. Citizenship and its trappings (i.e., wealth and power) confer upon Kuwaitis a privileged position within the country, and account for the subordinate (i.e., "weaker") position of noncitizens. During the class—and other classes—she never raised the possibility that her and her students' shared religious background with Kuwaitis, that is, that they were Muslim, did, or has the possibility of affecting or challenging this system. It simply went unspoken and unacknowledged as a possibility, underscoring the hegemonic nature of Kuwait's sociopolitical hierarchy predicated on ethnonational belongings. Being Muslim did not level these differences. Yet she invoked Islam as a critique of this system in stating Kuwaitis' ways are "wrong," and as the basis from which she and her students, and the da'wa movement more generally, are knitting together an alternative horizon of belonging that others, in particular Kuwaitis, might one day recognize and have to contend with, a system she strongly believed would be more just.

Fraught Intimacies

Another realm of repeated—and often absorbed—conversation among students centered on their romantic entanglements and intimate relationships. These discussions, in which they negotiated shifting understandings of gendered respectability and morality, did not occur during class time, but rather in their interstices: in whispered conversations before or after class; in small, hushed groups during break; or during special meetings students set up with teachers. Some of the younger students were not shy about publicly attesting their undying love for Shah Rukh Khan, Leonardo DiCaprio and other global celebrities, but discussions about their partners, boyfriends, fiancés, and husbands rarely occurred in larger group settings. Most of the students considered such matters "too personal" or inappropriate to discuss in public. Others worried about crying, losing face, or being judged by others. And many were concerned about potential gossip spreading about their situations and eventually finding the ears of family members or others concerned.

Perhaps more than any other, the issue of intimate relationships underscored the naram quality of how domestic workers and other converts were being taught and were beginning to practice Islam. Although Sister Zahida, Nasreen, Kulsum, and other teachers firmly believed premarital relations—in particular, sexual relations—and the marriage of Muslim women to non-Muslim men to be *haram*, or forbidden, they also recognized that it was difficult for many of their students to act in accordance with these restrictions given their circumstances. As Sister Zahida once explained:

> many of our ladies come from difficult home situations,
> their husbands do not respect them, and it is difficult to say what to do.
> Help their husbands be better, and hopefully they too will become Muslim?
> Leave their husbands? But what will happen to them then?
> Many of them, their fathers, brothers, families have left them,
> abandoned them,
> and they are alone here,
> vulnerable;
> but they also have opportunities for marriage,
> ones they often need help with.
> I try to protect them—tell them to be sensible and careful.
> I tell them to talk to me, to call me if something is troubling them.
> We do our best,
> may God help us.

Her comments highlight some of the major difficulties domestic workers encountered as they negotiated becoming Muslim with their existing or emergent intimate relationships. Women who were married, and whose husbands were generally not in Kuwait, had to work out how to tell their husbands about their adoption of Islam and deal with the potential consequences. Rather than counseling their students to divorce their non-Muslim husbands, or husbands who were opposed to their practice of Islam, the teachers generally advised their students to remain married and work through the problems that ensued in the hopes that their husbands and children might themselves eventually come to practice Islam. In situations of students already having difficulties with their husbands—for example, their husbands were not supporting their families financially, or they were engaged in extramarital affairs—the teachers generally counseled their students to try and resolve these problems. Only in extreme cases, for example, situations of abuse or financial exploitation, would they advocate separation or divorce.

The situation of unmarried women was also complicated and fraught. As one interlocutor described, domestic workers experienced a "mixed suitcase" when it came to marriage—a metaphor referencing not only their transnational status, but also the variability of what they came out with through their transnational journeys. Some found their social mobility and marriageability increased as a result of their migration, a situation they attributed to their improving financial situation. Others found themselves subject to the pervasive stigma associating transnational migration with sex work (see chapter 3). These women were regarded as morally suspect in their home communities, resulting in dwindling marriage opportunities. As a consequence of this, many domestic workers such as Ritu (discussed in chapter 2) hoped to find a potential spouse while they were abroad. Here again, the results varied, ranging from a few successful engagements and marriages (e.g., Chandani's marriage, discussed in the epilogue) to heartbreaking disappointment.

One of the most devastating stories was that of Maya, a Nepali domestic worker from Katmandu. Almost two years after she migrated to Kuwait, Maya married an Egyptian man. She "absconded," or left, her employers so that she could live with him. Her employers were furious but agreed to release her from her contract so long as they did not have to pay for her repatriation costs, in particular, her airline ticket back to Nepal. Maya's visa under their sponsorship about to expire, Maya's husband suggested she return to Nepal, after which he would sponsor her return. A month after she returned to Nepal, Sister Nasreen received a phone call from Maya: "She is worried, poor girl. She is worried something has happened to him. After the first week, she has not heard from him: no phone calls or letters . . . She asked me to try calling his mobile here, or his work number."

Over the next several weeks, Sister Nasreen called Maya's husband repeatedly, but was unable to get in touch with him. She then tried visiting him at his apartment, but found that he had moved out. When she visited his workplace, his coworkers told her he had returned to Egypt. The situation became increasingly desperate. Maya discovered she was pregnant, and her family had become increasingly hostile toward her. She had also learned that in Nepal (like Kuwait), citizenship was conferred through the father. Her child being fathered by a nonnational, he or she would not be granted Nepali citizenship. In addition, without her husband submitting the necessary paperwork, her child would not be granted Egyptian citizenship. Before I traveled to Nepal, Sister Nasreen gave me Maya's telephone number and address. She had not heard from her in several months, and hoped I would be able to locate her. My attempts to do so proved fruitless. Her family refused to speak to me when I tried visiting them at their home. Their neighbors and shopkeepers nearby informed me Maya had moved away several months earlier. No one knew where she had gone.

While some married, divorced, or, like Maya, were abandoned by their partners and spouses, most unmarried domestic workers who converted to Islam experienced what Hema described as "stagnant stillness" or fluid uncertainty with respect to finding a potential husband. Ritu's situation with Hari is illustrative. Despite her employers' policing of her activities and curtailing of her opportunities to meet a potential boyfriend, she and Hari had managed to meet and develop a relationship mediated through phone conversations and eventually through the exchange of letters (see chapter 2). Before Ritu returned to Nepal, she and Hari exchanged photographs with the understanding that they would show them to their family members, a necessary precursor to what they hoped would be the eventual arrangement of a marriage. Before she left Kuwait, Ritu sought Sister Nasreen's advice about Hari. Sipping tea in a small seating area in the center's main room, Ritu began by glossing over the details of how the two had met, intimating that they had been introduced by friends in Nepal. Several weeks later in Nepal, she told a similar story to her mother, except in that case Ritu indicated that she had met Hari through a trusted Nepali friend in Kuwait. Ritu had thought carefully about how to present her budding relationship with Hari to both Sister Nasreen and her mother. The fact that she told a similar story about how she met Hari to both women points to how, although of significantly different backgrounds—one being an Indian Muslim and educator at Kuwait's Islamic da'wa movement, the other a Hindu and chatelaine of a small subsistence farm in Nepal—both women shared overlapping understandings about gendered respectability and morality. Both women considered it inappropriate for young people, in particular young women, to solicit and develop relationships on their own. Where they differed was in how they responded to the fact Hari and Ritu practiced different religious traditions, and whether this constituted an impediment to their potential marriage.

Ritu's mother herself had married a man whose religious traditions were different from her own. She did not perceive the issue to be a problem in itself. Of more concern to her was how Hari's family might react to Ritu's practice of Islam. Ritu's mother had experienced a great deal of social ostracism from her husband's family and village, and was worried her daughter might be subject to the same treatment. In contrast to Ritu's mother, Sister Nasreen believed the difference in their religious traditions to be an inherent problem. In keeping with most schools of Islamic jurisprudence, she believed strongly that Muslim women were restricted from marrying non-Muslim men. However, during her discussions with Ritu, Sister Nasreen came to recognize there were other ethical considerations to take into account in assessing her situation. Ritu had explained that there were few if any Muslims in her home community and that Hari did not oppose her practice of Islam. Given this information, Ritu's situation raised a series of ethical conundrums Sister Nasreen struggled with. She believed marriage to be a virtue, what she had described numerous times in class or in conversation as the bedrock upon which proper Muslim lives were built. In consultation with her fellow teachers and other religious figures in Kuwait, she therefore deliberated about a series of interconnected questions: If Ritu returned to her home community where few (if any) Muslims resided, would it be better for her to remain unmarried or married to a non-Muslim man? Would marriage to a non-Muslim man offset other potential difficulties (e.g., financial, social ostracism) she might face upon her return to her community? If she married, might her husband convert, and/or could she ensure her children would be practicing Muslims? During their conversations Sister Nasreen told Ritu that given the circumstances she did not oppose the idea of her marrying Hari, but she counseled Ritu to try and seek out other Muslims in Nepal whom she could potentially marry or who could assist her in finding an eligible Muslim man. She also counseled Ritu to ascertain as much as she could about whether Hari or his family might oppose her ongoing practice of Islam, and her teaching of Islam to their children.

Ritu's situation with Hari illustrates the complications and difficulties domestic workers encounter as they seek potential spouses in the midst of the everyday conversions marking their transnational experiences. Sister Nasreen's counsel also points to the complex, often fraught nature of ethical deliberations related to these situations, ones in which different virtues and moral concerns are considered simultaneously. Ritu's circumstances, and the advice given to her by an Islamic da'wa teacher, underscores once again the processual nature of domestic workers' everyday conversions to Islam, the often porous boundaries between their existing and developing intimate relations and belongings, and how differences and commonalities, belongings and exclusions, are being reconfigured in fluid and often unpredictable ways.

In a region all too often glossed as salafi or Wahhabi, where the activities of Islamic groups are assumed to be diffusionary in nature—characterized by the spread of a particular, puritanical understanding of Islam—Kuwait's Islamic da'wa movement provides an important counterpoint. The movement's dialogical development underscores the vital role foreign residents and migrants have played in the development of religious movements and the novel forms of Muslim practice, belonging, and organizing that are emerging in the region. The cosmopolitanism cultivated by the da'wa movement is one that requires us to reassess our understanding of belonging. The movement promotes a form of belonging that is not predicated on identity—assumed similarities among Muslims by virtue of their practice of Islam, whether these Muslims are newly practicing or already practicing.[33] It is a form of belonging in which differences are not elided, erased or reinforced, but that exist alongside and are continually reconfigured through members' everyday Islamic practice. Belonging here is predicated on a commonality that develops through shared purposes and practices, not a univocal or universal design. Being Muslim is not understood simply as a form of identification, as a category of belonging that is binary or digital in its logic—something you either are or are not. Unlike citizenship or national belonging—or even how Muslim identity is treated as an ethnicity or racialized category within North America and Europe—as Sister Aisha's discussion of fitra points to, being Muslim is understood as intrinsic to everyone and it is conceived in fundamentally processual terms. Though a capacity latent in everyone, being Muslim is something that must be actualized and something that requires constant striving to maintain. One is not simply *a* Muslim; one must *be* Muslim, and being Muslim is something both new—and old—Muslims must constantly enact, work at, and produce every day. One becomes, and is in a state of constantly becoming, Muslim by learning Islamic precepts and practices and reengaging with one's life in relation to these.[34] The da'wa movement's classes for newly practicing Muslims were designed to be naram or adaptable and flexible spaces within which women can engage in this process and, in so doing, return back to their fitra. As Sister Zahida discovered through her experience of learning to teach this class—of learning the importance of enfolding, flexible, and naram rather than forceful and sakht speech—this process is neither unidirectional nor linear, but cyclical and recursive: one apprehends and approaches Islamic precepts and practices in and through cultural meanings and social relations that comprise one's daily lived experiences. Proficiency is achieved through constant striving, a constant tacking back and forth between Islamic precepts and practices and the stuff of everyday life through which these precepts and practices are apprehended, approached, and actualized. For the women of the class, the stuff of everyday life necessarily includes their preexisting languages, religious traditions, familial relations and other forms of belonging, including those based on ethnicity and nationality. Becoming Muslim is thus not conceived as a renouncing, rejection, or supplanting of one's existing belongings but as a reworking and reengagement thereof. It is a dynamic and encompassing process in which the boundaries between Islam and other forms of belonging are conceived as porous and fluid, where they are configured and reconfigured together. As embodied by the space of the da'wa movement's Hindi/Urdu Salat wa Tah'ara classes—where Nepali and Indian forms of belonging are reconstituted in and through Muslim idioms, practice and networks—this form of Muslim belonging works through and reconfigures other forms of belonging in complex and often seemingly contradictory ways. The implications of this form of belonging—as Sonia and Karima's reunion, and Mary/Maryam, Phoolan, and Ritu's situations poignantly underscore—remain incipient and uncertain. And as Jacintha's experience further illustrates, this Muslim cosmopolitanism is limited and conceived as a basis of critique in relation to sociopolitical contexts such as Kuwait, in which ethnonational belongings shape domestic workers' overall sociopolitical position and status.

ONGOING CONVERSIONS

On a trip to Kuwait several years after my primary fieldwork ended, I was engrossed in conversation with Sister Zahida, an eerie sense of familiarity prickling at me. Shifting in my chair, I knew the feeling creeping at the edges of my thoughts, tugging me away from Sister Zahida's words, was not from the strange juxtapositions that mark returns—in which understandings sedimented with time, and further smoothed by time away, butt up against the sharp realizations of change.

Sister Zahida and I were updating one another about the women we knew in common: Muslim converts, South Asian domestic workers, our interlocutors or students, and in some cases, our friends. I had the distinct feeling I had heard Sister Zahida's comments before, but not from her. Staring at Sister Zahida from across her desk, a computer screen illuminating one side of her face and hijab, the other side framed by her stacks of files and books, I tried to give some definition to that sense. Looking down at the tiny cup of qahwa I held in my hands, its grounds starting to break the smooth dark surface, I remembered another cup of coffee I had held a few months earlier, a much larger corrugated cup in a café thousands of miles away in New York.

There I had met with a recently hired program officer of a large international human rights organization. Curious about my research, the program officer had asked to meet to discuss my time in the Gulf region. I had been in the midst of describing how, based on letters and the odd garbled phone call, it seemed as though little had changed in my interlocutors' lives in the years since I had left Kuwait. The program officer's response was quick and decisive: "Of course, that makes sense. It's [conversions] a necessary convenience, a polite fiction 'til they leave, right? They'll do anything. . . . and who can blame them?"

Months and miles later, Sister Zahida's own response was eerily similar: "Alhumdullilah, Allah knows best. Inshallah they will see and understand. They are learning God's guidance and way. These journeys of learning, they take time."

Although the human rights program officer and Sister Zahida made sense of South Asian migrant domestic workers' Islamic conversions in radically different ways, the underlying logic of their understandings are strikingly similar. Both attributed, and read domestic workers' conversion experiences, in relation to broader sets of principles and discourses—liberal secularism or Islamic reform—that animated their own worlds, marshaling their concerns, actions, and everyday work. For the human rights program officer, domestic workers' Islamic conversions were a necessary "convenience" that offset and unsettle the problems these migrant women experience in Kuwait, subject as they are to deeply hierarchical relationships and acute dependence upon their employers. Sister Zahida understood domestic workers' becoming Muslim as a necessary outcome of their being immersed in Muslim households, where they come to learn and adopt Islamic precepts and practices. That South Asian migrant domestic workers' conversion experiences are marked by few overt or dramatic changes in their lives was not surprising to either the human rights program officer or Sister Zahida, confirming either the polite fiction of their conversions, or the gradual nature of their religious journeys. By reading domestic workers' experiences only in terms of power/agency, or religious striving, both the human rights officer and Sister Zahida glossed over and disregarded the very nature and substance of these migrant women's experiences of conversion: the everyday transnational and gendered circumstances, activities, discourses, subjectivities and belongings that are the site and means of—not merely the background to—their conversions.

South Asian migrant domestic workers' everyday conversions are centered on their household experiences, where they are positioned as dual agents of reproduction. Many develop deeply wrought if fraught relationships of care, patronage, loyalty, and intimacy with their employers in the face of (not in spite of) deeply entrenched processes of exclusion and hierarchical relations that exist between them.[1] Their very selves are implicated and shaped through the work they perform. Domestic workers' subjectivity—their comportment, gestures, tone of voice, mood—is part and parcel of their everyday work and relations in

Kuwait, activities infused with Islamic understandings and practices. Their everyday experiences within Kuwaiti households mark the confluence of affective and immaterial labor, Islamic ethical practice, and discourses of South Asian women's malleability—all of which reshape their subjectivities and affinities. South Asian domestic workers' Islamic conversions develop through and also point to how their everyday lives in Kuwait are not reducible to temporariness, suspension, work, and wages. These migrant women are crucial nodal points in the reproduction of citizens, households, and ethnonational belongings in both the Gulf and South Asia, and they are subject to an assemblage of processes that discipline their subjectivities, relations, and affinities in ways that produce and consolidate their role as dual agents of reproduction. Yet their everyday experiences do not simply reproduce these sociopolitical forms. Also interwoven are emergent possibilities and alternative trajectories that constitute forms of everyday conversions. The assemblages producing domestic workers' temporariness, engendering their sense of suspension, and gendered discourses of malleability facilitating their adjustment to their transnational circumstances, are also the conditions of possibility for their everyday conversions. The fluid and emergent forms of subjectivity and affinity they develop are often difficult to discern, or are disregarded within existing frameworks of understanding. Their conversions are not marked by a radical shift in their lives or by the rejection of previous understandings, practices, and relationships. They entail a stickier, more processual reworking of their lives, ones in which their familial relations and ethnonational belongings are not rejected but reworked and in which traditions of religious practice are not juxtaposed but experienced in entangled ways.

Rather than an either/or binary emphasizing the importance of political-economic processes *or* religious processes, domestic workers' everyday conversions mark the confluence and complex configuration of several processes simultaneously, including globalizing Islamic movements, the feminization of transnational labor migration, the commoditization of care and intimacy, gendered discourses of subjectivity, familial and kinship networks, and state-led (raced, gendered, classed) assemblages that produce regimes of ethnonational belongings and exclusions. Domestic workers' everyday conversions point to the everyday not just as a space of habit, routine and continuity—a space through which religious traditions, disciplinary apparatuses, discursive systems and neoliberal processes are produced and reproduced—but the everyday as "an intersecting space where many forces and histories circulate and become 'ready to hand' . . . for inventing new rhythms for living, rhythms that could, at any time, congeal into norms, forms, and institutions" as described by Lauren Berlant.[2] These women's conversions index emergent forms of subjectivity, affinity, and organizing that do not constitute an exception to everyday life, but rather, that constitute important forms thereof, ones anthropology increasingly needs to contend with in our contemporary world. Developing analyses of these emergent forms necessitates an anthropology that is as attentive to precariousness, possibility, and contingency as it is to process and continuity. Such an approach enables us to discern and develop analyses for phenomena that fit awkwardly within existing categories of analysis.

This ethnography examines domestic workers' everyday conversions through a consideration of moments that punctuated their lives and our fieldwork encounters. These moments help us to account for the affective register in which domestic workers experienced different aspects of their everyday conversions— of temporariness, of suspension, of being *naram*, of housetalk, of a "quiet space," of "a feeling"—ones this ethnography conveys through anecdotes, vignettes, and stories. Following a long tradition of feminist ethnography;[3] black, Chicana and postcolonial feminist scholars;[4] life history renderings of domestic workers' migration experiences;[5] work by and inspired by Walter Benjamin;[6] and evocative tracings of everyday affects,[7] I use storytelling to tease out and convey my interlocutors' experiences without stabilizing, foreclosing, or overgeneralizing their meaning and significance.[8] In contrast with "news" and "information"— forms that demand transparency in meaning and that attempt to be understandable in themselves[9]—stories are a supple form that index and illustrate the layered, multidimensional, and (irrepressibly) expansive nature of the everyday. If narratives have long been the preeminent form and medium of conversion, retellings in and through which conversions are enacted,[10] in this ethnography I have sought to tell a more modest and mundane set of stories that convey moments of slippage, tension, and traces of feelings, thoughts and impressions of everyday conversions. To this end, and to end this ethnography, I therefore return in brief to my interlocutors' stories, those further underlining the fluid nature of their everyday conversions and how they continue to develop in tandem or in tension, and are slowly reconfiguring their subjectivities, affinities, and belongings.

During one of my first visits back to Kuwait a few years after my primary fieldwork ended, I used the occasion to arrange for a meeting I had long sought. Mary/Maryam and Geeti were both excited to see me—to hear about how my "exams" had fared, and what it was like to be a newly minted "lady doctor." Emboldened by their goodwill, I pushed for us all to meet together. I had suggested the same several times while conducting fieldwork, but to no avail. I had (perhaps naively) thought that because of the striking similarities in their experiences, Mary/Maryam and Geeti might become friends. Both were part of the first wave of migrant domestic workers to come to Kuwait from India. Each had worked within their respective employers' households for decades, embedded positions from which they witnessed dramatic transformations in Kuwait's social and political landscapes. Through their everyday experiences in Kuwait, both women had come to adopt Islamic precepts and practices. Given the deep resonances in their experiences, I had thought they might find comfort and possible solidarity in each other's company—a hoped-for belief made more acute by the concern and guilt I felt about leaving them when my fieldwork ended. Yet every time I suggested a meeting, one of the two was busy, or something inevitably came up to scuttle our plans.

On the day that we finally met, both women clearly wanted to make an impression, or as Geeti put it, "to make a respectable showing." Geeti had arranged for us to travel to Mary/Maryam's home (whose health made it difficult to leave the house) in her employers' nicest car, a sleek sedan testifying to her employers' wealth and their regard toward her. Her hair carefully oiled and coiffed, she wore an embroidered *shalwar kameez* she had recently brought back from India. Not to be outdone, Mary/Maryam met us on the front steps of Fardous's home wearing a long sequined *thobe*. She ushered us into her seating room, and we could see she had prepared a lavish meal. I was grateful but also concerned about the trouble I was putting the women through. I hoped fervently that it would go well.

That day we spoke in polite generalities as the two became acquainted with one another. In subsequent correspondence and conversations, the news I heard from them began to intertwine, indicating that some sort of rapport, possibly friendship, had taken hold. Geeti told me of Mary/Maryam's trepidation as she planned her next trip to India. Upon Mary/Maryam's return, Geeti shared her thoughts about the "understanding" Mary/Maryam had come to with her family: that they would accept her conversion to Islam so long as she agreed not to make her practice of Islam apparent when she visited them in India. Mary/Maryam, in turn, told me of Geeti's indecisiveness or "double-mindedness" about whether she should retire in Kuwait with Mama Lulua's family or with her brother's family in India, who continued to grapple with her conversion to Islam. She also gave me her assessment of the *halaqa* Geeti had begun attending in her neighborhood—how her Arabic was improving, and what passages from the Qur'an she was learning. For both women, life continued much as it had when I was in Kuwait.

———

I also met with Phoolan and her son, Varshan, during my visits to Kuwait. Phoolan's family had been successful in jointly financing her son's migration. They hoped his presence in Kuwait would dissuade Phoolan from converting. Phoolan, in turn, hoped that by coming to Kuwait, her son would better understand her conversion, and if not convert himself at least become "softer" toward Islam. When we met, Varshan had only been in Kuwait for a few short months. It was clear he had been too preoccupied with adjusting to his new environment to be able to spend much time focusing on his mother's emergent practice of Islam. Before migrating, Varshan had formed a mental image of Kuwait, one largely shaped by glossy images of Dubai. Rather than the easy wealth he had envisioned, his more prosaic experiences of working as a sales assistant for an Indian-Kuwaiti chain of electronic stores and living in shared accommodations in a rundown building on the city's outskirts, had tempered his hopes of what he had set out to accomplish in the Gulf. His visits to his mother at Dalal's home had also surprised him. He had begun to situate his mother's conversion within a broader context and constellation of issues—of which he was trying to come to grips. As he mentioned during our meeting: "I thought they [employers] had forced Ma-ji, or that Ma-ji was maybe leaving us, abandoning us, her responsibilities and duties, but no. It is not what I thought. They [employers] don't seem to care much one way or another I think. Now . . . I just don't know." For her part, Phoolan was trying her best to help her son adjust to life in Kuwait so that he could pay off the lingering debts her family had incurred in sending him. She also hoped he would be able to save and eventually settle and marry in Kuwait. When I asked her if she thought he might eventually come to understand her conversion, her response was telling: "These things, they take time, no? His mind, his eyes . . . they are already too full. It takes time."

———

Chandani returned to India, but not entirely on the terms she had envisioned. With sizeable savings she had accrued from over two decades of work in Kuwait, she was returning to her home village an independent woman—but she was returning as a married rather than a single independent woman. A year after Chandani had taken *shahada*, she found herself the object of admiration of one of the drivers employed by a member of Ilham Bibi's extended family.

Qasim, a middle-aged man who had migrated to Kuwait many years earlier, a widower with no children, had long admired Chandani. Upon learning of her conversion to Islam, he had spent months mustering up the courage to make her an offer of marriage. Chandani rejected him, which, rather than quelling, redoubled Qasim's efforts. He began wooing Chandani with small gifts, followed by repeated offers of marriage, which she repeatedly rejected, until one day, for reasons neither she nor others could quite explain, she finally accepted. The two moved to an apartment at the back of Ilham Bibi's family's complex. After a year of marriage, they began planning their return to Southern India. Chandani had long invested in a small agricultural business her brothers maintained on her behalf. Newly married, she decided to return and tend to her business with her new husband's support. Chandani and Qasim were also returning with the intention of establishing a mosque in her home community, one Ilham Bibi and her family were providing funding for. I never had the opportunity to visit Chandani in India, but learned through our phone conversations and from meeting with Ilham Bibi in Kuwait that her business was doing relatively well and that she and her husband were in the midst of trying to coordinate the building of the mosque with other Muslims living in their community.

———

Both Ritu and Hema left Kuwait earlier than they anticipated or wanted: Ritu for health-related reasons; Hema because of the sudden, tragic death of her brother. Several months before the completion of her second contract cycle, Ritu became increasingly lethargic and started losing weight. At first she attributed her condition to all the traveling she had been doing with Yasmin Mama's family—going to Lebanon, Egypt, and Dubai over a few months. But when she did not recover in the weeks following their return, Yasmin Mama took her to the health clinic, where Ritu underwent a series of tests. They soon discovered a tumor developing in her abdomen, one necessitating surgery. In the ensuing weeks, a complicated network of transnational negotiations and arrangements took place. Yasmin Mama and her husband insisted Ritu have surgery in Kuwait, where she could be assured of quality care, and they contacted friends and their family doctor for advice. Ritu, at her mother's insistence, and her own (at least then) unspoken concern about dying in Kuwait, away from home, wanted to return to Nepal. Her sister, who lived in a district close to her mother, had been making inquiries to find the necessary facilities, and found one across the border, in India. Ritu was set on returning home. Within a few weeks, all the arrangements for her return to Nepal and her surgery had been made. When I visited Ritu in Nepal several months later, her tumor had been successfully removed, and though still underweight, she was on the mend. Yasmin Mama called regularly to check on her condition. She also wired money to help support Ritu during her convalescence. Yasmin Mama hoped Ritu would return after her recovery. With few economic opportunities in her home community, and her and her mother's financial situation as acute as ever, it was an expectation Ritu shared.

While home in Nepal, her practice of Islam was readily visible. During her convalescence, she stayed in the main room of her mother's house where she undertook her daily prayers and had hung her prayer mat and a poster of Mecca on the walls. These signs of her continued Islamic practice pointed to how Ritu's family, in particular how her mother, Sonali, responded to her conversion to Islam. Born into a Dalit family, Sonali's marriage to a Hindu man entailed her own religious conversion to what she described as a "high" form of Hinduism. Her marriage also entailed her relocation to her husband's large plot of land in a rich river valley, a region several hours to the south of the tea-terraced hills where her extended family lived. When her husband died, Sonali and her children were shunned by her husband's first wife, and kept at a wary distance by much of the surrounding community. In our discussions, her mother emphasized the similarities and continuities between her life experiences and those of her daughter. Although the particularities differed—Brahmanic Hinduism versus Islam, virilocal residence versus transnational labor migration—both had experienced religious conversion, migration, social dislocation, and upward social mobility. In conversation Sonali explained that she considered Hema's conversion to Islam to mark the changing circumstances of her life, changes she told me that women are especially susceptible to by virtue of their being naram.

Hema's situation contrasted markedly. If Ritu's Islamic practice took place in her room, Hema's was largely confined to her suitcase. Hema had returned home when her brother, who had been serving in the Indian army, was killed during a border skirmish in Kashmir. Utterly distraught at the death of her son, her mother would not countenance the idea of Hema's return to Kuwait—something her daughter was keen to do. Given her family circumstances—their grieving and the contentious issue of Hema's return—she had decided to wait before telling her parents about her conversion to Islam. As I was to observe when I visited her family home, Hema had kept her Qur'an, prayer mat, instructional booklets, and CDs of Qur'anic recitations locked securely in her suitcase. Only when she was alone in her room, her door locked, would she take them out and surreptitiously pray or read Nepali translations of Qur'anic passages. As Hema explained her circumstances to both Ritu and me during our impromptu reunion (see chapter 3), she emphasized how her actions were not only necessary, but appropriate. Echoing Sonali's comments, she emphasized that as the only daughter of her house, not only was she more flexible than the others, but that it was incumbent upon her to be naram. Eventually she hoped to come to an understanding with her family similar to the one Ritu had developed with her mother. Biding her time and being patient (*sabr*) was necessary to accomplishing this.

Deliberation also characterized Ritu's and Hema's initial outreach to other Muslims in their district. Unlike in the Katmandu Valley, the Pokhara District and other regions of the Terai, they lived in a district of the Terai region with relatively few Muslims.[11] Having encountered few if any Muslims since their return to Nepal, Hema and Ritu were delighted when they learned of a mosque in a nearby market village. A weather-beaten affair, the mosque was located in a liminal area of the town, between its market roads and residential streets. I was with them when they first visited the mosque. When we entered the front courtyard, we found the custodian asleep in a corner. Roused from his sleep, he was far from welcoming. Thinking he had misunderstood the intentions for our visit, and pointing to our covered heads, we explained that we were Muslims who had recently come from the Gulf—and we apologized profusely for waking him. The custodian's brow furrowed further. "Women," he declared, "do not come to mosques."

As in other parts of South Asia, the tradition of Islam practiced by members of this mosque was one in which women's religious activities took place in their households, not in mosques. Women undertook their daily prayers in private, and when young girls were taught the Qur'an, their teachers came to their homes. Ritu and Hema had learned and begun practicing Islam in a strikingly different context. Mosques in Kuwait—whether they were neighborhood mosques, or the grand mosque in the city center—had relatively large designated spaces where women could pray or gather. Other public spaces, such as shopping malls and bus stations, also had prayer spaces for women. Ritu and Hema had also regularly attended classes at the *da'wa* movement's women's center, a space where they had access to multiple sources of learning and the opportunity to meet and develop relations with other women. Given their experiences in the Gulf, a region often portrayed as restrictive to women, an Orientalist discourse that was pervasive in Nepal, the custodian's seeming interdiction clearly caught Ritu and Hema by surprise.

Their confusion was only slightly abated when the imam joined us. Offering us cold sodas in the front courtyard, he listened quietly as Ritu and Hema discussed their circumstances: how they had both migrated to Kuwait, converted to Islam while abroad, and now returned and living in the surrounding villages, wanted to learn more about the activities of the mosque. Shaking his head and looking pensive, he indicated that there were few activities at the mosque for women. Most Muslim women in the area, he told us, were illiterate and their knowledge of Islam limited. They could recite passages from the Qur'an they had memorized, and could pray, but little else.

Later that day as we lounged on Ritu's front porch, sipping tea into the lengthening shadows, I asked them about what they thought about our visit to the mosque. Both indicated that though they had not expected there to be the same facilities for Muslims in Nepal as there were in Kuwait, they had been surprised about the dearth of resources available to them. In Kuwait if they had any questions about Islamic precepts and practices, Ritu and Hema could turn to their teachers at the women's center, fellow domestic workers who had also converted to Islam, or their employers, or find pamphlets or audiovisual recordings. The imam's inability (at least initially) to respond to their questions was quite disconcerting to them. Ritu and Hema were not only worried about the imam being unaware about the particularities of gendered forms of Islamic practices, for example, veiling practices, the special ablutions they needed to undertake as women, and differences between women and men's prayer and fasting schedules. They were also concerned the imam would not be able to fully understand or appreciate the everyday naram ways in which, as "New Muslims" they were negotiating their sense of familial and community obligation with their emergent religious ones. "These things," Hema pointed out "may seem normal for him [the imam], for them [other people in general], nothing special, but for us, us people, it's so much more."[12]

APPENDIX 1. *Notes on Fieldwork*

I conducted three stages of fieldwork: preliminary fieldwork in Pakistan, the UAE, and Kuwait during the summer of 2003 and 2004; primary fieldwork in Kuwait from 2006–7, which included a visit to Nepal during the summer of 2007; and follow-up visits to Kuwait in 2008 and 2010.

Regardless of the plans and itineraries I charted before leaving for the field, my initial time in Kuwait was consumed with figuring out how to live and navigate the city-state as a single woman on a straightened budget (relatively speaking). I learned firsthand how living accommodations, transportation, and spaces of social interaction are highly segmented in Kuwait, divided between (1) those who belonged to, reside with and socialize through networks of households (including domestic workers, Kuwaitis, long-standing foreign residents); (2) recently arrived well-heeled foreign residents and expatriates living in housing complexes, individuals who largely socialize in commercially oriented public spaces (i.e., malls, restaurants, cafes); (3) so-called bachelor workers or migrant workers, who live in dormitories or building complexes located in neighborhoods on the outskirts of the city, or in parts of the city that have otherwise been abandoned by others, and who are bused to and from their housing accommodations to their work places by the companies with whom they work; and (4) others such as myself, service industry workers, nurses, teachers, lower-middle-class and middle-class foreign residents who existed in the interstices of these other spaces. In general, social interactions among different groups in Kuwait, and households and private spaces are largely channeled along national, ethnic, and linguistic lines. Important exceptions are private spaces and households of Kuwaitis and well-heeled foreign residents who employ migrant domestic workers. Interactions among peoples of different ethnonational and class-occupational backgrounds take place in public arenas such as (in certain cases) work spaces, elite private schools, commercially oriented public places, certain public parks, and religious centers.

Within this social matrix, at first there were few spaces where I could meet with and get to know domestic workers. My entry into Kuwait's myriad social worlds was hampered by my lack of substantive connections (i.e., in the form of family members, work colleagues or long-standing friendships). As I was experiencing firsthand, in addition to the paucity of spaces of plural interaction, most people in Kuwait tend to be wary of individuals, most especially would-be-researchers with an odd story and even odder requests, whom they do not have preexisting social connections with. In embarking on my research, it was therefore necessary for me to draw upon connections I had forged through my predissertation research, including longtime members of the Pakistani community who were linked to my own diasporic Pakistani friend and family networks, and Kuwaiti academics to whom I had been introduced in absentia by fellow scholars overseas. Through these connections, I was introduced to a quickly expanding and proliferating network of people to whom I explained my research topic, and whom I asked to introduce me to domestic workers they knew and/or members of the households these women work for or with. I was soon vetted by a panoply of sponsor-employers, and eventually introduced to the women working within their households. Only one employer made it difficult, and de facto impossible, for me to return to her or his household for reasons that were never explained to me. Overall, however, most acceded to my requests and did not place any overt restrictions on my access to the women working within their household so long as the women themselves were willing to meet and speak with me and I did not interfere with their duties and work.

My ability to access these spaces was predicated upon vetting processes (most notably ensuring I was a bona fide researcher affiliated with academic institutions in Kuwait and the United States—also being vouched for by acquaintances and contacts in my growing network). My ability to access these spaces was also facilitated by my gender, my religious background, and my interstitial ethnonational background. Employers generously granted me access to their household spaces for a myriad of reasons: they too were curious or concerned about their domestic workers' Islamic conversions, and they were acutely aware of popular perceptions—among foreign residents in Kuwait and in international news media reports—of Kuwaiti citizen-employers' exploitative and abusive treatment of migrant domestic workers. These employers were eager to have a "scientifically trained," "unbiased," and/or "open minded" scholar who could research the matter. Like the vast majority of ethnographic research, in particular research involving long-term and intensive participant-observation, my interlocutors were largely self-selecting, and amenable to my conducting research with them as long as I remained discreet in Kuwait about their family news/gossip and privacy, and as I did not disrupt or interfere with the functioning of their households. My research was further deepened by interviews and research I conducted about the migrant domestic work sector and with "outside" domestic workers (i.e., domestic workers who do not reside with their employers). Incidents of domestic workers' exploitation and abuse are relatively well documented in Kuwait and other countries of the Gulf. My research is not nor should be read as a refutation of the fact that fraught and conflictual relationships exist between migrant domestic workers and their employers in the Gulf. This book discusses and analyzes power relations, moments of frustration, and conflict between migrant domestic workers and their employers. It also underscores how other forms of relationships develop between migrant domestic workers and their employers in the face—and not despite, or as mitigating against—hierarchical relations of power existing between them.

I decided to focus on South Asian domestic workers not only because they constitute the overwhelming majority of domestic workers, but also because unlike male domestic workers, they reside within the household (rather than in separate quarters), and because of gender-based restrictions on social interactions.[1] I also decided to work with women who had migrated from India and Nepal.[2] I did so not only because I was able to communicate with them (many of these women spoke Hindi/Urdu).[3] I also worked with them because of the resonances and points of overlap in their sociocultural understandings and practices, and because of their different histories and structures of migration to Kuwait. Places and peoples in the Indian subcontinent have long-term connections with what are today the Arab Gulf states, and throughout the twentieth century, Indians have constituted a large population in Kuwait. The experiences of Indian nationals contrast markedly with those of the Nepalese, who began migrating in significant numbers to Kuwait beginning in the early 1990s.

As I started to learn about my interlocutors' experiences of Islamic conversion, I discovered that many of them had obtained informational and instructional materials about Islam, and had attended various study circles and classes organized through Kuwait's Islamic da'wa groups, and to a lesser degree, Islamic reform movements. To learn more about my interlocutors' experiences with these groups and movements, I therefore began attending activities organized by them, and interviewing their members. Over the course of my research, I also spent time with the Ministry of Awqaf's Women's Outreach center to learn about their Project Barira, a project focusing on raising awareness about the situation of domestic workers in Kuwait. I also spent time with an Islamic Inter-Cultural Awareness Center that caters largely to the country's expatriate population (i.e., from countries in North America and Europe), the women's center of an organization affiliated with Kuwait's *salafi* movement, and several weekly *halaqa* organized by women in my neighborhood (or adjacent areas). Most of my research, however, concentrated on the women's center of Kuwait's largest Islamic da'wa movement (henceforth referred to as the women's center), a movement with links to numerous Islamic groups in Kuwait, including a prominent transnational Islamic social reform group and the Ikhwan Muslimin (Muslim Brotherhood), as well as Islamic groups throughout the world (including Jamaat-i-Islam, the Tablighi Jamaat, the Islamic Charitable Centers of Nepal, Muslim Women's League in Sri Lanka, etc.). I focused on this women's center because it is most actively involved with Kuwait's foreign female migrant and resident populations. I attended the center's Hindi-Urdu "Salat wa Tah'ara classes for Newly Practicing Muslims" for over fourteen months. Simultaneously, as some of my interlocutors progressed with their learning, I followed them as they took the next level of courses, including ones that focused on *seera* (the biography of Prophet Muhammad), *tajwid* (pronunciation and recitation of the Qur'an), *fiqh* (often translated as Islamic jurisprudence, but in the context of these classes it was translated as Islamic etiquette and practice), and *tafsir* (Qur'anic exegesis and interpretation). I also attended the center's course on "The Practice of Da'wa" (in English), which was being taught for the first time. Through interviews and participant observation with these groups, I focused on learning their history, organization, and composition; the pedagogical techniques they employed; the resources they offered and how they distributed them to members; and the ways in which domestic workers accessed and engaged with them. Through all of these activities I also became acquainted with, and developed relations with, a further group of domestic workers who had converted to Islam. I also became part of a dense interconnected network of migrant women active in these Islamic groups.

Ten months into my research, I came to realize that few, if any, of my existing interlocutors had more than piecemeal information about other actors and groups (i.e., aside from domestic workers and their sponsor-employers) involved with Kuwait's domestic work sector. I was unable to find documentation or research on this sector.[4] I therefore undertook a short sectoral analysis of Kuwait's transnational domestic work sector: I met with officials at embassies, staff and owners of labor recruitment agencies, journalists, lawyers, and human rights workers to learn more about the demographic history of migrant domestic workers in Kuwait; visa, legal, and contract-related systems and procedures; and different systems by which their activities are governed and policed in Kuwait. Through these activities, I became acquainted with and learned more about the experiences of domestic workers who had been exploited and/or abused by their sponsor-employers. I also developed relations with a further group of domestic workers, many of whom worked part time and did not live with their sponsor-employers (commonly referred to as "outside workers") and who had not converted to Islam.

In addition to all these sources, I also developed relations and collected data from domestic workers residing in my neighborhood. Toward the end of my fieldwork, I also traveled to Nepal to visit with some of my interlocutors who had returned back, or who had traveled back to visit their families and communities temporarily. Most of my Nepalese interlocutors were from three regions in Nepal: the Katmandu valley, areas surrounding Pokhara, and the Jhapa District. I had hoped to meet with six interlocutors in total, two in each region; however, the two who were from the Katmandu valley were unreachable—one had disappeared, and one had migrated to Israel shortly before I arrived in the country.

In total I worked closely with twenty-four migrant domestic workers. When I was first introduced to them, and during our initial meetings, I often undertook structured and semistructured interviews with them. I did so not only to learn about their life and migration trajectories, but also because many of them expected me, as a "journalist," "book writer," and researcher to do so.[5] As I developed rapports and relationships with these women, our conversations became more informal. When possible, I met with and interviewed members of their household (i.e., sponsor-employers, fellow domestic workers), and their families and friends in Kuwait, and I conducted participant-observation in their households. With a few exceptions in which my interlocutors declined to do so, I tape-recorded our interviews and conversations.[6] I supplemented these recordings with notes and reflections recorded in my field journals.

My interactions and interrelations with my interlocutors varied widely, some of which related to age differences, facility with the language(s) we shared, and our respective circumstances and situations in Kuwait. I introduced myself as a researcher from Canada, studying in the United States, and part of diasporic Pakistani networks. I also was up front about my own religious background, and when asked, discussed with them the reasons I did not wear the hijab and abaya, or (in some cases) practice Islam in the same way that they, their sponsor-employers, or members of the Islamic movements practiced Islam. My situation and living conditions in Kuwait caught many of my interlocutors by surprise. Many of the women with whom I met, especially those I met early on, worked and resided in relatively affluent homes, and were driven by their employers or drivers if they were visiting friends or were out in public spaces. In contrast, except when using taxis at night, and except when some of my Kuwaiti interlocutors and friends made their family drivers' services available to me, I walked and used public transportation a great deal. I also resided in a modest apartment, one associated with male migrant workers (i.e., I lived in rooftop quarters formerly occupied by the building's maintenance workers and/or security guard). For domestic workers living and working "outside" Kuwaiti homes, my living situation was comprehensible and resonant with their own. Domestic workers residing and working within prosperous Kuwaiti households, however, were often shocked, dismayed, or pitying about how I lived (i.e., where I lived, and living "alone") and about how I commuted in Kuwait. Their assumptions about my situation and status—predicated on my being a doctoral student studying in the United States, and having citizenship in North America—were jarred, dashed, or tempered by seeing how I lived in Kuwait.[7] My living circumstances either provided a counterpoint, or were similar to my interlocutors' experiences in ways that helped me better foreground and understand how they experienced and navigated Kuwait.

AUNTIE ANJUM: Long-standing member of Kuwait's South Asian Muslim diasporic community who coordinates Al-Huda lessons and other Islamic *halaqa* (study circles) in Kuwait.

ROSA: Filipina domestic worker who took *shahada* during one of Auntie Anjum's *halaqa* gatherings.

SISTER HAWA: Egyptian woman who facilitates a series of *halaqa* hosted by Auntie Anjum.

NAUREEN: contact in Kuwait who put me in touch with Auntie Anjum.

GEETI (GERTRUDE): migrant domestic worker from India; part of a family with connections of many years with a merchant family in Kuwait.

MAMA LULUA: Geeti's Kuwaiti employer.

SAAD: Geeti's employer's grandson.

AL-ANOUD: Geeti's employer's daughter.

BILQUIS: Geeti's employer's daughter.

MARY/MARYAM: Migrant domestic worker from India.

UNCLE BOBBY: Mary/Maryam's uncle.

BABA IBRAHIM: Mary/Maryam's first male employer.

MAMA ALIA: Mary/Maryam's first female employer.

FARDOUS BIBI: Mama Alia's daughter; Mary/Maryam's second female employer.

KHALED: Fardous's son.

'ALIA: Fardous's daughter.

OMAR: Fardous's nephew.

ASHU: Domestic worker from India employed by Mama Alia and Fardous's extended family.

ROSHNI: Domestic worker from India employed by Mama Alia and Fardous's extended family.

PHOOLAN: Migrant domestic worker from India; widow.

DALAL: Phoolan's Kuwaiti employer.

NADIA: Dalal's daughter.

HAJIRA: Dalal's daughter.

ASAD: Dalal's son.

VARSHAN: Phoolan's son.

MADU: Phoolan's sister.

SAKINA: Dalal's mother.

CHANDANI: Migrant domestic worker from India; divorced and then remarried.

GUL NAR: Chandani's employer (mother).

UMM MUHAMMAD: Gul Nar's half-sister.

ILHAM BIBI: Chandani's employer (daughter).

VINOD: Chandani's ex-husband.

QASIM: Chandani's husband.

HISHAM: 'houseboy' from Yemen employed by Gul Nar's brother.

BILAL: gardener from Bangladesh employed by Ilham Bibi's family.

BIPASH: driver from Bangladesh employed by Ilham Bibi's family.

PAROMITA: Domestic worker from India employed by Ilham Bibi's family.

HEMA: Migrant domestic worker from Nepal.

SIHAM MAMA: Hema's employer.

YOUMMA FATIMA: Siham's mother.

YOUBBA ALI: Siham's father

FARAH: Siham's daughter.

SADIA: Siham's daughter.

RITU: Migrant domestic worker from Nepal.

SONALI: Ritu's mother.

HARI: Ritu's boyfriend.

YASMIN MAMA: Ritu's employer.

SONIA: Migrant domestic worker from Nepal, Karima's mother.

KARIMA: Migrant domestic worker from Nepal, Sonia's daughter.

ABU KHALID: Karima's employer.

UMM KHALID: Karima's employer.

NIRMALA: Migrant domestic worker from Sri Lanka, previously employed by Abu and Umm Khalid, Karima's employers.

OTHER MIGRANT DOMESTIC WORKERS AND EMPLOYERS

HEBA: Migrant domestic worker from India.

PRIYA ROSHNI: Migrant domestic worker from India.

AMITA: Migrant domestic worker from Nepal.

LAKSHMI: Migrant domestic worker from Nepal.

NEELI: Migrant domestic worker from India.

MEENA: Migrant domestic worker from Sri Lanka.

ALICE: Migrant domestic worker from the Philippines.

JACINTHA: Migrant domestic worker from India.

FATIMA: Kuwaiti employer of Shi'a background.

DA'WA MOVEMENT

SISTER KULSUM: Teacher at the women's center.

SISTER NASREEN: Teacher at the women's center.

SISTER ZAHIDA: Teacher at the women's center.

SISTER HANAN: Teacher at the women's center.

SISTER AISHA: One of the founders and teachers of the women's center.

SARA: Student at the women's center from Goa and of Christian background.

MADHU: student at the women's center from Mumbai.

PUSHPA: student at the women's center from Nepal.

MAYA: student at the women's center from Nepal.

All words are Arabic unless otherwise indicated.

a'adi
normal

abaya
cloak or long, loose overgarment (plural: *abayat*)

Ahl al-Kitab
people of the book; used to refer to Jews and Christians

al-Huda
an Islamic women's movement that initially developed in Pakistan

alhumdullilah
phrase: "thanks be to God"

Angrez
English or "white" people

'aqida
creed or tenets of faith

astaghfirallah
phrase: "I seek forgiveness from God"; used when abstaining from doing wrong

---

baat
word or talk

bakala
corner store

banda (Urdu/Hindi)
man or male person

bandh (Urdu/Hindi)
strike

baraka
blessings

basti (Urdu/Hindi)
neighborhood, often connotation of slum

bayt
house or home

beti (Urdu/Hindi)
daughter

bibi (Urdu/Hindi)
used as a respectful title or honorific for women and is added to the first name

―――――

chalo (Urdu/Hindi)
(let's) go

―――――

dars (pl.: durus)
lessons or class

da'iya
those who call people to Islam (feminine)

da'wa
to call or invite

dharam (Urdu/Hindi)
religion

din
often translated as "religion" but carries the broader meaning of way of life

dishdasha
floor-length tunic, often white in the Greater Arabian Peninsula

diwaniyya
gathering or place of gathering; room often at the periphery of a house in the Greater
Arabian Peninsula where people, usually men, assemble for regular gatherings (plural:
diwaniyyat; colloquial Kuwaiti: diwawin)

du'a
prayer; act of supplication; means 'invocation'

―――――

fajr
first of the five daily prayers (salat) performed before sunrise

fiqh
Islamic jurisprudence

fitra
disposition or human nature

————

gharmi (Urdu/Hindi)
hot (weather)

ghar (Urdu/Hindi)
house or home

————

hadith
traditions of Prophet Muhammad

halaqa
Islamic study circle

hajj
annual pilgrimage to Mecca; one of the five pillars of faith

haram
forbidden

hijab
clothing such as the veil or headscarf that covers a person's hair

hotel (Urdu/Hindi)
word often used among South Asians to refer to a restaurant

Husseniyya
congregation space for Shi'a religious ceremonies, especially commemoration ceremonies

————

iftar
evening meal when Muslims break their fast at sunset

ijma'
consensus or agreement of the community

iman
faith

inshallah
phrase: "God willing"

iqama
Gulf residency visa and identification card

————

jao (Urdu/Hindi)
(you) go

jalabiyya
floor-length tunic

jam'ayya
local cooperative grocery store and complex

-ji (Urdu/Hindi)
honorific added to the end of a name or word

jinsiyya
nationality

juma'a
Friday; Friday afternoon prayers

––––––––

ka'ba
square stone building in the center of the Great Mosque of Mecca

kaam (Urdu/Hindi)
work

kafala
sponsorship and guarantor system

kafeel
sponsor and guarantor

Khaliji
of the "Gulf"

khawf
fearfulness

Kuwaiti bil-asl
Kuwaiti by "origin"

Kuwaiti bil-tajanus
Kuwaiti by "naturalization"

––––––––

lawg (Urdu/Hindi)
people

––––––––

madhhab
school of jurisprudence (plural: *madhahib*)

maghrib
the fourth of the five daily prayers (salat) performed just after sunset

majlis
place of sitting; often used to refer to a council or legislature

marja'iyya
traditional forms of Shi'a clerical authority

mashallah
phrase: "Whatever God wills"; often used to congratulate someone's achievement or
good deed

mazbut (Arabic)
correct or right

mazbut (Urdu/Hindi)
strong

mehram
male guardian

----

nakba
catastrophe; word used to refer to the displacement of Palestinians brought about by
the creation of Israel

naram (Urdu/Hindi)
softness, malleability

nikab
veil covering the face, often with the eyes left uncovered

----

panjabi
word used for shalwar kameez or loose tunic and pants in parts of South Asia and the
Greater Arabian Peninsula

----

qahwa
Arabic coffee

----

riba
interest

----

sabr
patience

sadaqa
voluntary charity

sahaba
companions of Prophet Muhammad

sahwa
awakening, term used to refer to Islamic revival and reformist movements

sakht (Urdu/Hindi)
hard, tough, brittle

salaam
peace; greeting

salaf
community of Muslims at the time of Prophet Muhammad

salafiyyun (salafi)
Islamic reform movement with worldwide networks

salat
prayer; daily prayer

seera
biographies of the prophets

shalwar kameez (Urdu/Hindi)
loose tunic or pants

shahada
testament of faith

shughl
work

shurta
police

sirif (Urdu/Hindi)
only

sura (pl.: suwar)
passage from the Quran

─────────

tafsir
Qur'anic exegesis

tah'ara
purification

tajwid
Qur'anic recitation

taqlid
to follow, term used with reference to following a school of jurisprudence

tawhid
oneness of God

thobe
floor-length tunic

tori (Urdu/Hindi)
Urdu/Hindi word meaning 'a little'

———

umma
community of believers

umra
lesser pilgrimage to Mecca that is not time specific

———

Wahhabi
reform and revivalist Islamic movement founded by Abd-al Wahhab in the mid-eighteenth century

wallah
phrase: "I swear by God"

-wallah (Urdu/Hindi)
suffix added to a noun or an agentive sense with a verb; surname or suffix indicating a person involved with some type of activity

wasta
connections and influence

———

yalla
go

———

zabaan (Urdu/Hindi)
tongue, language

zakat
almsgiving; one of the five pillars of Islam

INTRODUCTION: EVERYDAY CONVERSIONS

1 Giorgio Agamben, *Homer Sacer*, and *Means without End*.

2 Migrants here include current migrants, returning migrants, and secondary migrants.

3 Shifts in veiling practices include adoption of abaya and nikab. Changes in everyday language practices include shifts in greetings (e.g., from "marhaba" to "as-Sala'm 'Alekum"), and good-byes (e.g., "Khuda Hafiz" to "Allah Hafiz"). An example of shifts in gendered relations is the gendered segregation of wedding ceremonies. An example of shifts in religious ceremonies include the burgeoning of *halaqa* that often replaced "Qur'an Khanis" and "Khatme Qur'an."

4 English translation: There is no God but God, and Muhammad is the Messenger of God.

5 Domestic workers of a myriad of ethnonational backgrounds develop Islamic pieties in Kuwait and the Gulf. I focused on South Asian domestic workers for reasons I discuss in appendix 1.

6 T. Asad, "Comments on Conversion," 263.

7 Agrama, *Questioning Secularism*, 9.

8 Weber, *The Protestant Ethic and the Spirit of Capitalism*.

9 Casanova, *Public Religions in the Modern World*.

10 Viswanathan, *Outside the Fold*.

11 Said, *Orientalism*.

12 For works that critique these understandings, see Deeb, *An Enchanted Modern*; Kurtzman, *Modernist Islam, 1840–1940*; Lawrence, *Shattering the Myth*; Mamdani, *Good Muslim, Bad Muslim*; Said, *Orientalism*, and *Culture and Imperialism*.

13 Foucault, *The History of Sexuality*, 34.

14 Mahmood, "Feminist Theory," "Rehearsed Spontaneity and the Conventionality of Ritual," "Ethical Formation and Politics of Individual Autonomy in Contemporary Egypt," *Politics of Piety*; and "Secularism, Hermeneutics, and Empire." Also see Hirschkind, "The Ethics of Listening," and *The Ethical Soundscape*; and Henkel,

"Between Belief and Unbelief Lies the Performance of Saat," and "The Location of Islam."

15 Trouillot, *Global Transformations*.

16 Grewal, *Transnational America*; Grewal and Kaplan, *Scattered Hegemonies*; Mintz, *Sweetness and Power*; Stoler, *Race and the Education of Desire*, and *Carnal Knowledge and Imperial Power*; Trouillot, *Global Transformations*; Van der Veer, "Syncretism, Multiculturalism and the Discourse of Tolerance," and *Imperial Encounters*; Visweswaran, *Fictions of Feminist Ethnography*, and *Uncommon Cultures*.

17 Materialist approaches to the study of Islam include the works of Beinin and Stork, *Political Islam*; Eickelman and Piscatori, *Muslim Politics*; and Rodinson, *Muhammad*. Idealist approaches include the works of Geertz, *Islam Observed*; Gellner, *Muslim Society*; and Weber, *The Protestant Ethic and the Spirit of Capitalism*.

18 Information gathered from memos, reports, and interviews conducted with officials and volunteers of human rights and domestic work organizations in Kuwait, including Al-Haqooq, the Kuwait Union of Domestic Labor Organizations, the Kuwait Human Rights Society, the Kuwait Friendship Society; U.S. Department of State; Kuwait Annual "Bureau of Democracy, Human Rights, and Labour" reports 2006, 2007; interviews with officials at the Indian, Bangladeshi, Sri Lankan, Filipino, and Indonesian embassies, as well as the then unofficial representative of Nepali government (in the absence of a consulate, embassy, or official representation at the time my primary fieldwork was being conducted).

19 Al-Hijji, *Kuwait and the Sea*; Anscombe, *The Ottoman Gulf*, and "An Anational Society"; Bose, "Space and Time on the Indian Ocean Rim," and *A Hundred Horizons*; Fuccaro, "Mapping the Transnational Community," and *Histories of the City and State in the Persian Gulf*; Ho, *The Graves of Tarim*; Onley, "Transnational Merchants in the Nineteenth-Century Gulf," and *The Arabian Frontier of the British Raj*.

20 Dresch, "Debates on Marriage and Nationality in the United Arab Emirates."

21 I use *race*, *raced*, and *racialization* to refer to sociohistorical processes through which (a) differences are produced and reproduced between actors and groups, (b) generalized characteristics are attributed to these actors and groups that are/become naturalized, and (c) these differences articulate asymmetrical power relations among actors and groups. Histories of racialization in the Gulf are distinctive in relation to other sociohistorical contexts (e.g., North America). In the Gulf racialization occurs along ethnonational lines: where ethnonational belongings are sutured to and conflated with occupations and sociopolitical status. Systems of racialization in the Gulf have developed through transnational imperial and colonial histories in which racializing labor regimes were developed and implemented by the British and Americans with the complicity of particular sets of local actors (see Secombe and Lawless, "Foreign Worker Dependence in the Gulf, and the International Oil Companies"; Vitalis, "Black Gold, White Crude," and *America's Kingdom*; and also see chapter 1). Racialized differences articulated in terms of ethnonationalism are also produced by the kafala system (see chapter 1 for further discussion of this) and, in the case of migrant domestic workers, through their everyday relations with their employers (see chapters 1 and 2).

22 Limbert, "Caste, Ethnicity and the Politics of Arabness in Southern Arabia."

23 Crystal, *Kuwait*, 52.

24 Dresch, "Debates on Marriage and Nationality in the United Arab Emirates."

25 This assemblage comprises migration and residency laws in both the Gulf and migrant-sending countries, as well as labor recruitment agencies, embassies, consulates, and state institutions, which include the police, border patrols, and ministries of the interior, foreign affairs, and social affairs. See Crystal, *Kuwait*, and "Public Order and Authority"; Longva, *Walls Built on Sand*.

26 Crystal, *Oil and Politics in the Gulf*; *Kuwait*; and "Public Order and Authority"; Gardner, *City of Strangers*; Longva, "Keeping Migrant Workers in Check Gulf"; "Citizenship in the Gulf States"; "Neither Autocracy nor Democracy but Ethnocracy."

27 Crystal, *Kuwait*.

28 Nagy, "'This Time I Think I'll Try a Filipina'"; "The Search for Miss Philippines Bahrain."

29 Vora, "Producing Diasporas and Globalization," and *Impossible Citizens*.

30 Vora, "Producing Diasporas and Globalization," and *Impossible Citizens*.

31 Gardner, *City of Strangers*; Longva, "Keeping Migrant Workers in Check"; and "Neither Autocracy nor Democracy but Ethnocracy," 114–35.

32 On June 24, 2015, the Kuwaiti government passed a new law giving domestic workers enforceable labor rights. At the time I was conducting fieldwork, domestic workers did not fall under existing labor laws; however, like all other citizens and noncitizens in Kuwait, they could seek recourse through civil and criminal laws. It is also worth noting that with few exceptions (most notably the United Kingdom, and Kuwait more recently), domestic workers are excluded from most countries' labor laws. I discuss these matters further in chapter 1.

33 These groups include Kuwait's diverse noncitizen populations, members of the country's self-styled liberal movement, local and international human rights organizations, labor agencies, and foreign embassies.

34 Information gathered from reports, memos, and interviews that were conducted with members of the Islamic Presentation Committee Ministry of Awqaf officials, including Project Barira members and Grand Mosque of Kuwait's outreach workers, Revival of Islamic Heritage Society, and the Aware Center.

35 Lacroix, *Awakening Islam*, 4.

36 Mitchell, *Carbon Democracy*.

37 Lacroix, *Awakening Islam*, 4.

38 Agrama, *Questioning Secularism*; T. Asad, *Genealogies of Religion*, and *Formations of the Secular*.

39 Al-Moqatei, "Introducing Islamic Law in the Arab Gulf States."

40 Ghabra, *Palestinians in Kuwait*; Louer, *Transnational Shia Politics*, 2.

41 Ghabra, *Palestinians in Kuwait*.

42 Al-Moqatei, "Introducing Islamic Law in the Arab Gulf States"; Bill, "Resurgent Islam in the Persian Gulf"; Ghabra, *Palestinians in Kuwait*; Louer, *Transnational Shia Politics*; Rizzo, *Islam, Democracy, and the Status of Women*.

43 N. Brown, *The Rule of Law in the Arab World*, 5–6; Ghabra, *Palestinians in Kuwait*; Louer, *Transnational Shia Politics*; Rizzo, *Islam, Democracy, and the Status of Women*.

44 Ghabra, *Palestinians in Kuwait*; Rizzo, *Islam, Democracy, and the Status of Women*, 19.

45 Louer, *Transnational Shia Politics*, 85.

46 Louer, *Transnational Shia Politics*, 85.

47 Ghabra, *Palestinians in Kuwait*; Rizzo, *Islam, Democracy, and the Status of Women*, 19.

48 Al-Rasheed, *Contesting the Saudi State*, 2; Haykel, *Revival and Reform in Islam*, 42.

49 Haykel, *Revival and Reform in Islam*, 38; Meijer, *Global Salafism*, 4.

50 Haykel, *Revival and Reform in Islam*, 36; Lacroix, *Awakening Islam*.

51 Lacroix, *Awakening Islam*; Meijer, *Global Salafism*, 29.

52 Al-Moqatei, "Introducing Islamic Law in the Arab Gulf States"; Bill, "Resurgent Islam in the Persian Gulf"; N. Brown, *The Rule of Law in the Arab World*.

53 Ghabra, *Palestinians in Kuwait*.

54 Rizzo, *Islam, Democracy, and the Status of Women*, 19.

55 El Shakry, "Schooled Mothers and Structured Play"; McLarney, "Private Is Political" and "The Islamic Public Sphere and the Discipline of Adab."

56 As discussed in appendix 1, I worked closely with twenty-four South Asian migrant domestic workers, and to varying extents with members of their employers' households, their friends and family members in Kuwait, and in a few cases, in Nepal. My ability to access these spaces was predicated upon vetting processes (most notably ensuring I was a bona fide researcher affiliated with academic institutions in Kuwait and the United States, as well as being vouched for by acquaintances and contacts in my growing network). My ability to access these spaces was also facilitated by my gender, my religious background, and my interstitial ethnonational background. Only in one circumstance was my request to engage with a domestic worker and members of the employers' household declined—for reasons that were not made clear to me. With that exception, employers generously granted me access to their household spaces for myriad reasons: they too were curious or concerned about their domestic workers' Islamic conversions, and they were acutely aware of popular perceptions of Kuwaiti citizen-employers' exploitative and abusive treatment of migrant domestic workers among foreign residents in Kuwait and in international news media reports. These employers were eager to have a "scientifically trained," "unbiased," or "open-minded" scholar who could research the matter. Like the vast majority of ethnographic research—in particular that involving long-term and intensive participant-observation—my interlocutors were largely self-selecting, and amenable to my conducting research with them so long as I remained discreet in Kuwait about their family news, gossip and privacy, and so long as I did not disrupt or interfere with the functioning of their households. My research was further deepened by interviews and research I conducted about the migrant domestic work sector and with "outside" domestic workers (i.e., domestic workers who do not reside with their employers). Incidents of domestic workers' exploitation and abuse are relatively well documented in Kuwait and other countries of the Gulf. My research is not nor should be read as a refutation of the fact that fraught and conflictual relationships exist between migrant domestic workers and their employers in the Gulf. This book discusses and analyzes power relations, moments of frustration, and conflict between migrant

domestic workers and their employers. It also underscores how other forms of relationships develop between migrant domestic workers and their employers in the face—and not despite, or as mitigating against—of hierarchical relations of power existing between them. My work, which includes immersive participant-observation, complements and extends existing research on migrant domestic workers in the region, which is largely based on interviews and interactions with domestic workers outside the households of their employers, and/or has been conducted with the assistance of embassies, human rights organizations, and international organizations.

57 Bloch, *The Principle of Hope*; de Certeau, *The Practice of Everyday Life*; Deleuze, *Difference and Repetition*; Lefebvre, *Critique of Everyday Life*.

58 On race, see endnote 21.

59 T. Asad, *The Idea of an Anthropology of Islam*, and *Genealogies of Religion*; Henkel, "Between Belief and Unbelief Lies the Performance of Salat"; Hirschkind, *The Ethical Soundscape*; Mahmood, "Ethical Formation and Politics of Individual Autonomy in Contemporary Egypt," and *Politics of Piety*.

60 Clough and Halley, *The Affective Turn*; Gregg, *The Affect Theory Reader*; Lazzarato, "Immaterial Labor"; Parrenas, *Intimate Labors*; Weeks, "Life within and against Work," and *The Problem with Work*.

61 Asad, "Comments on Conversion," 266; Austin-Broos, "The Anthropology of Conversion," 2; Buckser and Glazier, *The Anthropology of Religious Conversion*; Krstic, "Illuminated by the Light of Islam and the Glory of the Ottoman Sultanate," and *Contested Conversions to Islam*; Morrison, *Understanding Conversion*, xii; van Nieuwkerk, "Gender, Conversion, and Islam," and "Islam Is Your Birthright," 151; Viswanathan, *Outside the Fold*.

62 Morrison, *Understanding Conversion*, xii.

63 Deleuze, *Nietzsche and Philosophy*, 48.

64 Foucault, *The Hermeneutics of the Subject*, 205–27.

65 Foucault, "About the Beginnings of the Hermeneutic of the Self," 162.

66 In other words, Foucault is indicating that his writing on "ethics" is not reintroducing or reinscribing the sovereign subject.

67 Foucault, "The Ethic of Care for the Self as a Practice of Freedom," 11.

68 Deleuze, *Bergsonism*.

69 Sedgwick, *Touching Feeling*, 5.

70 Sedgwick, *Touching Feeling*, 5, 9.

71 While it is debatable whether Butler's understanding of performance is "essentialist," Sedgwick's critique underscores how Butler's understanding of performance is not as encompassing and individuated as the one Austin presents us with. See Sedgwick, *Touching Feeling*, 6.

72 Sedgwick, *Touching Feeling*, 126, 134.

73 Sedgwick, *Touching Feeling*, 8; also see Berlant, *Cruel Optimism*, 8–10.

74 Grewal and Kaplan, *Scattered Hegemonies*; Stoler, *Race and the Education of Desire*, and *Carnal Knowledge and Imperial Power*; Visweswaran, *Fictions of Feminist Ethnography*, and *Uncommon Cultures*.

75 Masuzawa, *The Invention of World Religions.*
76 Eaton, *The Rise of Islam and the Bengal Frontier, 1204–1760*; Ho, *The Graves of Tarim*; Ricci, *Islam Translated*; Shaw and Stewart, "Introduction: Problematizing Syncretism"; Simpson and Kress, "Introduction: Cosmopolitanism Contested."
77 Flood, *Objects of Translation.*
78 Metcalf, "Presidential Address."
79 Flueckiger, *In Amma's Healing Room*; also see Langford, *Fluent Bodies.*
80 Butalia, *The Other Side of Silence*; Hasan, "Introduction: Memories of a Fragmented Nation"; Menon and Bhasin, *Borders and Boundaries.*
81 de Certeau, *The Practice of Everyday Life*; Lefebvre, *Critique of Everyday Life.*
82 These accounts include how these transnational migrations (1) mark reconfiguration between global capitalism, gendered relations and roles, household or "private" spaces, and state development and policies (Cheng, *Serving the Household and the Nation*; Huang et al., "Introduction: Asian Women as Transnational Domestic Workers"; Lan, *Global Cinderellas*; Robinson, "Gender, Islam and Nationality"; Sanjek and Colen, *At Work in Homes*; (2) index the increasing global prominence of emotional, affective, and immaterial forms of labor (Anderson, *Doing the Dirty Work*; Hochschild, *The Time Bind*, and "Global Care Chains and Economic Surplus Value"; Parrenas, *Intimate Labors*, 3; K. Weeks, "Life within and against Work," and *The Problem with Work*); (3) produce an international division of reproductive labor (Parrenas, "Migrant Filipina Domestic Workers and the International Division of Reproductive Labour," and *Servants of Globalization*); and "global care chains" (Hochschild, "Global Care Chains and Economic Surplus Value," and *Global Woman*); labor diasporas articulated in ethnonational terms (Parrenas, *Servants of Globalization*); and transnational families (Parrenas, *Children of Global Migration*); (4) underscore the gendered nature of migration policies and laws (Oishi, *Women in Motion*); wage-based market labor regimes (Anderson, *Doing the Dirty Work*); and state development programs (Cheng, *Serving the Household and the Nation*; Silvey, "Transnational Migration and the Gender Politics of Scale, 1997–2000"); (5) both reflect and produce hierarchical gendered, ethnoracial, and class subjectivities and relationships (see Adams and Dickey, "Introduction: Negotiating Homes, Hegemonies, Identities and Politics"; Cheng, *Serving the Household and the Nation*; Constable, "At Home but Not at Home"; Hondagneu-Sotelo, *Domestica*; Lan, *Global Cinderellas*; Ray and Qayum, *Cultures of Servitude*; Silvery, "Transnational Domestication"); (6) engender ambiguous personalistic/professional and fictive or pseudokinship relationships between domestic workers and their employers (Adams and Dickey, "Introduction: Negotiating Homes, Hegemonies, Identities and Politics"; Anderson, *Doing the Dirty Work*; Cheng, *Serving the Household and the Nation*; Constable, *Maid to Order in Hong Kong*; Hondagneu-Sotelo, *Domestica*; Jureidini and Moukarbel, "Female Sri Lankan Domestic Labour in Lebanon"; Moors, "Migrant Domestic Workers"; Robinson, "Gender, Islam and Nationality"); (7) rework and mark mixed forms of gendered, familial, and socioeconomic empowerment (Gamburd, *The Kitchen Spoon's Handle*; Lan, *Global Cinderellas*; Parrenas, *The Force of Domesticity*); (8) produce and reinscribe normative gender and

sexual relations as well as heteronormative familial forms that are in turn repli-
cated and reinscribed by existing scholarship (Manalansan, "Queering the Chain
of Care Paradigm"); and (9) are either animated by religious motivations (Liebelt,
Caring for the Holy Land; Silvey, "Transnational Migration and the Gender Politics of
Scale, 1997–2000," and "Mobilizing Piety"), or engender forms of religious support
and solidarity in the face of transnational dislocations (Constable, *Maid to Order in
Hong Kong*; Johnson, "Diasporic Dreams, Middle Class Moralities" and "Migrant
Domestic Workers among Muslim Filipinos in Saudi Arabia").

83 Notable examples are the works of Parrenas, *Servants of Globalization*; and Lan,
Global Cinderellas.

84 T. Asad, *Genealogies of Religion*; W. Brown, *States of Injury*, 145–51, 181–84; Cheng,
Serving the Household and the Nation; El Shakry, "Schooled Mothers and Structured
Play," and *The Great Social Laboratory*; McLarney, "Private Is Political," and "The
Islamic Public Sphere and the Discipline of Adab"; Silvey, "Power, Difference,
and Mobility," "Transnational Domestication: Indonesian Domestic Workers in
Saudi Arabia," and "Transnational Migration and the Gender Politics of Scale,
1997–2000."

85 W. Brown, *States of Injury*.

86 Jayawardena, *Feminism and Nationalism in the Third World*; Kandiyoti, *Women, Islam
and the State*; Pollard, *Nurturing the Nation*; El Shakry, "Schooled Mothers and
Structured Play."

87 L. Abu-Lughod, *Veiled Sentiments*; al-Mughni, *Women in Kuwait*; El Shakry, *The
Great Social Laboratory*; Kandiyoti, *Women, Islam and the State*; Pollard, *Nurturing
the Nation*.

88 Oishi, *Women in Motion*.

89 Freeman, "Is Local:Global as Feminine:Masculine?"; also see Basch, Glick-Schiller,
and Blanc, *Nations Unbound*; Grewal and Kaplan, *Scattered Hegemonies*; Silvey,
"Power, Difference, and Mobility," "Transnational Domestication," "Transnational
Migration and the Gender Politics of Scale, 1997–2000"; Tadiar, *Things Fall Away*.

90 Basch, Glick-Schiller, and Blanc, *Nations Unbound*; Freeman, "Is Local:Global as
Feminine:Masculine?"; Grewal and Kaplan, *Scattered Hegemonies*; Silvey, "Power,
Difference, and Mobility," "Transnational Domestication," "Transnational Migra-
tion and the Gender Politics of Scale, 1997–2000"; Tadiar, *Things Fall Away*.

91 Osella, "Muslim Entrepreneurs in Public Life between India and the Gulf"; Tadiar,
Things Fall Away.

92 Cheng, *Serving the Household and the Nation*; Oishi, *Women in Motion*; Silvey,
"Power, Difference, and Mobility," "Transnational Domestication: Indonesian
Domestic Workers in Saudi Arabia," and "Transnational Migration and the Gender
Politics of Scale, 1997–2000."

93 Oishi, *Women in Motion*; Shah, "Relative Success of Male Workers in the Host
Country, Kuwait"; Shah and Menon, "Violence against Women Migrant Workers."

94 Cheng, *Serving the Household and the Nation*; Silvey, "Power, Difference, and
Mobility."

95 Parrenas, *Servants of Globalization*.

96　Constable, *Maid to Order in Hong Kong*, 92.

97　Parrenas, *Servants of Globalization*; Tadiar, *Things Fall Away*.

98　Hondagneu-Sotelo, "Introduction: Gender and Contemporary US Immigration"; Oishi, *Women in Motion*; Silvey, "Transnational Domestication," 499.

99　Lan, *Global Cinderellas*, 17.

100　Anderson, *Doing the Dirty Work*.

101　Adams and Dickey, "Introduction: Negotiating Homes, Hegemonies, Identities and Politics," 2; also see Anderson, *Doing the Dirty Work*; Hondagneu-Sotelo, *Domestica*, 171; Lan, *Global Cinderellas*, 3, 5, 17; Ray and Qayum, *Cultures of Servitude*; Silvey, "Transnational Domestication."

102　Similarly, Lan, in *Global Cinderellas*, refers to migrant domestic workers as a "provisional diaspora"; Constable, "At Home but Not at Home."

103　Parrenas, *Servants of Globalization*, 37–38; Silvey, "Transnational Domestication," 494.

104　Parrenas, *Servants of Globalization*.

105　Nagy, "The Search for Miss Philippines Bahrain."

106　Constable, "At Home but Not at Home"; Manalansan, "Queering the Chain of Care Paradigm."

107　See chapter 3 for a fuller discussion of this gendered discourse of South Asian women being naram; also see Lamb, *White Saris and Sweet Mangoes*; Raheja and Gold, *Listen to the Heron's Words*.

108　T. Asad, *Formations of the Secular*, 227–28.

109　El Shakry, "Schooled Mothers and Structured Play," 127–28; McLarney, "Private Is Political," 135.

110　Hondagneu-Sotelo, *Domestica*; Lan, *Global Cinderellas*; Oishi, *Women in Motion*; Parrenas, *Servants of Globalization*.

111　Geertz, *The Interpretation of Culture*.

112　L. Abu-Lughod, *Veiled Sentiments*.

113　Tsing, *In the Realm of the Diamond Queen*.

114　Both Ernst Bloch and Michel Foucault point to how possibilities of an event or experience are difficult to recognize at the time. In his discussion of the event, Bloch points to their paradoxical nature. The "newness" of events, he tells us, involves both absence and presence, the here-and-now and not-yet, clarity and obscurity. He explains that this has to do with the immediacy and proximity of an event, or "the darkness" of the lived moment, which makes it difficult to recognize or assess its nature at the time (see Geoghegan's discussion in *Ernst Bloch*, 35–36). In his discussion of the experience of writing his books, in *Remarks on Marx* Foucault tells us that "an experience is something you come out of changed" (27) and that experiences are neither true or false, but constructions and fictions that exist only after they are made (36).

CHAPTER 1: TEMPORARINESS

1　Lan, *Global Cinderellas*; also see Constable, "At Home but Not at Home"; Parrenas, *Servants of Globalization*.

2 Trade consisted of the circulation of dates and pearls from the Gulf; rice, coffee, tea, spices, wood, cotton, and smuggled gold from India; wood for the construction of boats and houses (including mangrove poles used for house construction whose length determined the size of rooms) from the East Coast of Africa; and later, manufactured goods including guns form Europe (Crystal, *Kuwait*, 32).

3 See J. Abu-Lughod, *Before European Hegemony*; Al-Rasheed, "Introduction: Localizing the Transnational and Transnationalizing the Local"; Anscombe, *The Ottoman Gulf*, and "An Anational Society"; Bose, "Space and Time on the Indian Ocean Rim," and *A Hundred Horizons*; Chaudhuri, *Asia before Europe*; Ghosh, *In An Antique Land*; Ho, *The Graves of Tarim*; Magnus, "Societies and Social Change in the Persian Gulf"; Onley, "Transnational Merchants in the Nineteenth-Century Gulf."

4 Crystal, *Oil and Politics in the Gulf*, 2–5, 166.

5 Crystal, *Oil and Politics in the Gulf*, 48–60.

6 Crystal, *Oil and Politics in the Gulf*, and *Kuwait*.

7 He murdered his brothers in claiming the throne. These events were omitted from Kuwaiti history books and classes until relatively recently. Some of my Kuwaiti interlocutors mentioned learning about the death of Mubarak's brothers when reading about Kuwaiti history overseas.

8 Longva, *Walls Built on Sand*, 183–84.

9 Crystal, "Public Order and Authority," 167.

10 Crystal, *Oil and Politics in the Gulf*, and *Kuwait*, 78.

11 Crystal, "Public Order and Authority," 167.

12 Of Kuwait's population 92 percent were employed by the state.

13 Crystal, *Oil and Politics in the Gulf*, and *Kuwait*.

14 This agreement was undocumented but widely understood/acknowledged and practiced; see Crystal, *Kuwait*, 8, 75.

15 Crystal, *Kuwait*, 7.

16 Crystal, *Kuwait*, 75.

17 Crystal, *Kuwait*, 8.

18 The commercial companies law of 1960 required that 51 percent of all companies belong to Kuwaitis and stipulated that only Kuwaitis could own businesses or property outright. Foreign residents were banned from finance and banking. Import businesses, the ownership of commercial agencies, and the right to establish businesses were restricted to Kuwaitis. In addition, preference was given to locally produced goods and to Kuwaiti companies when it came to bids for state contracts. In general, this law primarily benefited the merchant class of Kuwait; see Crystal, *Kuwait*, 8, 90.

19 Crystal, *Kuwait*, 8, 76, 90.

20 Longva, "Citizenship in the Gulf States," 185.

21 State of Kuwait 1948, Order no. 3, 23–30.

22 State of Kuwait 1948, Law no. 2, 35–49.

23 The year 1920 date marks the Battle of Jahra, an important event in Kuwait history, when residents of the city repelled the Al-Saud-led Ikhwan armies, thus preserving the city-state's independence from who are now the rulers of present-day Saudi Arabia; Longva, "Citizenship in the Gulf States," 185.

24 Longva, "Citizenship in the Gulf States," 185.

25 Some argue the Al-Sabah granted citizenship to the Bedouin to redress the widening demographic gap between citizens and foreign residents in Kuwait, and to build their popular base of support against the increasingly vocal liberal opposition led by members of the merchant class. Longva, "Citizenship in the Gulf States," 187.

26 Research has yet to be conducted about the reasons and circumstances whereby Kuwait's Jewish community migrated to Israel in the late 1940s.

27 Longva, "Citizenship in the Gulf States," 193.

28 Longva, "Citizenship in the Gulf States," 192.

29 Al-Mughni, *Women in Kuwait*; Leonard, "South Asian Women in the Gulf"; Shryock, *Nationalism and the Genealogical Imagination*; Tetreault, *Stories of Democracy*.

30 Most notably with reference to the Bedouin and to individuals granted citizenship by emiri decree (usually because of their service to the Al-Sabah and to the Kuwaiti state).

31 Dresch, "Debates on Marriage and Nationality in the United Arab Emirates," 31.

32 Onley, "Transnational Merchants in the Nineteenth-Century Gulf," 62.

33 Al-Rasheed, "Introduction: Localizing the Transnational and Transnationalizing the Local," 8; Crystal, *Kuwait*, 52; Onley, "Transnational Merchants in the Nineteenth-Century Gulf: The Case of the Safar Family," 60, 62.

34 Crystal, *Kuwait*, 52.

35 Secombe and Lawless, "Foreign Worker Dependence in the Gulf, and the International Oil Companies," 565.

36 Secombe and Lawless, "Foreign Worker Dependence in the Gulf, and the International Oil Companies," 568.

37 Secombe and Lawless, "Foreign Worker Dependence in the Gulf, and the International Oil Companies," 568.

38 For a discussion of how American companies implemented Jim Crow–style labor systems in Saudi Arabia, see Vitalis, "Black Gold, White Crude," and *America's Kingdom*.

39 Secombe and Lawless 1999: 569.

40 Reports mention workers being housed in tents, subject to sandstorms and Kuwait's intense heat. Secombe and Lawless, "Foreign Worker Dependence in the Gulf, and the International Oil Companies," 568.

41 Secombe and Lawless, "Foreign Worker Dependence in the Gulf, and the International Oil Companies," 569–70.

42 Kapiszewski, *Nationals and Expatriates*, 62.

43 Arnold and Shah, *Asian Labor Migration*, 15; also see Nagi 1986: 54.

44 Nagi, "Determinants of Current Trends in Labor Migration and the Future Outlook," 49–50; also see Birks and Sinclair, *International Migration and Development in the Arab Region*.

45 Nagi, "Determinants of Current Trends in Labor Migration and the Future Outlook," 50–54.

46 The only exceptions were in the aftermath of the first Gulf War, when the majority of Kuwait's Palestinian population, estimated at 300,000 were expelled, and just

before other migrants and foreign residents who had fled the war had returned back, or were replaced by other migrants.

47 Ahmad, "Explanation Is Not the Point: South Asian Migrant Domestic Workers' Newfound Islamic Pieties in Kuwait," "Cosmopolitan Islam in a Diasporic Space: Foreign Resident Muslim Women's Halaqa in Kuwait," and "Labour's Limits: Foreign Residents in the Gulf"; Longva, *Walls Built on Sand: Migration, Exclusion and Society in Kuwait*, 44; Nagi, "Determinants of Current Trends in Labor Migration and the Future Outlook," 50; Osella and Osella, "'I am Gulf'"; "Muslim Entrepreneurs in Public Life between India and the Gulf: Making Good and Doing Good"; Vora, *Impossible Citizens*.

48 This amount has decreased. In 2004, the minimum threshold was 400 dinars. To get a sense of the scale of this amount, public-sector employees in Kuwait earn 90 dinars per month, the average salary of a domestic worker is 45 dinars per month, and for construction or semiskilled laborers it is 60 dinars. Schoolteachers are a notable exception in their exemption from this law.

49 Leonard, "South Asian Women in the Gulf: Families and Futures Reconfigured," 217; Nagi, "Determinants of Current Trends in Labor Migration and the Future Outlook," 52.

50 The system has been abolished in Bahrain, and although the governments of Kuwait and Saudi Arabia have considered doing so, no laws to the effect have been drafted.

51 See Longva, *Walls Built on Sand*, and "Keeping Migrant Workers in Check"; see also Crystal, "Public Order and Authority."

52 Foster, "The Islamic Law of Guarantees."

53 Longva, "Keeping Migrant Workers in Check," 20–21.

54 Crystal, "Public Order and Authority: Policing Kuwait," 158–68.

55 Gardner, *City of Strangers*; Longva, *Walls Built on Sand*, "Keeping Migrant Workers in Check," and "Neither Autocracy nor Democracy but Ethnocracy."

56 Kapiszewski, *Nationals and Expatriates*; Longva, "Neither Autocracy nor Democracy but Ethnocracy," 126.

57 Crystal, "Public Order and Authority," 169.

58 Foreign residents who meet certain criteria, in particular a salary threshold, are also permitted to sponsor domestic workers.

59 Longva, "Neither Autocracy nor Democracy but Ethnocracy," 120.

60 Crystal, *Kuwait*, 8–9, 75.

61 Dresch, "Introduction: Societies, Identities, and Global Issues," 23–24.

62 Unless kafeels are found to be complicit, few are actually prosecuted; however, the possibility remains/looms and acts as a deterrent. In winter 2009, the government passed more stringent laws related to this issue.

63 These limitations did not necessarily halt migrants' and foreign residents' potential return. At the time I was conducting research, I learned of many instances in which previously deported migrants and foreign residents had obtained black market passports with new identification information, enabling them to reenter Kuwait. This has led many government officials in Kuwait to advocate for the implementation

of biometric scans (in particular of eyes) at the airports and migrant-processing centers, similar to those in the United Arab Emirates.

64 This outcome usually occurs if the migrant is found to be guilty of a crime, but the procedures by which this occurs remain vague (Longva, "Keeping Migrant Workers in Check," 21).

65 Also see Crystal, "Public Order and Authority," 170; Longva, "Keeping Migrant Workers in Check," 21–22.

66 Switching their kafeel or finding jobs in-country usually involves entering into gray markets of visa trading and verbal (as opposed to written) contractual agreements.

67 Longva, "Keeping Migrant Workers in Check," 22.

68 Longva, "Keeping Migrant Workers in Check," 22.

69 See *Kuwait Times*, February 3, 2009, and *Asia News*, February 13, 2009.

70 On June 24, 2015, Kuwaiti legislators passed a new law (Law no. 6 of 2010 on Labor in the Private Sector) giving domestic workers enforceable labor rights.

71 There existed a system whereby well-to-do families would nominally adopt or foster a young child from an impoverished family. The child would be responsible for household tasks, and status distinctions would be made between them and the "blood children" of the family. Complex sets of relationships and reciprocity would develop over time. For example, one Kuwaiti family I met had a branch of the family comprising descendants (children and grandchildren) of a "houseboy" whom the family had adopted from an impoverished Arab family (Yemeni-Saudi). The descendants were treated, and regarded themselves as part of their Kuwaiti family (i.e., had the family name, socially interacted with the rest of the family regularly, and had begun intermarrying with other branches of the larger extended family).

72 It is worth noting that few Kuwaitis I met with mentioned this to me. Those who did were usually older Kuwaitis, unconcerned about admitting to their family's and country's previously less-affluent past. The younger generation tended to be unaware or unwilling to speak about members of their families who might have undertaken this work in the past.

73 There is a gap in demographic information for the 1990s due to the events of the first Gulf War. With regard to the population numbers of the mid- to late 2000s, some estimate as many as 200,000 domestic workers (of a total population of 500,000 domestic workers) are said to be in flux, either working "outside" or remaining in Kuwait despite the expiration of their work and residency visas (interviews, human rights and labor agency officials).

74 Alajami, "House-to-House Migration."

75 N. Brown, *The Rule of Law in the Arab World*, 209; Shah et al., "Foreign Domestic Workers in Kuwait."

76 In the 1960s and early 1970s Goans accounted for the overwhelming majority of migrant domestic workers, with some sources estimating that they comprised 95 percent of migrant domestic workers. Their preponderance led to the widespread sense/speculation among labor agents and migrants in South Asia that Kuwaitis are favorably disposed towards Christian maids—a discourse that contin-

ued until the mid-2000s when I was conducting fieldwork. Secombe and Lawless, "Foreign Worker Dependence in the Gulf, and the International Oil Companies: 1910–50," 565.

77 A ban, instituted by the Pakistani government in the late 1970s, ended that country's residents' participation. See Shah et al., "Asian Women Workers in Kuwait" and Shah et al., "Foreign Domestic Workers in Kuwait."

78 See Shah et al., "Asian Women Workers in Kuwait"; Shah et al., "Foreign Domestic Workers in Kuwait."

79 W. Brown, *States of Injury*; El Shakry, "Schooled Mothers and Structured Play," and *The Great Social Laboratory*; Silvey, "Power, Difference, and Mobility," "Transnational Domestication," and "Transnational Migration and the Gender Politics of Scale, 1997–2000."

80 These explanations were presented to me by human rights officials, legal scholars (including a former dean of Kuwait's Law School), and labor agency officials.

81 During one interview, a labor agent described the process of domestic workers' recruitment as follows: (1) the labor agent establishes contact and agreements with labor-sending agencies; (2) the labor agent undertakes a job order with the embassy of labor-sending countries; (3) the embassy in turn processes the job order, sends it to the labor department in its country, waits for the country's approval and when approved, the embassy and labour agent subsequently draft a contract; (4) the labor agency receives the biodata (resumes) of domestic workers recruited by agents in the labor-sending country and then markets them in Kuwait; (5) the marketing usually takes place in the agency's front office—where prospective employers can look through catalogues of potential domestic workers and where initial agreements with employers are reached; (6) the employer chooses the employee and obtains a visa from the Ministry of Interior; (7) the contract is signed by the employer and labor agent and sent to labor agent and prospective domestic worker in the labor-sending country; (8) the contract needs to be processed by ministry / government body in labor-sending country; (9) medical procedures are undertaken in the labor-sending country; (10) the contract, medical forms, and visa form are taken to the Kuwaiti embassy or consulate for processing and approval; (11) the domestic worker travels to Kuwait; (12) the labor agent receives the domestic worker at the airport, who is then brought to the agency (usually back rooms where there are showering and rest facilities); (13) the employer is contacted and comes to pick up the employee; (14) the employer signs the "receiving of worker" document, receives documents of the worker needed for obtaining an *iqama*, the residency visa and identification card; (15) the agent receives the commission; (16) there is a two-month waiting period while the domestic worker and employer-sponsor decide whether they will continue with their contractual agreement.

82 Lindquist et al., "Introduction: Opening the Black Box of Migration"; Silvey, "Mobilizing Piety."

83 Brown notes that there are two types of criminal offenses: (1) *junha*, crimes punished by fewer than three years in prison, are handled by the police and usually involve arbitration or dispute resolution (this is encouraged); and (2) *jinaya*, a

crime punishable by more than three years in prison, is handled by the *niyaba* or state prosecutors (N. Brown, *The Rule of Law in the Arab World*, 212).

84 Not just Kuwaiti, but state institutions in general.

85 N. Brown, *The Rule of Law in the Arab World*, 213.

86 Silvey, "Power, Difference, and Mobility," "Transnational Domestication," and "Transnational Migration and the Gender Politics of Scale, 1997–2000."

87 See Oishi, *Women in Motion*; Shah et al., "Asian Women Workers in Kuwait."

88 Oishi, *Women in Motion*.

89 Oishi, *Women in Motion*.

90 This process has become formalized. For a domestic worker to file charges or pursue a legal case against their kafeel, they must do so through their embassy. In addition, if a domestic worker "absconds" for this reason, they must report to their embassy within twenty-four to forty-eight hours to ensure they are not blacklisted (i.e., officially listed in Kuwait's police registry as absconded). Embassy grounds also became makeshift shelters for domestic workers who did not want to or could not return to their kafeel and who had nowhere else to go. Some embassies began establishing more formally run shelters on the embassy premises or in other rented buildings. The facilities offered by the different embassies vary widely. The Filipino Embassy has a smoothly run shelter. The Indian Embassy once established a shelter, but it was shut down after it was discovered that the "madam" of the house was contracting out domestic workers to do part-time work and pocketing some of, if not most of, their wages. The Sri Lankan Embassy has reserved the basement for "runaways"; however its facilities are quite rudimentary. When I spoke to embassy officials, many mentioned how difficult it became for them to look after and monitor the movements of their nationals, and how many of the women were understandably anxious about languishing at the embassy and not being able to earn an income. As a result, some embassy officials would quietly suggest that domestic workers live off the premises or not stop those who wanted to (i.e., by doing so workers could possibly work part-time and earn an income before being deported or repatriated back).

91 For example, during an interview with the foremost migration expert in Nepal, he mentioned that despite the country's civil war and economic downturn, the GDP of the country had actually remained the same or even increased, largely due to remittances. He further noted that much of these remittances were being sent by migrant domestic workers.

92 During the time of my primary fieldwork, this included the following: (1) Filipino government in November 2003, set a minimum wage of 120 KD (versus 40–45 KD set by the Kuwaiti government); migrant domestic workers need to undertake pre- and in-country orientation sessions; migrant domestic workers and their employers must register with the labor attaché's division in Kuwait; penalties were stipulated for non-compliant recruitment agencies. (2) Indian government in October 2007, set a minimum wage of USD $300–350/month (in comparison with Kuwait's minimum wage of USD$146–64); migrant domestic workers have to be paid through banks; migrant domestic workers must have mobile phone connectivity; employers

need to provide a bank guarantee of $2,500 if a domestic worker is recruited directly (i.e., not through a labor agency; it is unclear who would keep possession of the guarantee); the minimum wage of the employer must be USD$2,723/month; domestic workers need to be at least thirty years old; contracts must be approved by the embassy in-country and overseen by the Ministry of Overseas Indian Affairs; employers must purchase a life insurance policy for migrant domestic workers. (3) Sri Lankan and Indonesian governments in fall 2007, both set a minimum wage of KD60.

93 And vice-versa: there is no Kuwaiti Embassy in Nepal.

94 The Nepalese government was unaware of this until alerted by a labor agent *two weeks after* the ban had been implemented.

CHAPTER 2: SUSPENSION

1 Parrenas, *Servants of Globalization*, 197.

2 Parrenas discusses four forms of dislocation: noncitizenship, the pain of family separation, contradictory class mobility, and alienation in the migrant community; see *Servants of Globalization*, 30, 197.

3 Parrenas, *Servants of Globalization*, 197.

4 Constable, "At Home but Not at Home"; also see Parrenas, *Servants of Globalization*, 56.

5 This includes how domestic workers' migration is a source of independence, freedom and pleasure: they migrate to get (and stay) away from their family members or difficult situations at "home"; they develop a new sense of self through their migration; they become accustomed to the lifestyles of the places they migrate to; they become alienated from the places they've migrated from after having been away for long stretches of time; and at "home" they have no source of income and are anxious about providing for themselves and their loved ones.

6 Ahmad, "Cosmopolitan Islam in a Diasporic Space," and "Labour's Limits"; Leonard, "South Asian Women in the Gulf"; Nagy, "The Search for Miss Philippines Bahrain"; Osella and Osella, " 'I am Gulf,' " and "Muslim Entrepreneurs in Public Life between India and the Gulf"; Vora, "Producing Diasporas and Globalization," and *Impossible Citizens*.

7 Ali, *Dubai*; Ahmad, "Cosmopolitan Islam in a Diasporic Space," and "Labour's Limits"; Gardner, *City of Strangers*; Longva, *Walls Built on Sand*, "Keeping Migrant Workers in Check," "Citizenship in the Gulf States," and "Neither Autocracy nor Democracy but Ethnocracy"; Mahdavi, *Gridlock*.

8 I will use the form Mary/Maryam for two reasons: my accounts about her experiences track periods before and after she insisted on being called Maryam; also, in Kuwait there remained people who continued calling her Mary despite her oft-stated preference to be called Maryam. I discuss her experiences of Islamic conversion in chapter 4.

9 All three words mean *work*: the first in Arabic, the second Hindi/Urdu, and the third English. Her utterances, like those of many of my interlocutors, underscore how polylingual and creolized conversations were in Kuwait.

10 Adams and Dickey, "Introduction: Negotiating Homes, Hegemonies, Identities and Politics," 2–3; Anderson, *Doing the Dirty Work*, 113; Ray and Qayum, *Cultures of Servitude*; Silvey, "Transnational Domestication: Indonesian Domestic Workers in Saudi Arabia," 493.

11 Examples are Asian women as domestic workers or sales associates, Arab women as teachers, Egyptian men as cab drivers, Western expatriates as white-collar workers, and Kuwaitis as owners, bosses, or "untouchable (i.e., cannot be fired) workers."

12 Many domestic workers wore *panjabis* and Western clothes, both of which their employers also wore but with a different aesthetic; some domestic workers also wore uniforms and hand-me-down clothes from their employers.

13 In contrast, houseboys lived in small buildings separate from or adjoined to houses.

14 Whether this was her intention or not, the effect of her actions was similar to what Ann Stoler has discussed with respect to domestic workers in colonial Java—where intimate relations were managed to ensure the ongoing social reproduction of the Dutch, and the simultaneous purification and production of difference between the Dutch and the local population (Stoler, *Race and the Education of Desire*, and *Carnal Knowledge and Imperial Power*).

15 Stoler, *Race and the Education of Desire*, and *Carnal Knowledge and Imperial Power*.

16 Adams and Dickey, "Introduction: Negotiating Homes, Hegemonies, Identities and Politics," 4; Anderson, *Doing the Dirty Work*, 122–23; Cheng, *Serving the Household and the Nation*, 118; Constable, *Maid to Order in Hong Kong*, 111; Lan, *Global Cinderellas*, 20; Moors, "Migrant Domestic Workers," 390–91; K. Robinson, "Gender, Islam and Nationality," 258.

17 Adams and Dickey, "Introduction: Negotiating Homes, Hegemonies, Identities and Politics"; Anderson, *Doing the Dirty Work*, 122–23; Cheng, *Serving the Household and the Nation*; Constable, *Maid to Order in Hong Kong*; Hondagneu-Sotelo, *Maid to Order in Hong Kong*; Lan, *Global Cinderellas*; Moors, "Migrant Domestic Workers," 391; Parrenas, "Migrant Filipina Domestic Workers," 18, 252.

18 Also see Anderson, *Doing the Dirty Work*, 122.

19 Constable, *Maid to Order in Hong Kong*, 27; Moors, "Migrant Domestic Workers," 389–90.

20 We were speaking Hindi/Urdu, and she used the modified English word *sorry*.

21 Cheng, *Serving the Household and the Nation*; Hondagneu-Sotelo, *Domestica*; Lindquist et al., "Introduction: Opening the Black Box of Migration"; Silvey, "Mobilizing Piety."

22 As part of their contract stipulations, domestic workers are entitled to a paid month of holiday per year, and a return ticket home every two years at the end of a contract cycle. Most deferred taking their holiday time until the end of their contract cycle, when they would spend a two-month holiday, or return two months before their contracts officially expired.

23 Adams and Dickey, "Introduction: Negotiating Homes, Hegemonies, Identities and Politics," 14.

24 For discussions of how family relations have increasingly become commodified, and/or articulated through commodities, also see Lan, *Global Cinderellas*, 20;

M. B. Mills, "Gender and Inequality in the Global Labor Force," 50; Moors, "Migrant Domestic Workers," 392; Parrenas, *Servants of Globalization*, 149.

25 For a resonant discussion about how migration affects their status within their family, see Mills and Grafton, *Conversion*, 46; for a somewhat contrasting discussion, see Gamburd, *The Kitchen Spoon's Handle*, 237–39. The difference in my account with that of Gamburd's may be because my discussion is based on the accounts provided by my interlocutors in Kuwait, as opposed to when they were in the communities from which they had migrated, and thus at a spatial and temporal remove from their employers and life in Kuwait.

26 Lan, *Global Cinderellas*, 20; Moors, "Migrant Domestic Workers," 392; Parrenas, *Servants of Globalization*, 149.

27 Lan, *Global Cinderellas*, 20; Moors, "Migrant Domestic Workers," 392; Parrenas, *Servants of Globalization*, 149.

28 Adams and Dickey, "Introduction: Negotiating Homes, Hegemonies, Identities and Politics," 14.

29 Parrenas, *Servants of Globalization*, 149.

30 For discussions about restrictions on migrant domestic workers' sociospatial mobility, see Jureidini and Moukarbel, "Female Sri Lankan Domestic Labour in Lebanon"; Lan, *Global Cinderellas*, 3; Moors, "Migrant Domestic Workers," 387–38; Robinson, "Gender, Islam and Nationality," 258.

31 The few expatriate women I met who walked in Kuwait also had similar experiences, but as directed by guidebooks and embassy officials, if threatened they would take out their cell phones or yell back that they would call their embassy officials and/or the police.

32 Some newspaper and human rights reports argued domestic workers did not go to the police or engage with Kuwait's juridical system because they perceived these institutions to be biased toward Kuwaitis. In addition, many indicated that they were wary of these state institutions based on their experiences in Nepal and India, where accessing these institutions required connections and bribes.

33 Moors, "Migrant Domestic Workers," 387–38; Robinson, "Gender, Islam and Nationality," 257.

34 Many people I met in Nepal referred to the Gulf region and the Middle East as "Saudi"—a quick gloss referring to the region.

35 Heba was a domestic worker from Youmma's household whom they were friends with.

36 Rose was a reference to Kate Winslet's character, the heroine of *Titanic*. The movie, and Leonardo "Leo" DiCaprio were favorites of theirs.

37 At this point, she isn't quite as disapproving. It might be because the exchange of photographs often takes place when engagements are being decided on. For Hema, this act might have indicated to her that Hari's intentions were proper and honorable.

38 The word *Ritu* is used to refer to the restaurant where he worked; among many South Asians, *hotel* is used to refer to what North Americans typically call a restaurant.

39 The manager of this hotel was a Nepali man who hired many other Nepalis. The hotel was jokingly called "Nepali Central 2" by Hema. "Nepali Central 1" was a

Nepali restaurant, a second-floor hole-in-the-wall in the city center, owned by a Nepali man who has lived in Kuwait since the early 1990s, and in the absence of an embassy, was the intermediary/representative that Kuwaiti police, human rights and governmental officials went to for help with translation, and who facilitated the activities of embassy officials from the Nepali Embassy in Saudi Arabia.

40 Hema spoke in Hindi/Urdu (neither Heba nor I speak Nepali, and Ritu speaks Hindi/Urdu as well). There were a few exceptions, though: *bayt* and *shurta* were spoken in Arabic; *detention* was spoken in English. *Bayt-surta* means "house" of "police," that is, police station.

CHAPTER 3: NARAM

1 Interview with high-placed official at the Kuwait Union of Domestic Labour Organizations.

2 For example, a UN report states that in 2006 fewer than 1 percent of Nepali migrants were women. The report later indicates a disjuncture between the United Nations Development Fund for Women's (UNIFEM) estimates of the number of Nepali domestic workers abroad (70,000) versus the official Department of Labour and Statistics that states that only 161 women migrated abroad from 1985–2001 as domestic workers. See Siddiqui, "Migration and Gender in Asia."

3 Bose, "Sons of the Nation"; Chatterjee, *The Nation and Its Fragments*.

4 In 2003 this ban was modified, allowing women to work in formal sectors in the Gulf. The migration of domestic workers, however, remained illegal throughout the period in which I conducted primary fieldwork. It was partially lifted in 2008.

5 Since the late 1970s a series of labor bans on the outmigration of domestic workers to the Gulf have been passed by a number of countries (see chapter 1). The only effective ban appears to be one passed by the Pakistani government in 1979.

6 In Kuwait, a Nepali consulate or embassy was not established until 2010, three years after my primary fieldwork ended.

7 This also applies to Indian women who have been subject to periodic migration bans leading them to travel to the Gulf via Sri Lanka or other intermediary countries.

8 It is illegal for women under the age of eighteen to migrate to and work in Kuwait.

9 Daniel, *Fluid Signs*; Inden and Nicholas, *Kinship in Bengali Culture*; Marriott, "Hindu Transactions."

10 Raheja and Gold, *Listen to the Heron's Words*, 77; also see Lamb, *White Saris and Sweet Mangoes*.

11 Donner, *Domestic Goddesses*, 2008; Lamb, *White Saris and Sweet Mangoes*; Raheja and Gold, *Listen to the Heron's Words*.

12 Lamb, *White Saris and Sweet Mangoes*, 207.

13 Hermez, unpublished paper; Vora, "Domestic Work, Affective Labor, and Social Reproduction in South Asian America."

14 That is, my research was generative of social encounters and interactions that were otherwise unusual/unprecedented.

15 For a discussion of the familial-like relations between migrant domestic workers and their employers, see chapter 2.

16 Anderson, *Doing the Dirty Work*, 3; Weeks, "Life within and against Work," 239, 241; Yan, *New Masters, New Servants*, 168.

17 Engels, *Origins of the Family, Private Property and the State*; Weeks, "Life within and against Work," and *The Problem with Work*.

18 Engels, *Origins of the Family, Private Property and the State*; Weeks, "Life within and against Work, and *The Problem with Work*.

19 Hardt and Negri, *Labor of Dionysus*; Lazzarato, "Immaterial Labor," and *Signs and Machines*; Weeks "Life within and against Work," and *The Problem with Work*.

20 Constable, *Maid to Order in Hong Kong*, 90; also see Lazzarato, *Signs and Machines*; Weeks, "Life within and against Work," 239–40.

21 Weeks, "Life within and against Work," 241–42; also see Hochschild, *The Time Bind*, and "Global Care Chains and Economic Surplus Value"; Moors, "Migrant Domestic Workers," 390.

22 Filipina women included fellow domestic workers in their neighborhoods or hired by friends of their employers, as well as sales clerks and food servers encountered in shopping centers and malls.

23 For example, Filipina domestic workers were widely perceived to be better educated, more knowledgeable about household appliances and technologies, and so on.

24 A Panjabi consists of a long tunic and loose trousers. An abaya is a long loose cloak.

25 Manalansan, "Queering the Chain of Care Paradigm."

CHAPTER 4: HOUSETALK

1 As discussed by Crystal, *Oil and Politics in the Gulf*, and *Kuwait*, and by Al-Mughni and Tetreault, "Political Actors without the Franchise," these social organizations (e.g., Graduates Society, Women Social and Cultural Society) were important sociopolitical activist centers that played a role in lobbying the government and shaping public opinion.

2 For example, Hardt and Negri, *Labor of Dionysus*; Hochschild, "Global Care Chains and Economic Surplus Value," and *Global Woman*; Weeks, "Life within and against Work."

3 Constable, *Maid to Order in Hong Kong*; Johnson, "Diasporic Dreams, Middle Class Moralities and Migrant Domestic Workers among Muslim Filipinos in Saudi Arabia"; Libelt, *Caring for the Holy Land*; Pignol, "Filipino Women Workers in Saudi"; Silvey, "Mobilizing Piety."

4 Latour, *We Have Never Been Modern*.

5 Understanding promulgated by Arthur Darby Nock and G. Stanley Hall (see Buckser and Glazier, *The Anthropology of Religious Conversion*; and Morrison, *Understanding Conversion*).

6 Morrison, *Understanding Conversion*, xiv.

7 Austin-Broos, "The Anthropology of Conversion: An Introduction"; Coleman, *The Globalization of Charismatic Christianity*.

8 DeWeese, *Islamicization and Native Religion in the Golden Horde*; Eaton, *The Rise of Islam and the Bengal Frontier*; Ricklefs, "Six Centuries of Islamicization in Java."

9 Morrison, *Understanding Conversion*.

10 T. Asad, "Comments on Conversion."

11 T. Asad, *The Idea of an Anthropology of Islam*, *Genealogies of Religion*, *Formations of the Secular*; Henkel, "Between Belief and Unbelief Lies the Performance of Salat"; Hirschkind, "The Ethics of Listening," and *The Ethical Soundscape*; Mahmood, "Feminist Theory," "Rehearsed Spontaneity and the Conventionality of Ritual: Disciplines of Salat," "Ethical Formation and Politics of Individual Autonomy in Contemporary Egypt," and *Politics of Piety*.

12 Mauss, *The Gift*.

13 Foucault, "The Ethic of Care for the Self as a Practice of Freedom," and "About the Beginnings of the Hermeneutic of the Self."

14 Clough and Halley, *The Affective Turn*; Gregg, *The Affect Theory Reader*; Lazzarato, "Immaterial Labor"; Parrenas, *Intimate Labors*; Weeks, *The Problem with Work*.

15 Non-Muslims are ordinarily not permitted to enter Mecca. Mary/Maryam's employers, through connections in Saudi Arabia, were able to procure a visa for Mary/Maryam under the condition she would not enter holy sites such as the Al-Har'am Al-Sharif, the compound in which the Ka'aba is located.

16 There exists general consensus among Muslims that a pilgrimage to Mecca is incumbent upon all able-bodied Muslims. The pilgrimage to Mecca involves a fair amount of physical activity and exertion.

17 Over one-third of marriages end in divorce in Kuwait. According to the Kuwait Central Statistics Bureau, divorce rates increased by over 10 percent per year in the mid-2000s.

18 Kuwaiti women were outperforming their male compatriots both in terms of grades as well as enrollment and graduation rates.

19 In a few cases, some Kuwaiti men married domestic workers, usually as second wives or after divorcing their first wife. These women had previously worked in their husbands' households or those of their family members. They were often ostracized from their husbands' families. Women who were of the Ahl al-Kitab were usually not expected to convert to Islam, but those who fell outside this category (e.g., Hindus and Buddhists) could not marry a Muslim man unless they converted. Like all other noncitizen women who marry Kuwaiti men, these women might be granted citizenship, usually if they bore their husbands a child and were married to their husbands for over ten years (duration of "waiting period" varied according to periodic changes in legal amendments).

20 I should also note that although happy with the development, Bilquis was also mystified by Geeti's conversion. Aware of her mother's ambivalence toward her own deepening piety, she had been discreet about her religious practice, careful to keep her "practice contained to my room and to me [i.e., her own personal practice, listening to Qur'anic recitations in her room and car]." She never discussed the issue directly with Geeti: "It just never occurred to me she'd be interested."

21 That is, Bedouins, many of whom were formerly citizens of Saudi Arabia and had been naturalized in the late 1970s and early 1980s.

22 The *Ikhwan* refers to the Muslim Brotherhood, a group that initially developed in Egypt and spread into the Gulf during the mid-twentieth century (see discussion in chapter 1).

23 While I was conducting fieldwork from 2004 to 2010, the Ministry of Religious Affairs undertook a public campaign, consisting of pamphlets, public presentations, billboard advertisements, and lectures to promote what they termed a "reasonable" or "moderate" form of Islam, one they argued characterized the overall practice of Islam in Kuwait historically.

24 Although no systematic research exists on employers' preferences, based on over two years of conducting fieldwork in Kuwait, I found that most employers indicated that an ability to learn, competence, and loyalty were what they most sought and valued in domestic workers. Employers moreover expressed racialized preferences for domestic workers in ways intertwining ethnonational backgrounds with particular types of work—for example, that they preferred to hire South Asian domestic workers as cooks because of their traditions of cuisine and presumed culinary skills, and to hire Filipina domestic workers for childcare work because they were perceived to be more patient and gentle with children.

25 Dutton, "Conversion to Islam"; also see Anway, *Daughters of Another Path*; T. Arnold, *The Spread of Islam in the World*; M. Asad, *The Road to Mecca*; Calasso, "Récits de conversion, zèle dévotionnel et instruction religieuse dans les biographies des 'gens de Basra' due Kitab al-Tabaqat d'Ibn Sa'd"; Garcia-Arenal, Introduction to *Conversions Islamiques*, and "Dreams and Reason"; Gilliat-Ray, "Rediscovering Islam"; Kose, *Conversion to Islam*; McGinty, *Becoming Muslim*; Minkov, *Conversion to Islam in the Balkans*; Morony, "The Age of Conversions"; van Nieuwkerk, "Gender, Conversion, and Islam," and "Islam Is Your Birthright."

26 The process requires applicants to complete and submit a "declaration of conversion to Islam" form to the Ministry of Justice. The prospective convert is then called to recite the shahada in front of a judge.

27 This includes knowledge of the five pillars of faith, the 'aqida, and how to perform the daily prayers.

28 For discussions about consumerism, gendered subjectivities, and piety in relation to hijab fashions, see Gökariksel, "Feminist Geography of Veiling"; Gökariksel and Secor, "Between Fashion and Tesettür," and "Islamic-ness in the Life of a Commodity"; Moors, "Discover the Beauty of Modesty"; Moors and Ünal, "Format, Fabrics and Fashions."

29 Mahmood, "Feminist Theory," and *Politics of Piety*.

30 One way in which people surreptitiously flirted or sent messages to one another in public spaces was through messages sent on cell phones via Bluetooth.

31 My interlocutors often described Bon Buddhism as a "mixed religion," one incorporating Tibetan Buddhism, Hinduism, ancestor worship, animism, and Hinduism.

1 Translations: Arabic: correct/right; Urdu: strong.

2 Translation from Arabic: testament of faith.

3 Members of the organization rarely use the term *convert* to refer to people who have taken shahada and developed newfound Islamic pieties. They prefer to use the terms *reverts* or *newly practicing Muslims*. They use the term *convert* when speaking to someone they assume conceives of religious transformation in these terms.

4 Deleuze, *Difference and Repetition*, and *Nietzsche and Philosophy*; Grosz, *The Nick of Time*, and *Time Travels*.

5 Until the mid-2000s this was the da'wa movement's only women's center; however, over the subsequent two years, several others were established throughout Kuwait.

6 The roads are a series of highways fanning out from the city-state's historic center.

7 A shalwar kameez is a large tunic and baggy trousers. A jalabiyya is a floor-length tunic.

8 A *diwaniyya* is a large open room, typically towards the front of the house or in the basement in which guests are received and hosted, in particular gatherings of men.

9 Al-Hijji, *Kuwait and the Sea*; Anscombe, *The Ottoman Gulf*, and "An Anational Society"; Fuccaro, "Mapping the Transnational Community" and *Histories of the City and State in the Persian Gulf*; Onley, "Transnational Merchants in the Nineteenth-Century Gulf," and *The Arabian Frontiers of the British Raj*.

10 Some just used the term *liberal* to indicate that the term superseded or was not reducible to Western practice. Others used both *liberal* and *Westernized* to point to how liberal practice was synonymous/reducible to Western forms and practice. I should also note that while Kuwait has developed through long-standing colonial and postcolonial relations with the British and Americans, prior to the Gulf War, many Kuwaitis conceived of the process of modernity upon which they had embarked as inflected and developed as much in relation to other parts of the Arab world as it was to the "West." Many of my interlocutors—citizens and noncitizens, young and old, who have resided in Kuwait for a long period of time—pointed to the aftermath of the Gulf War as leading to Kuwait's greater integration into an American-led globalism / American-driven form of globalization, and to them revisioning their prior development in and through these terms.

11 For a discussion of the salafi movement, please see the Introduction. Many of Kuwait's Bedouin groups were naturalized by Emiri decree in the late 1970s and early 1980s (Crystal, *Oil and Politics in the Gulf*, *Kuwait*, and "Public Order and Authority").

12 Exceptions were, for example, Kuwaitis who, through kinship and trade ties to India, were able to speak Hindi/Urdu.

13 For example, several mentioned "rice" conversions in the Indian subcontinent, and in Kuwait, Christian groups were involved in setting up the first modern hospitals and schools in the region.

14 As an illustration of an exceptional case of coercion, several members mentioned the third part of what was then a widely circulating PBS documentary *An Empire of Faith*, which details the conquest and coercion of Ottoman leaders.

15 Translation of 'aqida: Tenets of faith/belief.
16 Hafez, *An Islam of Her Own*; Henkel, "Between Belief and Unbelief Lies the Performance of Salat," and "The Location of Islam"; Hirschkind, "The Ethics of Listening," and *The Ethical Soundscape*; Mahmood, "Feminist Theory," "Rehearsed Spontaneity and the Conventionality of Ritual," "Ethical Formation and Politics of Individual Autonomy in Contemporary Egypt," and *Politics of Piety*.
17 Van der Veer, *Imperial Encounters*.
18 Pollock et al., "Cosmopolitanisms"; Vertovec and Cohen, *Conceiving Cosmopolitanism*.
19 For an incisive discussion about recent scholarship on cosmopolitanism, please see *Inhuman Conditions* by Cheah. Cheah cautions against accounts of cosmopolitanism that posit it as an inevitable and ineluctable outcome of contemporary processes of globalization, and as a necessarily emancipatory or progressive alternative to ethnonationalism. Cheah discusses the erasures and unexamined assumptions upon which these understandings are based. See also Mignolo, "The Many Faces of Cosmo-Polis; and Pollock et al., "Cosmopolitanisms."
20 What Mahmood ("Feminist Theory: Embodiment, and the Docile Agent," "Rehearsed Spontaneity and the Conventionality of Ritual: Disciplines of Salat," and *Politics of Piety*) has discussed in terms of pious cultivation, and Foucault ("The Ethic of Care for the Self as a Practice of Freedom," and "About the Beginnings of the Hermeneutic of the Self") refers to as the ethical formation of the self. Also see Lambek ("The Anthropology of Religion and the Quarrel between Poetry and Philosophy").
21 Arabic translation: tenets of faith and belief. The approach of the 'Salat wa Tah'ara' classes contrasts with the da'wa classes offered by other Islamic reformist groups in Kuwaiti, most notably ones that are organized by salafi networks.
22 Term used to refer to resume or curriculum vitae.
23 Arabic translation: praises and thanks to Allah (God).
24 T. Asad, *The Idea of an Anthropology of Islam*; Henkel, "The Location of Islam: Inhabiting Istanbul in a Muslim Way"; Hirschkind, *The Ethical Soundscape*; Lambek, "The Anthropology of Religion and the Quarrel between Poetry and Philosophy"; Mahmood, *Politics of Piety*.
25 Note: this is not fully apparent in my transcription, in which most of the words she uttered were translated into English.
26 Arabic translation of *kafeel*: Kuwaiti sponsor and guarantor of foreign residents in Kuwait. They obtain work and residency permits for the foreign residents they sponsor to come to Kuwait.
27 Arabic translation: every district in Kuwait has at least one *jam'ayya*, a cooperative shopping area in which profits get redistributed to the citizens residing in the district in proportion to the amount they spend every year. The jam'ayya is usually located close to artisanal workshops, restaurants, and health care centers.
28 Employers and domestic workers have a three-month probationary period, during which employers could send back or domestic workers choose to return to the recruitment agency.

29 Prior to migrating to Kuwait, Sonia and Karima (both of whom are from Nepal's Tamang ethnic community) practiced what they told me was a form of "everything" religion, one that incorporated elements of Tibetan Buddhism, Hinduism, animism, and ancestor worship. Also see chapter 4.

30 Mahmood, "Feminist Theory," "Rehearsed Spontaneity and the Conventionality of Ritual," and *Politics of Piety*.

31 Hirschkind, *The Ethical Soundscape*.

32 Hirschkind, *The Ethical Soundscape*.

33 Deleuze, *Difference and Repetition*, and *Nietzsche and Philosophy*.

34 This form of Muslim belonging resonates with what Gilles Deleuze refers to as an "ontology of becoming." See discussion of Deleuze and Muslim becomings and belongings in the introduction.

EPILOGUE: ONGOING CONVERSIONS

1 Stoler, *Race and the Education of Desire*, and *Carnal Knowledge and Imperial Power*.

2 Berlant, *Cruel Optimism*, 9.

3 L. Abu Lughod, *Writing Women's Worlds: Bedouin Stories*; Behar and Gordon, *Women Writing Culture*; Lutz, "The Gender of Theory."

4 Devi, *Imaginary Maps*; Lorde, *Sister Outsider*; Moraga and Anzaldúa, *This Bridge Called My Back*.

5 Constable, *Maid to Order in Hong Kong*; Gamburd, *The Kitchen Spoon's Handle*.

6 Benjamin, "The Storyteller."

7 Sedgwick, *Touching Feeling*; Stewart, *Ordinary Affects*.

8 L. Abu-Lughod, *Writing Women's Worlds: Bedouin Stories*.

9 Benjamin, "The Storyteller."

10 Hindmarsh, *The Evangelical Conversion Narrative*; Rouse, *Engaged Surrender*; van Nieuwkerk, "Gender, Conversion, and Islam," and "Islam Is Your Birthright."

11 Sijapati, *Islamic Revival in Nepal*; also see Dastider, *Understanding Nepal*; Gaborieau, "Nepal"; Sharma, "Lived Islam in Nepal."

12 In her comments, Hema switched between Arabic (using the word *a'adi* meaning "normal"), and Hindi/Urdu (using the term *kohoi khaas nahin* meaning "nothing special").

APPENDIX 1: NOTES ON FIELDWORK

1 I met with and developed ongoing conversations and rapport with a host of drivers and gardeners, including those who were fellow rooftop dwellers. I lived in a masculine space—in the rented former guard's rooftop quarters of a small apartment complex. From my rooftop perch I could often see and sometimes speak with guards, caretakers, and drivers living on other rooftops. On the street, however, these individuals were circumspect about speaking with me for fear of damaging their reputations and my own.

2 I met and interacted with domestic workers who had migrated from other places besides India and Nepal, most notably the Philippines and Sri Lanka, some of

whom had converted to Islam, others who were self-styled secularists or practiced a different religious tradition (i.e., Catholics, Baptists, Hindus and Buddhists).

3 Although they may not have been our first languages. Many Nepali women had learned Hindi through Bollywood films and other Indian media.

4 With the exception of Dr. Nasra Shah's extremely informative and important demographic research.

5 I explained the nature of my project and my position as a doctoral student several times to my interlocutors; however, many continued to interpellate me as a journalist, writer, or book writer.

6 Many of my interlocutors allowed me to record our conversations so long as I promised not to let anyone else listen to these recordings, and to destroy them once I no longer needed them.

7 This, of course, in no way mitigates the deeply entrenched privileges and access to resources I have as a doctoral student and Canadian citizen. I should also qualify that all domestic workers are subject to deeply entrenched asymmetrical relations with their sponsor-employers in Kuwait, and not all domestic workers live in large rooms or suites as did some of my interlocutors.

Abu-Lughod, Janet. *Before European Hegemony: The World System* A.D. *1250–1350*. New York: Oxford University Press, 1989.

Abu-Lughod, Lila. *Remaking Women: Feminism and Modernity in the Middle East*. Princeton, NJ: Princeton University Press, 1998.

———. *Veiled Sentiments: Honor and Poetry in a Bedouin Society*. Berkeley: University of California Press, 1986.

———. *Writing Women's Worlds: Bedouin Stories*. Berkeley: University of California Press, 1993.

Adams, Kathleen M., and Sara Dickey. "Introduction: Negotiating Homes, Hegemonies, Identities and Politics." In *Home and Hegemony: Domestic Service and Identity Politics in South and Southeast Asia*, ed. Kathleen M. Adams and Sara Dickey. Ann Arbor: University of Michigan Press, 2000.

Addleton, Jonathan S. *Undermining the Center: The Gulf Migration and Pakistan*. Karachi: Oxford University Press, 1992.

Agamben, Giorgio. *Homo Sacer: Sovereign Power and Bare Life*. Stanford, CA: Stanford University Press, 1998.

———. *Means without End: Notes on Politics*. Minneapolis: University of Minnesota Press, 2000.

Agrama, Hussein A. *Questioning Secularism: Islam, Sovereignty, and the Rule of Law in Modern Egypt*. Chicago: University of Chicago Press, 2012.

Ahmad, Attiya. "Cosmopolitan Islam in a Diasporic Space: Foreign Resident Muslim Women's Halaqa in Kuwait." In *Islamic Reform in South Asia*, ed. F. Osella and C. Osella. Cambridge: Cambridge University Press, 2012.

———. "Explanation Is Not the Point: South Asian Migrant Domestic Workers' Newfound Islamic Pieties in Kuwait." *Asian and Pacific Journal of Anthropology* 11, nos. 3–4 (2010): 293–310.

———. "Labour's Limits: Foreign Residents in the Gulf." In *Migrant Labor in the Persian Gulf*, ed. M. Kamrav and Z. Babar. New York: Columbia University Press, 2012.

Ahmed, Akbar S. "The Arab Connection: Emergent Models of Social Structure among Pakistan Tribesmen." *Asian Affairs* 12, no. 2 (1981): 167–72.

―――. "Dubai Chalo: Problems in the Ethnic Encounter between Middle Eastern and South Asian Muslim Societies." *Asian Affairs* 15, no. 3 (1984): 262–76.

Alajami, Abdullah M. "House-to-House Migration: The Hadrami Experience in Kuwait." *Journal of Arabian Studies: Arabia, the Gulf, and the Red Sea* 2, no. 1 (2012): 1–17.

Al-Azmeh, Aziz. *Islam and Modernities*. New York: Verso Books, 1996.

Al-Hijji, Yacoub. *Kuwait and the Sea: A Brief Social and Economic History*. London: Arabian Publishing, 2010.

Ali, Syed. *Dubai: Gilded Cage*. New Haven, CT: Yale University Press, 2010.

Al-Moqatei, Mohammad. "Introducing Islamic Law in the Arab Gulf States: A Case Study of Kuwait." *Arab Law Quarterly* 4, no. 2 (1989): 138–48.

al-Mughni, Haya. *Women in Kuwait: The Politics of Gender*. London: Saqi Books, 1993.

al-Mughni, Haya, and Tetreault, Mary Ann. "Political Actors without the Franchise: Women and Politics in Kuwait." In *Monarchies and Nations: Globalisation and Identity in the Arab States of the Gulf*, ed. Paul Dresch and James Piscatori. New York: I. B. Taurus, 2005.

Al-Rasheed, Madawi. *Contesting the Saudi State: Islamic Voices from a New Generation*. Cambridge: Cambridge University Press, 2007.

―――. "Introduction: Localizing the Transnational and Transnationalizing the Local." In *Transnational Connections and the Arab Gulf*, ed. Madawi Al-Rasheed. New York: Routledge, 2005.

―――. *Kingdom without Borders: Saudi Arabia's Political, Religious, and Media Frontiers*. New York: Columbia University Press, 2008.

―――. "Saudi Religious Transnationalism in London." In *Transnational Connections and the Arab Gulf*, ed. Madawi Al-Rasheed. New York: Routledge, 2005.

Anderson, Bridget. *Doing the Dirty Work: The Global Politics of Domestic Labour*. New York: Zed Books, 2000.

Anscombe, Frederick F. "An Anational Society: Eastern Arabia in the Ottoman Period." In *Transnational Connections and the Arab Gulf*, ed. Madawi Al-Rasheed. New York: Routledge, 2005.

―――. *The Ottoman Gulf: The Creation of Kuwait, Saudi Arabia, and Qatar*. New York: Columbia University Press, 1997.

Anway, Carol Anderson. *Daughters of Another Path: Experiences of American Women Choosing Islam*. Lee's Summit, MO: Yawna Publications, 1996.

Arab Times Report. "More Women Convert to Islam: Maids Looked After: Panel. *Arab Times*, September 27, 2015. Accessed November 8, 2015. www.arabtimesonline.com.

Arnold, Fred, and Nasra M. Shah. *Asian Labor Migration: Pipeline to the Middle East*. Boulder, CO: Westview Press, 1986.

Arnold, Thomas. *The Spread of Islam in the World: A History of Peaceful Preaching*. New Delhi: Goodword Books, [1896] 2005.

Asad, Muhammad. *The Road to Mecca*. New York: Simon and Shuster, 1954.

Asad, Talal. "Are There Histories of People without Europe?" *Comparative Studies in Society and History* 29 (1987): 594–607.

―――. "Comments on Conversion." In *Conversions to Modernity: The Globalization of Christianity*, ed. Peter van der Veer. New York: Routledge, 1996.

———. *Formations of the Secular: Christianity, Islam and Modernity*. Stanford, CA: Stanford University Press, 2003.

———. *Genealogies of Religion: Discipline and Reasons of Power in Christianity and Islam*. Baltimore: Johns Hopkins University Press, 1993.

———. *The Idea of an Anthropology of Islam*. Washington, DC: Center for Contemporary Arab Studies, Georgetown University, 1986.

———. "Religion, Nation-State, Secularism." In *Conversions to Modernity: The Globalization of Christianity*, ed. Peter van der Veer. Princeton, NJ: Princeton University Press, 1999.

Austin-Broos, Diane. "The Anthropology of Conversion: An Introduction." In *The Anthropology of Religious Conversion*, ed. Andrew Buckser and Stephen Glazier. Oxford: Rowman and Littlefield, 2002.

Aydin, Cemil. *The Politics of Anti-Westernism in Asia: Visions of World Order in Pan-Islamic and Pan-Asian Thought*. New York: Columbia University Press, 2007.

Bachelard, Gaston. *The Dialectic of Duration*. Manchester: Clinamen Press Limited, [1950] 2000.

———. *Poetics of Space*. Boston, MA: Beacon Press, 1994.

Baer, Marc. "The Double Bind of Race and Religion: The Conversion of the Donme to Turkish Secular Nationalism." *Society for Comparative Study of Society and History* 46, no. 4 (2004): 678–712.

———. *Honored by the Glory of Islam: Conversion and Conquest in Ottoman Europe*. New York: Oxford University Press, 2008.

———. "Islamic Conversion Narratives of Women: Social Change and Gendered Religious Hierarchy in Early Modern Ottoman Istanbul." *Gender and History* 6, no. 2 (2004): 425–58.

Bakhtin, M. M. *The Dialogic Imagination: Four Essays*. Austin: University of Texas Press, 1981.

Balibar, Etienne, and Immanuel Wallerstein. *Race, Nation, Class: Ambiguous Identities*. New York: Verso, 1991.

Basch, Linda, Nina Glick-Schiller, and Szanton Blanc. *Nations Unbound: Transnational Projects, Postcolonial Predicaments and Deterritorialized Nations-States*. Langhorne, PA: Gordon and Breach, 1994.

Bayly, C. A., and Leila Fawaz. "Introduction: The Connected World of Empires." In *Modernity and Culture: From the Mediterranean to the Indian Ocean*, ed. C. A. Bayly and Leila Fawaz. New York: Columbia University Press, 2002.

Becker, Gary S. *Human Capital: A Theoretical and Empirical Analysis, with Special Reference to Education*. New York: Columbia University Press, 1975.

Behar, Ruth, and Deborah Gordon, eds. *Women Writing Culture*. Berkeley: University of California Press, 1996.

Beinin, Joel, and Joe Stork. *Political Islam: Essays from the Middle East Report*. Berkeley: University of California Press, 1997.

Benjamin, Walter. "The Storyteller." In *Illuminations*. New York: Harcourt, [1936] 1996.

Berlant, Lauren. *Cruel Optimism*. Durham, NC: Duke University Press, 2011.

Bill, James A. "Resurgent Islam in the Persian Gulf." *Foreign Affairs*, fall 1984, 108–27.

Birks, J .S., and C. A. Sinclair. *International Migration and Development in the Arab Region.* Geneva: International Labour Organization, 1980.

Birt, Jonathan. "Wahhabism in the United Kingdom: Manifestations and Reactions." In *Transnational Connections and the Arab Gulf*, ed. Madawi Al-Rasheed. New York: Routledge, 2005.

Blanchot, Maurice. *The Infinite Conversation.* Minneapolis: University of Minnesota Press, 1992.

Bloch, Ernst. *The Principle of Hope.* Vol. 1. Cambridge, MA: MIT Press, [1959] 1986.

Boris, Eileen, and Elisabeth Prugl. 1996. *Homeworkers in Global Perspective: Invisible No More.* New York: Routledge, 1996.

Bose, P. K. "Sons of the Nation: Child Rearing in the New Family." In *Texts of Power: Emerging Disciplines in Colonial Bengal*, ed. P. Chatterjee. Calcutta: Samya, 1995.

Bose, Sugata. *A Hundred Horizons: The Indian Ocean in the Age of Global Empire.* Cambridge, MA: Harvard University Press, 2006.

———. "Space and Time on the Indian Ocean Rim: Theory and History." In *Modernity and Culture: From the Mediterranean to the Indian Ocean*, ed. C. A. Bayly and Leila Fawaz. New York: Columbia University Press, 2002.

Bosworth, C. Edmund. "The Nomenclature of the Persian Gulf." In *Persian Gulf States: A General Survey*, ed. Alvin J. Cottrell. Baltimore: Johns Hopkins University Press, 1980.

Boyarin, Jonathan, and Daniel Boyarin. *Powers of Diaspora: Two Essays on the Relevance of Jewish Cultures.* Minneapolis: University of Minnesota Press, 2002.

Brodkin, Karen. 2000. "Global Capitalism: What's Race Got to Do with It?" *American Ethnologist* 27, no. 2 (2000): 237–56.

Brown, Jacqueline Nassy. 1998. "Black Liverpool, Black America, and the Gendering of Diasporic Space." *Cultural Anthropology* 13, no. 3 (1998): 291–325.

Brown, Nathan J. *The Rule of Law in the Arab World: Courts in Egypt and the Gulf.* Cambridge: Cambridge University Press, 1997.

Brown, Norman O. *Apocalypse and/or Metamorphosis.* Berkeley: University of California Press, 1991.

Brown, Wendy. *States of Injury: Power and Freedom in Late Modernity.* Princeton, NJ: Princeton University Press, 1995.

Buckser, Andrew, and Stephen Glazier. *The Anthropology of Religious Conversion.* Oxford: Rowman and Littlefield, 2002.

Bulliet, Richard. 1979. "Conversion Stories in Early Islam." In *Conversion and Continuity: Indigenous Christian Communities in Islamic Lands 8th to 18th centuries*, ed. Michael Gervers and Ramzi Jibra Bikhazi. Toronto: Pontifical Institute of Medieval Studies, 1990.

———. *Conversion to Islam in the Medieval Period: An Essay in Quantitative History.* Cambridge, MA: Harvard University Press, 1979.

Butalia, Urvashi. *The Other Side of Silence.* Durham, NC: Duke University Press, 2000.

Calasso, Giovanna. "Récits de conversion, zèle dévotionnel et instruction religieuse dans les biographies des 'gens de Basra' due Kitab al-Tabaqat d'Ibn Sa'd." In *Conversion and Continuity: Indigenous Christian Communities in Islamic Lands 8th to 18th Centuries*, ed. Mercedes Garcia-Arenal. Paris: Maisonneuve, 2001.

Campt, Tina, and Deborah Thomas. "Gendering Diaspora: Transnational Feminism, Diaspora and Its Hegemonies." *Feminist Review* 90, no. 1 (2008): 1–8.

Casanova, Jose. *Public Religions in the Modern World*. Chicago: University of Chicago Press, 1984.

Chakrabarty, Dipesh. *Provincializing Europe: Postcolonial Thought and Historical Difference*. Princeton, NJ: Princeton University Press, 2000.

Chatterjee, P. *The Nation and Its Fragments*. Princeton, NJ: Princeton University Press, 1993.

Chaudhuri, K. N. *Asia before Europe: Economy and Civilization of the Indian Ocean from the Rise of Islam to 1750*. Cambridge: Cambridge University Press, 1989.

Cheah, Pheng. *Inhuman Conditions: On Cosmopolitanism and Human Rights*. Cambridge, MA: Harvard University Press, 2007.

Chen, Mel. *Animacies: Biopolitics, Racial Mattering, and Queer Affect*. Durham, NC: Duke University Press, 2012.

Cheng, Shu-ju Ada. *Serving the Household and the Nation: Filipina Domestics and the Politics of Identity in Taiwan*. Oxford: Lexington Books, 2006.

Clark, Brian D. "Tribes of the Persian Gulf." In *Persian Gulf States: A General Survey*, ed. Alvin J. Cottrell. Baltimore: Johns Hopkins University Press, 1980.

Clifford, James. "Diasporas." *Cultural Anthropology* 9, no. 3 (1994): 302–38.

Clough, Patricia Ticento, and Jean Halley. *The Affective Turn: Theorizing the Social*. Durham, NC: Duke University Press, 2007.

Coleman, Simon. *The Globalization of Charismatic Christianity*. Cambridge: Cambridge University Press, 2007.

Constable, Nicole. "At Home but Not at Home: Filipina Narratives of Ambivalent Returns." *Cultural Anthropology* 14, no. 2 (1999): 203–28.

———. *Maid to Order in Hong Kong: Stories of Migrant Workers*. 2d ed. Ithaca, NY: Cornell University Press, [1997] 2007.

Coronil, Fernando. *The Magical State: Nature, Money, and Modernity in Venezuela*. Chicago: University of Chicago Press, 1997.

Cottrell, Alvin J. *The Persian Gulf States: A General Survey*. Baltimore: Johns Hopkins University Press, 1980.

Crystal, Jill. *Kuwait: The Transformation of an Oil State*. Boulder, CO: Westview Press, 1992.

———. *Oil and Politics in the Gulf: Rulers and Merchants in Kuwait and Qatar*. Cambridge: Cambridge University Press, 1990.

———. "Public Order and Authority: Policing Kuwait." In *Monarchies and Nations: Globalisation and Identity in the Arab States of the Gulf*, ed. Paul Dresch and James Piscatori. New York: I. B. Taurus, 2005.

Daiber, Hans. "Abu Hatim ar-Razi (10th century AD) on the Unity and Diversity of Religions." In *Monarchies and Nations: Globalisation and Identity in the Arab States of the Gulf*, ed. Jerald D. Gort et al. Grand Rapids, MI: W. B. Eerdmans, 1989.

Daniel, E. Valentine. *Fluid Signs: Being a Person The Tamil Way*. Berkeley: CA: University of California Press, 1984.

Daniel, Jamie Owen, and Tom Moylan. "Why Not Yet, Now?" In *Not Yet: Reconsidering Ernst Bloch*, ed. Jamie Owen Daniel, and Tom Moylan. New York: Verso Books, 2007.

Dastider, Mollica. *Understanding Nepal: Muslims in a Plural Society*. Har Anand Publications, 2010.

de Certeau, Michel. *The Practice of Everyday Life*. Berkeley: University of California Press, 1984.

Deeb, Laura. *An Enchanted Modern: Gender and Public Piety in Shi'I Lebanon*. Princeton: Princeton University Press, 2006.

De Genova, Nicholas. "Migrant 'Illegality' and Deportability in Everyday Life." *Annual Review of Anthropology* 31 (2002): 419–47.

Deleuze, Gilles. *Bergsonism*. New York: Zone Books, 1988.

———. *Difference and Repetition*. New York: Columbia University Press, 1994.

———. *Nietzsche and Philosophy*. New York: Columbia University Press, 2006.

———. *Spinoza: Practical Philosophy*. San Francisco: City Lights Books, 1988.

Deleuze, Gilles, and Felix Guattari. *A Thousand Plateaus: Capitalism and Schizophrenia*. Minneapolis: University of Minnesota Press, 1987.

Derrida, Jacques. *Of Hospitality: Anne Dufourmantelle Invites Jacques Derrida to Respond*. Stanford, CA: Stanford University Press, 2000.

Devi, Mahashweta. *Imaginary Maps*. New York: Routledge, 1994.

DeWeese, Devin. *Islamicization and Native Religion in the Golden Horde: Baba Tukles and Conversion to Islam in Historical and Epic Tradition*. University Park: Pennsylvania State University Press, 1994.

Diederich, Mathias. "Indonesians in Saudi Arabia: Religious and Economic Connections." In *Transnational Connections and the Arab Gulf*, ed. Madawi Al-Rasheed. New York: Routledge, 2005.

Donner, H. *Domestic Goddesses: Maternity, Globalization and Middle-Class Identity in Contemporary India*. Burlington, VT: Ashgate Publishing, 2008.

Dougherty, James E. "Religion and Law." In *Persian Gulf States: A General Survey*, ed. Alvin J. Cottrell. Baltimore: Johns Hopkins University Press, 1980.

Doumato, Eleanor Abdella. *Getting God's Ear: Women, Islam, and Healing in Saudi Arabia and the Gulf*. New York: Columbia University Press, 2000.

Dowling, Emma et. al. "Immaterial and Affective Labour: Explored." *Ephemera: Theory & Politics in Organization* 7, no. 1 (2007): 1–7.

Dresch, Paul. "Debates on Marriage and Nationality in the United Arab Emirates." In *Monarchies and Nations: Globalisation and Identity in the Arab States of the Gulf*, ed. Paul Dresch and James Piscatori. New York: I. B. Taurus, 2005.

———. "Introduction: Societies, Identities, and Global Issues." In *Monarchies and Nations: Globalisation and Identity in the Arab States of the Gulf*, ed. Paul Dresch and James Piscatori. New York: I. B. Taurus, 2005.

Dubois, Colette. "The Red Sea Ports during the Revolution in Transportation, 1800–1914." In *Modernity and Culture: From the Mediterranean to the Indian Ocean*, ed. C. A. Bayly and Leila Fawaz. New York: Columbia University Press, 2002.

Dutton, Yasin. "Conversion to Islam: the Qur'anic paradigm." In *Religious Conversions: Contemporary Practices and Controversies*, ed. Christopher Lamb and M. Darrol Bryant. New York: Cassell, 1999.

Eaton, Richard. *The Rise of Islam and the Bengal Frontier, 1204–1760*. Berkeley: University of California Press, 1993.

Edwards, Brent Hayes. "The Uses of Diaspora." *Social Text* 19, no. 1 (2001): 45–66.

Eickelman, Dale, and James Piscatori. *Muslim Politics*. Princeton, NJ: Princeton University Press.

———. 1999. *New Media in the Muslim World: The Emerging Public Sphere*. Bloomington: Indiana University Press, 1996.

El Shakry, Omnia. *The Great Social Laboratory: Subjects of Knowledge in Colonial and Postcolonial Egypt*. Stanford, CA: Stanford University Press, 2007.

———. "Schooled Mothers and Structured Play: Child Rearing in the Turn of the Century Egypt." In Remaking Women: Feminism and Modernity in the Middle East, ed. Lila Abu-Lughod. Princeton, NJ: Princeton University Press, 1998.

Engels, Friedrich. *Origins of the Family, Private Property and the State*. New York: International Publishers, 1972.

Ewing, Katherine. "Ambiguity and *Shari'at*: A Perspective on the Problem of Moral Principles in Tension." In *Shari'at and Ambiguity in South Asian Islam*, ed. Katherine Ewing. Berkeley: University of California Press, 1988.

———. *Arguing Sainthood: Modernity, Psychoanalysis and Islam*. Durham, NC: Duke University Press, 1997.

Facey, William, and Grant, Gillian. *Kuwait by the First Photographers*. New York: I. B. Taurus, 1998.

Fattah, Hala. "Islamic Universalism and the Construction of Regional Identity in Turn-of-the-Century Basra: Sheikh Ibrahim al-Haidari's Book Revisited." In *Modernity and Culture: From the Mediterranean to the Indian Ocean*, ed. C. A. Bayly and Leila Fawaz. New York: Columbia University Press, 2002.

Fischer, Michael M. J. "Competing Ideologies and Social Structure in the Persian Gulf." In *Persian Gulf States: A General Survey*, ed. Alvin J. Cottrell. Baltimore: Johns Hopkins University Press, 1980.

Flinn, Frank K. "Conversion: Up From the Evangelicalism or the Pentecostal and Charismatic Experience." In *Religious Conversions: Contemporary Practices and Controversies*, ed. Christopher Lamb and M. Darrol Bryant. New York: Cassell, 1999.

Flood, Finbarr. *Objects of Translation: Material Culture and Medieval 'Hindu-Muslim' Encounter*. Princeton, NJ: Princeton University Press, 2009.

Flueckiger, Joyce. *In Amma's Healing Room: Gender and Vernacular Islam in South India*. Bloomington: Indiana University Press, 2006.

Fortunati, Leopoldina. *The Arcane of Reproduction: Housework, Prostitution, Labour and Capital*. Brooklyn, NY: Autonomedia, 1995.

———. "Immaterial Labor and Its Mechanization." *Ephemera: Theory and Politics in Organization* 7, no. 1 (2007): 139–57.

Foster, Nicholas H. D. 2001. "The Islamic Law of Guarantees." *Arab Law Quarterly* 16, no. 2 (2001): 133–57.

Foucault, Michel. "About the Beginnings of the Hermeneutic of the Self." In *Religion and Culture: Michel Foucault*, ed. Jeremy R. Carrette. New York: Routledge, 1999.

———. *The Archaeology of Knowledge and Discourse on Language.* New York: Pantheon Books, 1972.

———. *Discipline and Punish.* New York: Vintage Books, 1977.

———. "The Ethic of Care for the Self as a Practice of Freedom." In Rasmussen, David. (Ed.). *The Final Foucault.* Cambridge, MA: MIT Press, 1991.

———. *The Hermeneutics of the Subject: Lectures at the College de France 1981–1982.* New York: Palgrave Macmillan, 2001.

———. *The History of Sexuality.* New York: Vintage Books, 1978.

———. *Remarks on Marx.* New York, NY: Semiotexte, 1991.

———. *Society Must Be Defended: Lectures at the College de France, 1975–1976.* New York: Picador, 2003.

Freeman, Carla. "Is Local:Global as Feminine:Masculine? Rethinking the Gender of Globalization." In *Gender Relations in Global Perspective*, ed. Nancy Cook. Toronto: Canada Scholars' Press, 2007.

Friedman, Maurice. "The Dialogue of Touchstones as an Approach to Interreligious Dialogue." In *Dialogue and Syncretism: An Interdisciplinary Approach*, ed. Jerald D. Gort et al. Grand Rapids, MI: W. B. Eerdmans, 1989.

Friedmann, Yohanan. *Tolerance and Coercion in Islam: Interfaith Relations in the Muslim Tradition.* New York: Cambridge University Press, 2003.

Fuccaro, Nelida. *Histories of the City and State in the Persian Gulf.* Cambridge: Cambridge University Press, 2009.

———. "Mapping the Transnational Community: Persians and the Space of the City in Bahrain, c. 1869–1937." In *Transnational Connections and the Arab Gulf*, ed. Madawi Al-Rasheed. New York: Routledge, 2005.

Gaborieau, Marc. "Nepal." In *Encyclopedia of Islam*, ed. P. Bearman et al. Leiden: Brill, 2007.

Gamburd, Michelle. *The Kitchen Spoon's Handle: Transnationalism and Sri Lanka's Migrant Housemaids.* Ithaca, NY: Cornell University Press, 2000.

Garcia-Arenal, Mercedes. "Dreams and Reason: Autobiographies of converts in religious polemics." In *Conversions Islamiques: Identitiés religieuses en Islam méditerranéen / Islamic Conversions: Religious Identities in Mediterranean Islam*, ed. Mercedes Garcia-Arenal. Paris: Maisonneuve, 2001.

———. "Introduction." In *Conversions Islamiques: Identitiés religieuses en Islam méditerranéen / Islamic Conversions: Religious Identities in Mediterranean Islam*, ed. Mercedes Garcia-Arenal. Paris: Maisonneuve, 2001.

Gardener, Andrew. *City of Strangers: Gulf Migration and the Indian Community in Bahrain.* Ithaca, NY: Cornell University Press, 2010.

———. "Strategic Transnationalism: The Indian Diasporic Elite in Contemporary Bahrain." *City and Society* 20, no. 1 (2008): 54–78.

Geertz, Clifford. *The Interpretation of Culture.* New York: Basic Books, 1973.

———. *Islam Observed.* Chicago: University of Chicago Press, 1971.

Gellner, Ernest. *Muslim Society.* Cambridge: Cambridge University Press, 1983.

Geoghegan, Vincent. *Ernst Bloch.* New York: Routledge, 1996.

Ghabra, Shafiq. *Palestinians in Kuwait: The Family and the Politics of Survival.* Boulder, CO: Westview Press, 1987.

Ghosh, Amitav. *In An Antique Land.* New York: Granta Books, 1992.

Gilliat-Ray, Sophie. "Rediscovering Islam: A Muslim Journey of Faith." In *Religious Conversions: Contemporary Practices and Controversies,* ed. Christopher Lamb and M. Darrol Bryant. New York: Cassell, 1999.

Gilsenan, Michael. *Recognizing Islam: Religion and Society in the Modern Arab World.* New York: Pantheon Books, 1982.

Glissant, Edouard. *Poetics of Relation.* Ann Arbor: University of Michigan Press, 1997.

Gökarıksel, Banu. "Feminist Geography of Veiling: Gender, Class and Religion in the Making of Modern Spaces and Subjects in Istanbul," in *Women, Religion, and Space,* ed. Karen Morin and Jeanne Kay Guelke. Syracuse, NY: Syracuse University Press, 2007.

Gökarıksel, Banu, and Anna Secor, "Between Fashion and Tesettür: Marketing and Consuming Women's Islamic Dress." *Journal of Middle East Women's Studies* 6, no. 3 (2010): 118–48.

———. "Islamic-ness in the Life of a Commodity: Veiling-Fashion in Turkey." *Transactions of the Institute of British Geographers* 35, no. 3 (2010): 313–33.

Gregg, M. *The Affect Theory Reader.* Durham, NC: Duke University Press, 2010.

Grewal, Inderpal. *Transnational America: Feminisms, Diaspora, Neoliberalisms.* Durham, NC: Duke University Press, 2005.

Grewal, Inderpal, and Caren Kaplan. *Scattered Hegemonies: Postmodernity and Transnational Feminist Practices.* Minneapolis: University of Minnesota Press, 1994.

Grosz, Elizabeth. *The Nick of Time: Politics, Evolution, and the Untimely.* Durham, NC: Duke University Press, 2004.

———. *Time Travels: Feminism, Nature, Power.* Durham, NC: Duke University Press, 2005.

Gupta, Akil, and James Ferguson. *Anthropological Locations: Boundaries and Grounds of a Field Science.* Berkeley: University of California Press, 1997.

———. *Culture, Power, Place: Explorations in Critical Anthropology.* Durham, NC: Duke University Press, 1997.

Hafez, Sherine. *An Islam of Her Own: Reconsidering Religion and Secularism in Women's Islamic Movements.* New York: New York University Press, 2011.

Hardt, Michael, and Antonio Negri. *Labor of Dionysus: A Critique of the State Form.* Minneapolis: University of Minnesota Press, 1994.

Hardy, Peter. "Modern European and Muslim Explanations of Conversion to Islam in South Asia: A Preliminary Survey of the Literature." In *Conversion to Islam,* ed. Nehemia Levtzion. New York: Holmes and Meier Publishers, 1979.

Hasan, Mushirul. "Introduction: Memories of a Fragmented Nation: Rewriting the Histories of India's Partition." In *Inventing Boundaries: Gender, Politics and the Partition of India,* ed. Mushirul Hasan. New Delhi: Oxford University Press, 2000.

Haykel, Bernard. *Revival and Reform in Islam: The Legacy of Muhammad al-Shawkani.* Cambridge: Cambridge University Press, 2003.

Hegghammer, Thomas. *Jihad in Saudi Arabia: Violence and Pan-Islamism since 1979.* Cambridge: Cambridge University Press, 2010.

Henkel, Heiko. "Between Belief and Unbelief Lies the Performance of Salat: Meaning and Efficacy of a Muslim Ritual." *Royal Anthropological Institute* 11, no. 3 (2005): 487–507.

———. "The Location of Islam: Inhabiting Istanbul in a Muslim Way." *American Ethnologist* 34, no. 1 (2007): 57–70.

Hermez, Sami. Untitled. Unpublished paper presented at the SSHRC Inter-Asian Connections Conference in Dubai, spring 2008.

Hindmarsh, D. Bruce. *The Evangelical Conversion Narrative: Spiritual Autobiography in Early Modern England*. New York: Oxford University Press, 2005.

Hirschkind, Charles. *The Ethical Soundscape: Cassette Sermons and Islamic Counterpublics*. New York: Columbia University Press, 2006.

———. "The Ethics of Listening: Cassette-Sermon Audition in Contemporary Egypt." *American Ethnologist* 28, no. 3 (2001): 623–49.

Ho, Engseng. *The Graves of Tarim: Genealogy and Mobility across the Indian Ocean*. Berkeley: University of California Press, 2006.

Hochschild, A. R. "Global Care Chains and Economic Surplus Value." In *On the Edge: Living with Global Capitalism*, ed. W. Hutton and A. Giddens. London: Jonathan Cape, 2000.

———. *The Time Bind: When Work Becomes Home and Home Becomes Work*. New York: Metropolitan Books, 1997.

Hochschild, Arlie Russell, ed. *Global Woman: Nannies, Maids, and Sex Workers in the New Economy*. New York: Holt, 2002.

Holes, Clive. "Dialect and National Identity: The Cultural Politics of Self-Representation in Bahrain Musalsalat." In *Monarchies and Nations: Globalisation and Identity in the Arab States of the Gulf*, ed. Paul Dresch and James Piscatori. New York: I. B. Taurus, 2005.

Hondagneu-Sotelo, P. *Domestica: Immigrant Workers Cleaning and Caring in the Shadows of Affluence*. Berkeley: University of California Press, [2001] 2007.

———. "Introduction: Gender and Contemporary US Immigration." *American Behavioral Scientist* 24, no. 2 (1998): 565–76.

Huang, Shirlena et al. "Introduction: Asian Women as Transnational Domestic Workers." In *Asian Women as Transnational Domestic Workers*, ed. Shirlena Huang et al. Singapore: Marshall Cavendish Academic, 2005.

Inden, R., and R. Nicholas. *Kinship in Bengali Culture*. Chicago: University of Chicago Press, 1977.

Ingham, Bruce. "Languages of the Persian Gulf." In *Persian Gulf States: A General Survey*, ed. Alvin J. Cottrell. Baltimore: Johns Hopkins University Press, 1980.

Iqbal, Muhammad. *Javad Nama*. Lahore: Iqbal Academy Pakistan, 1932.

———. *Reconstruction of Religious Thought in Islam*. Lahore: Ashraf Press, 1934.

Jansen, Willy. "Conversion and Gender, Two Contested Concepts." In *Women Embracing Islam*, ed. Karin van Nieuwkerk. Austin: University of Texas Press, 2006.

Jawad, Haifaa. "Female Conversion to Islam: The Sufi Paradigm." In *Women Embracing Islam*, ed. Karin van Nieuwkerk. Austin: University of Texas Press, 2006.

Jayawardena, Kumari. *Feminism and Nationalism in the Third World*. New York: Zed Books, 1986.

Johnson, Mark. "Diasporic Dreams, Middle Class Moralities and Migrant Domestic Workers among Muslim Filipinos in Saudi Arabia." *Asian and Pacific Journal of Anthropology* 11, nos. 3–4 (2011): 428–48.

Jureidini, Ray, and Nayla Moukarbel. "Female Sri Lankan Domestic Workers in Lebanon: A Case of Contract Slavery." *Journal of Ethnic and Migration Studies* 30, no. 4 (2004): 581–607.

Kandiyoti, Deniz. *Women, Islam and the State.* Philadelphia: Temple University Press, 1991.

Kanna, Ahmed. *Dubai: The City as Corporation.* Minneapolis: University of Minnesota Press, 2011.

Kapiszewski, Andrzej. *Nationals and Expatriates: Population and Labour Dilemmas of the Gulf Cooperation Council States.* Reading, UK: Ithaca Press, 2001.

Katakura, Motoko. *Bedouin Village: A Study of a Saudi Arabian People in Transition.* Tokyo: University of Tokyo Press, 1997.

Kose, Ali. *Conversion to Islam: A Study of Native British Converts.* New York: Kegan Paul International, 1996.

Krstic, Tijana. *Contested Conversions to Islam: Narratives of Religious Change in the Early Modern Ottoman Empire.* Stanford, CA: Stanford University Press, 2011.

——. "Illuminated by the Light of Islam and the Glory of the Ottoman Sultanate: Self-Narratives of Conversion to Islam in the Age of Confessionalization." *Comparative Studies in Society and History* 5, no. 1 (2009): 35–63.

Kurtzman, Charles. *Modernist Islam, 1840–1940: A Sourcebook.* Oxford: Oxford University Press, 2002.

Lacroix, Stephane. *Awakening Islam: The Politics of Contemporary Religious Dissent in Contemporary Saudi Arabia.* Cambridge, MA: Harvard University Press, 2011.

Lamb, S. *White Saris and Sweet Mangoes: Aging, Gender and Body in North India.* Berkeley: University of California Press, 2000.

Lambek, Michael. "The Anthropology of Religion and the Quarrel between Poetry and Philosophy." *Current Anthropology* 41, no. 3 (2000): 309–20.

Lan, Pei-Chia. *Global Cinderellas: Migrant Domestics and Newly Rich Employers in Taiwan.* Durham, NC: Duke University Press, 2006.

Langford, Jean. *Fluent Bodies: Ayurvedic Remedies for Postcolonial Imbalance.* Durham, NC: Duke University Press, 2002.

Latour, Bruno. *We Have Never Been Modern.* Cambridge, MA: Harvard University Press, 1993.

Lawrence, Bruce. *Shattering the Myth: Islam beyond Violence.* Princeton, NJ: Princeton University Press, 2000.

Lazzarato, Maurizio. "Immaterial Labor." In *Radical Thought in Italy: A Potential Politics,* ed. P. Virno and M. Hardt. Minneapolis: University of Minnesota Press, 1996.

——. *Signs and Machines: Capitalism and the Production of Subjectivity.* New York: Semiotext(e), 2014.

Lefebvre, Henri. *Critique of Everyday Life.* New York: Verso, 1991.

——. *The Production of Space.* Oxford: Blackwell Publishers, 1991.

——. *Rhythmalaysis: Space, Time and Everyday Life.* New York: Continuum Books, 2004.

Leonard, Karen. "South Asian Women in the Gulf: Families and Futures Reconfigured." In *Trans-Status Subjects: Gender in the Globalization of South and Southeast Asia,* ed. Sonita Sarker and Esha Niyogi De. Durham, NC: Duke University Press, 2000.

Levy, Ze'ev. "Utopia and Reality in the Philosophy of Ernst Bloch." In *Not Yet: Reconsidering Ernst Bloch*, ed. Jamie Owen Daniel and Tom Moylan. New York: Verso Books, 2007.

Liebelt, Claudia. *Caring for the Holy Land: Filipina Domestic Workers in Israel*. Oxford, NY: Berghahn Books, 2011.

Limbert, Mandana. "Caste, Ethnicity and the Politics of Arabness in Southern Arabia." *Comparative Studies in South Asia, Africa and the Middle East* 34, no. 3 (2014): 590–98.

———. "Gender, Religious Knowledge and Education in Oman." In *Monarchies and Nations: Globalisation and Identity in the Arab States of the Gulf*, ed. Paul Dresch and James Piscatori, 182–202. New York: I. B. Taurus, 2005.

———. *In the Time of Oil: Piety, Memory and Social Life in an Omani Town*. Stanford, CA: Stanford University Press, 2010.

Lindquist, J., et al. "Introduction: Opening the Black Box of Migration: Brokers, the Organisation of Transnational Mobility, and the Changing Political Economy in Asia." *Pacific Affairs* 85, no. 1 (2012): 7–18.

Longva, Anh Nga. "Citizenship in the Gulf States: Conceptualization and Practice." In *Citizenship and State in the Middle East: Approaches and Applications*, ed. Nils A. Butenschan et al. Syracuse: Syracuse University Press, 2000.

———. "Keeping Migrant Workers in Check: The Kafala System in the Gulf." In *Middle East Report* 211 (1999): 20–22.

———. "Neither Autocracy nor Democracy but Ethnocracy: Citizens, Expatriates and the Socio-Political System in Kuwait." In *Monarchies and Nations: Globalisation and Identity in the Arab States of the Gulf*, ed. Paul Dresch and James Piscatori. New York: I. B. Taurus, 2005.

———. *Walls Built on Sand: Migration, Exclusion and Society in Kuwait*. Boulder, CO: Westview Press, 1997.

Lorde, Audre. *Sister Outsider: Essays and Speeches*. New York: Crossing Press, 2007.

Louer, Laurence. *Transnational Shia Politics: Religious and Political Networks in the Gulf*. London: Hurst and Company, 2008.

Lutz, Catherine. "The Gender of Theory." In *Women Writing Culture*, ed. Ruth Behar and Deborah Gordon. Berkeley: University of California Press, 1996.

Magnus, Ralph H. "Societies and Social Change in the Persian Gulf." In *Persian Gulf States: A General Survey*, ed. Alvin J. Cottrell. Baltimore: Johns Hopkins University Press, 1980.

Mahdavi, Pardis. *Gridlock: Labor, Migration, and Human Trafficking in Dubai*. Stanford, CA: Stanford University Press, 2011.

Mahmood, Saba. "Ethical Formation and Politics of Individual Autonomy in Contemporary Egypt." *Social Research* 70, no. 3 (2003): 837–61.

———. "Feminist Theory: Embodiment, and the Docile Agent: Some Reflections on the Egyptian Islamic Revival." *Cultural Anthropology* 16, no. 2 (2001): 202–36.

———. *Politics of Piety: The Islamic Revival and the Feminist Subject*. Princeton, NJ: Princeton University Press, 2005.

———. "Rehearsed Spontaneity and the Conventionality of Ritual: Disciplines of Salat." *American Ethnologist* 28, no. 4 (2001): 827–53.

———. "Secularism, Hermeneutics, and Empire: The Politics of Islamic Reformation." *Public Culture* 18, no. 2 (2006): 323–47.

Mamdani, Mahmood. *Good Muslim, Bad Muslim: America, the Cold War and the Roots of Terror.* New York: Three Leaves Press, 2005.

Manalansan, M., IV. "Queering the Chain of Care Paradigm." *Scholar & Feminist Online* 6, no. 3 (2008): 1–5.

Marchal, Roland. "Dubai: Global City and Transnational Hub." In *Transnational Connections and the Arab Gulf*, ed. Madawi Al-Rasheed. New York: Routledge, 2005.

Marchand, Marianne H., and Anne Sisson Runyan. "Introduction: Feminist Sightings of Global Restructuring: Conceptualizations and Reconceptualizations." In *Gender and Global Restructuring: Sightings, Sites and Resistances*, ed. Marianne H. Marchand and Anne Sisson Ruyan. New York: Routledge, 2000.

Marcus, George. "Ethnography in/of the World System: The Emergence of Multi-Sited Ethnography." *Annual Review of Anthropology* 24 (1995): 95–117.

Marriott, McKim. "Hindu Transactions: Diversity without Dualism." In *Transaction and Meaning: Directions in the Anthropology of Exchange and Symbolic Behavior*, ed. B. Kapferer. Philadelphia: Institute for the Study of Human Issues, 1976.

Masuzawa, Tomoko. *The Invention of World Religions: Or, How European Universalism Was Preserved in the Language of Pluralism.* Chicago: University of Chicago Press, 2005.

Mauss, Marcel. *The Gift.* London: Kegan Paul, 1954.

May, Todd. *Gilles Deleuze: An Introduction.* Cambridge: Cambridge University Press, 2005.

———. *Reconsidering Difference: Nancy, Derrida, Levinas, and Deleuze.* University Park: Pennsylvania State University Press, 1997.

McGinty, Anna Mansson. *Becoming Muslim: Western Women's Conversion to Islam.* New York: Palgrave Macmillan, 2006.

McLarney, Ellen. "The Islamic Public Sphere and the Discipline of Adab." *International Journal of Middle East Studies* 43, no. 3 (2011): 429–49.

———. "Private Is Political: Women and Family in Intellectual Islam." *Feminist Theory* 11, no. 2 (2010): 129–48.

McLauchlan, Keith. "Oil in the Persian Gulf Area." In *Persian Gulf States: A General Survey*, ed. Alvin J. Cottrell. Baltimore: Johns Hopkins University Press, 1980.

McPherson, Kenneth. "Port Cities as Nodal Points of Change: The Indian Ocean 1890–1920s." In *Modernity and Culture: From the Mediterranean to the Indian Ocean*, ed. C. A. Bayly and Leila Fawaz. New York: Columbia University Press, 2002.

Meijer, Roel. *Global Salafism: Islam's New Religious Movement.* New York: Columbia University Press, 2009.

Meneley, Ann. *Tournaments of Value: Sociability and Hierarchy in a Yemeni Tribe.* Toronto: University of Toronto Press, 1996.

Menon, Ritu, and Kamla Bhasin. *Borders and Boundaries: Women in India's Partition.* New Delhi: Kali for Women, 1998.

Messick, Brinkley. *The Calligraphic State: Textual Domination and History in a Muslim Society.* Berkeley: University of California Press, 1993.

Metcalf, Barbara. *Islamic Revival in British India: Deoband, 1860–1900.* Princeton, NJ: Princeton University Press, 1982.

———. 1995. "Presidential Address: Too Little, Too Much: Reflections on Muslims in the History of India." *Journal of Asian Studies* 54 (1995): 951–67.

Mies, Maria. *Patriarchy and Accumulation on a World Scale.* New Jersey: Zed Books, 1986.

Mignolo, W. "The Many Faces of Cosmo-Polis: Border Thinking and Critical Cosmopolitanism." *Public Culture* 12, no. 3 (2000): 721–48.

Mills, Kenneth, and Anthony Grafton, eds. *Conversion: Old Worlds and New.* Rochester, NY: University of Rochester Press, 2003.

Mills, Mary Beth. 2003. "Gender and Inequality in the Global Labor Force." *Annual Review of Anthropology* 32 (2003): 41–62.

Minkov, Anton. *Conversion to Islam in the Balkans: Kisve bahasi petitions and Ottoman social life, 1670–1730.* Boston: Brill, 2004.

Mintz, Sidney. *Sweetness and Power.* New York: Viking-Penguin Press, 1985.

Mitchell, Timothy. *Carbon Democracy: Political Power in the Age of Oil.* New York: Verso Books, 2011.

———. *Colonizing Egypt.* Berkeley: University of California Press, 1990.

Moghissi, Haideh, ed. *Muslim Diaspora: Gender, Culture and Identity.* New York: Routledge, 2006.

Moors, Annelies. "Discover the Beauty of Modesty: Islamic Fashion Line." In *Modest Fashion: Styling bodies, Mediating faith,* ed. R. Lewis. London: I. B. Tauris, 2013.

———. "Migrant Domestic Workers: Debating Transnationalism, Identity Politics, and Family Relations. A Review Essay." *Society for Comparative Study of Society and History* 45, no. 2 (2003): 386–94.

Moors, Annelies, and R. A. Ünal. "Format, Fabrics and Fashions: Muslim Headscarves Revisited." *Material Religion* 8, no. 3 (2012): 308–29.

Moraga, Cherríe, and Gloria Anzaldúa, eds. *This Bridge Called My Back: Writings by Radical Women of Colour.* New York: Kitchen Table Press, 1983.

Morony, Michael G. "The Age of Conversions: A Reassessment." In *Conversion and Continuity: Indigenous Christian Communities in Islamic Lands 8th to 18th Centuries,* ed. Michael Gervers and Ramzi Jibra Bikhazi. Toronto: Pontifical Institute of Medieval Studies, 1990.

Morrison, Karl F. *Understanding Conversion.* Charlottesville: University Press of Virginia, 1992.

Nagi, Mostafa. "Determinants of Current Trends in Labor Migration and the Future Outlook." In *Asian Labor Migration: Pipeline to the Middle East,* ed. Fred Arnold and Nasra M. Shah. Boulder, CO: Westview Press, 1986.

Nagy, Sharon. "The Search for Miss Philippines Bahrain: Possibilities for Representation in Expatriate Communities." *City and Society* 20, no. 1 (2008): 79–104.

———. "'This Time I Think I'll Try a Filipina': Global and Local Influences on Relations between Foreign Household Workers and Their Employers in Doha, Qatar." *City and Society,* Annual Review (1998): 83–103.

Oishi, Nana. *Women in Motion: Globalization, State Policies and Labor Migration in Asia*. Stanford, CA: Stanford University Press, 2005.

Ong, Aihwa. *Neoliberalism as Exception: Mutations in Citizenship and Sovereignty*. Durham, NC: Duke University Press, 2006.

Onley, James. *The Arabian Frontiers of the British Raj: Merchants, Rulers and the British in the Nineteenth-Century Gulf*. New York: Oxford University Press, 2008.

———. "Transnational Merchants in the Nineteenth-Century Gulf: The Case of the Safar Family." In *Transnational Connections and the Arab Gulf*, ed. Madawi Al-Rasheed. New York: Routledge, 2005.

Osella, Filippo, and Caroline Osella. "'I am Gulf': The Production of Cosmopolitanism in Kozhikode, Kera, India." In *Struggling with History: Islam and Cosmopolitanism in the Western Indian Ocean*, ed. Edward Simpson and Kai Kresse. London: Hurst/Columbia University Press, 2008.

———. "Muslim Entrepreneurs in Public Life between India and the Gulf: Making Good and Doing Good." *Journal of the Royal Anthropological Institute* 15 (2009): 202–21.

Parrenas, Rhacel Salazar. 2000. *Children of Global Migration: Transnational Families and Gendered Woes*. Stanford, CA: Stanford University Press, 2005.

———. *The Force of Domesticity: Filipina Migrants and Globalization*. New York: New York University Press, 2008.

———. *Intimate Labors: Cultures, Technologies, and the Politics of Care*. Palo Alto, CA: Stanford University Press, 2010.

———. "Migrant Filipina Domestic Workers and the International Division of Reproductive Labour." *Gender and Society* 14 (4): 560–80.

———. *Servants of Globalization: Women, Migration and Domestic Work*. Stanford, CA: Stanford University Press, 2001.

Patton, Paul. *Deleuze and the Political*. New York: Routledge, 2000.

Pignol, Alicia. "Filipino Women Workers in Saudi: Making Offering for the Here and Now and the Hereafter." *Asian and Pacific Journal of Anthropology* 11, no. 3–4 (2010): 394–409.

Piscatori, James. "Managing God's Guests: The Pilgrimage, Saudi Arabia and the Politics of Legitimacy." In *Monarchies and Nations: Globalisation and Identity in the Arab States of the Gulf*, ed. Paul Dresch and James Piscatori. New York: I. B. Taurus, 2005.

Pollard, Lisa. *Nurturing the Nation: The Family Politics of Modernizing, Colonizing and Liberating Egypt, 1805–1923*. Berkeley: University of California Press, 2005.

Pollock, S., et al. "Cosmopolitanisms." *Public Culture* 12, no. 3 (2000): 577–89.

Poston, Larry. *Islamic Da'wah in the West: Muslim Missionary Activity and the Dynamics of Conversion to Islam*. New York: Oxford University Press, 1992.

Povinelli, Elizabeth. 2001. *The Cunning of Recognition: Indigenous Alterities and the Making of Australian Multiculturalism*. Durham, NC: Duke University Press, 2002.

———. "Radical Worlds: The Anthropology of Incommensurability and Inconceivability." *Annual Review of Anthropology* 30 (2001): 319–34.

Raheja, G., and Gold, A. *Listen to the Heron's Words: Reimagining Gender and Kinship in North India*. Berkeley: University of California Press, 1994.

Rahman, Fazlur. *Islam*. Chicago: Chicago University Press, 1966.

Ray, Raka, and Seemin Qayum. *Cultures of Servitude: Modernity, Domesticity, and Class in India.* Stanford, CA: Stanford University Press, 2009.

Raymond, Andre. 2002. "A Divided Sea: The Cairo Coffee Trade in the Red Sea Area during the Seventeenth and Eighteenth Centuries." In *Modernity and Culture: From the Mediterranean to the Indian Ocean,* ed. C. A. Bayly and Leila Fawaz. New York: Columbia University Press.

Ricci, Ronit. 2011. *Islam Translated: Literature, Conversion, and the Arabic Cosmopolis of South and Southeast Asia.* Chicago: University of Chicago Press.

Ricklefs, M. C. "Six Centuries of Islamicization in Java." In *Conversion to Islam,* ed. Nehemia Levtzion. New York: Holmes and Meier Publishers, 1979.

Riles, Annelise. *The Network Inside Out.* Ann Arbor: University of Michigan Press, 2001.

Rizzo, Helen Mary. *Islam, Democracy, and the Status of Women: The Case of Kuwait.* New York: Routledge, 2005.

Roald, Anne Sofie. "The Shaping of a Scandinavian 'Islam': Converts and Gender Equal Opportunity." In *Women Embracing Islam,* ed. Karin van Nieuwkerk. Austin: University of Texas Press, 2006.

Robbins, Joel. 2004. "The Globalization of Pentecostal and Charismatic Christianity." *Annual Review of Anthropology* 33 (2004): 117–43.

Robinson, Francis. *Islam and Muslim History in South Asia.* New Delhi: Oxford University Press, 2000.

Robinson, Kathryn. "Gender, Islam and Nationality: Indonesian Domestic Servants in the Middle East." In *Home and Hegemony: Domestic Service and Identity Politics in South and Southeast Asia,* ed. Kathleen A. Adams and Sara Dickey. Ann Arbor: University of Michigan Press, 2000.

Rodinson, Maxime. *Muhammad.* New York: I. B. Taurus, 2002.

Rodrigue, Aron. 1996. "Interview: Difference and Tolerance in the Ottoman Empire." *SEHR* 5, no. 1 (1996): interview conducted by Nancy Reynolds.

Rouse, Carolyn. *Engaged Surrender: African American Women and Islam.* Berkeley, CA: University of California Press, 2004.

Said, Edward. *Culture and Imperialism.* New York: Vintage Press, 1994.

———. *Orientalism.* New York: Vintage Press, 1979.

Salamandra, Christa. "Cultural Construction, the Gulf and Arab London." In *Monarchies and Nations: Globalisation and Identity in the Arab States of the Gulf,* ed. Paul Dresch and James Piscatori, 73–95. New York: I. B. Taurus, 2005.

Sanjek, Roger, and Shellee Colen, eds. *At Work in Homes: Household Workers in World Perspective.* Washington, DC: American Anthropological Association, 1990.

Sayyid, S. "Beyond Westphalia: Nations and Diasporas: The Case of Muslim Umma." In *Un/settled Multi-Culturalisms: Diasporas, Entanglements, "Transruptions,"* ed. Barnor Hesse. London: Zed Books, 2001.

Scott, David, and Charles Hirschkind, eds. *Powers of the Secular Modern: Talal Asad and His Interlocutors.* Stanford, CA: Stanford University Press, 2006.

Secombe, I. J., and R. I. Lawless. "Foreign Worker Dependence in the Gulf, and the International Oil Companies: 1910–50." *International Migration Review* 20, no. 3 (1999): 548–74.

Sedgwick, Eve. *Touching Feeling: Affect, Pedagogy, Performativity*. Durham, NC: Duke University Press, 2003.

Shah, Nasra. "Relative Success of Male Workers in the Host Country, Kuwait: Does the Channel of Migration Matter?" *International Migration Review* 34, no. 1 (2000): 59–78.

Shah, Nasra, et al. "Asian Women Workers in Kuwait." *International Migration Review* 25, no. 3 (1991): 464–86.

Shah, Nasra, et al. "Foreign Domestic Workers in Kuwait: Who Employs How Many." *Asian and Pacific Migration Journal* 11, no. 2 (2002): 247–69.

Shah, Nasra, and Indu Menon. "Violence against Women Migrant Workers: Issues, Data and Partial Solutions." *Asian and Pacific Migration* 6, no. 1 (1997): 5–30.

Sharma, Sudhindra. "Lived Islam in Nepal." In *Lived Islam in South Asia: Adaptation, Accommodation and Conflict*, ed. Imtiaz Ahmed and Helmut Reifeld. Delhi: Social Science Press, 2004.

Shaw, Rosalind, and Charles Stewart. "Introduction: Problematizing Syncretism." In *Syncretism/Anti-Syncretism: The Politics of Religious Synthesis*, ed. Rosalind Shaw and Charles Stewart. New York: Routledge, 1994.

Shryock, Andrew. *Nationalism and the Genealogical Imagination: Oral History and Textual Authority in Tribal Jordan*. Berkeley: University of California Press, 1997.

Siddiqui, T. "Migration and Gender in Asia." Bangkok, Thailand: Report given to the UN Expert Group Meeting on International Migration and Development in Asia and the Pacific, September 20–21, 2008.

Sijapati, Megan. *Islamic Revival in Nepal: Religion and a New Nation*. New York: Routledge, 2013.

Silverblatt, Irene. *Modern Inquisitions: Peru and the Colonial Origins of the Civilized World*. Durham, NC: Duke University Press, 2004.

Silverstein, Paul A. "Immigrant Racialization and the New Savage Slot: Race, Migration, and Immigration in the New Europe." *Annual Review of Anthropology* 34 (2005): 363–84.

Silvey, Rachel. "Mobilizing Piety: Gendered Morality and Indonesian-Saudi Transnational Migration." *Mobilities* 2, no. 2 (2007): 219–29.

———. "Power, Difference, and Mobility: Feminist Advances in Migration Studies." *Progress in Human Geography* 28, no. 4 (2004): 490–506.

———. "Transnational Domestication: Indonesian Domestic Workers in Saudi Arabia." *Political Geography* 23, no. 3 (2004): 245–64.

———. "Transnational Migration and the Gender Politics of Scale, 1997–2000." *Singapore Journal of Tropical Geography* 25, no. 2 (2004): 141–55.

Simpson, Edward, and Kai Kress. "Introduction: Cosmopolitanism Contested: Anthropology and History in the Western Indian Ocean." In *Struggling with History: Islam and Cosmopolitanism in the Western Indian Ocean*, ed. Edward Simpson and Kai Kresse. London: Hurst/Columbia University Press, 2008.

Stewart, Kathleen. *Ordinary Affects*. Durham, NC: Duke University Press, 2007.

Stoler, Ann. *Race and the Education of Desire: Foucault's History of Sexuality and the Colonial Order of Things*. Durham, NC: Duke University Press, 1995.

———. *Carnal Knowledge and Imperial Power: Race and the Intimate in Colonial Rule.* Berkeley: University of California Press, 2002.

Tadiar, N. *Things Fall Away: Philippine Historical Experience and the Making of Globalization.* Durham, NC: Duke University Press, 2009.

Taylor, Charles. "Religious Mobilizations." *Public Culture* 18, no. 2 (2006): 281–300.

———. *A Secular Age.* Cambridge, MA: Belknap Press, 2007.

Taylor, Donald. "Conversion: Inward, Outward and Awkward." In *Religious Conversions: Contemporary Practices and Controversies,* ed. Christopher Lamb and M. Darrol Bryant. New York: Cassell, 1999.

Tetreault, Mary Ann. "Divided Communities of Memory: Diasporas Come Home." In *Muslim Diaspora: Gender, Culture and Identity,* ed. Haideh Moghissi. New York: Routledge, 2006.

———. *Stories of Democracy: Politics and Society in Contemporary Kuwait.* New York: Columbia University Press, 2000.

Thomas, Deborah A., and Kamari M. Clarke. "Introduction." In *Globalization and Race: Transformations in the Cultural Production of Blackness,* ed. Deborah A. Thomas and Kamari M. Clarke. Durham, NC: Duke University Press, 2006.

Trouillot, Michel-Rolph. "The Anthropology of the State in the Age of Globalization." *Current Anthropology* 42, no. 1 (2001): 125–39.

———. *Global Transformations: Anthropology and the Modern World.* New York: Palgrave Macmillan, 2003.

———. *Silencing the Past.* Boston: Beacon Press, 1997.

Tsing, Anna-Lowenhaupt. *Friction: An Ethnography of Global Connection.* Princeton, NJ: Princeton University Press, 2005.

———. *In the Realm of the Diamond Queen: Marginality in an Out-of-the-Way Place.* Princeton, NJ: Princeton University Press, 1993.

Tuchscherer, Michael. 2002. "Trade and Port Cities in the Red Sea: Gulf of Aden Region in the Sixteenth and Seventeenth Century." In *Modernity and Culture: from the Mediterranean to the Indian Ocean,* ed. C. A. Bayly and Leila Fawaz. New York: Columbia University Press, 2002.

van der Veer, Peter. "Conversion and Coercion: The Politics of Sincerity and Authenticity." In *Cultures of Conversion,* ed. Jan M. Bremmer et al. Leuven, Belgium: Peters, 2006.

———, ed. *Conversions to Modernity: the Globalization of Christianity.* New York: Routledge, 1996.

———. *Imperial Encounters: Religion and Modernity in India and Britain.* Princeton, NJ: Princeton University Press, 2001.

———. "Syncretism, Multiculturalism and the Discourse of Tolerance." In *Syncretism/Antisyncretism: The Politics of Religious Synthesis,* ed. Rosalind Shaw and Charles Stewart. New York: Routledge, 1994.

van der Veer, Peter, and J. Lehmann, eds. *Nation and Religion: Perspectives on Europe and Asia.* Princeton, NJ: Princeton University Press, 1999.

van Nieuwkerk, Karin. "Gender, Conversion, and Islam: A Comparison of Online and Offline Conversion Narratives." In *Women Embracing Islam,* ed. Karin van Nieuwkerk. Austin: University of Texas Press, 2006.

———. "Islam Is Your Birthright: Conversion, Reversion and Alteration: The Case of New Muslimas in the West." In *Cultures of Conversion*, ed. Jan M. Bremmer et al. Leuven, Belgium: Peters, 2006.

Vertovec, V., and R. Cohen. *Conceiving Cosmopolitanism: Theory, Context and Practice.* Oxford: Oxford University Press, 2002.

Viswanathan, Gauri. "Beyond Orientalism: Syncretism and the Politics of Knowledge." *SEHR* 5, no. 1 (1996). http://www.stanford.edu/group/SHR/5-1/text/viswanathan.html.

———. "Ethnographic Politics and the Discourse of Origins." *SEHR* 5, no. 1 (1996). http://www.stanford.edu/group/SHR/5-1/text/viswanathan2.html.

———. *Outside the Fold: Conversion, Modernity and Belief.* Princeton, NJ: Princeton University Press, 1998.

Visweswaran, Kamala. *Fictions of Feminist Ethnography.* Minneapolis: University of Minnesota Press, 1994.

———. *Uncommon Cultures: Racism and the Rearticulation of Cultural Difference.* Durham, NC: Duke University Press, 2010.

Vitalis, Robert. 2002. *America's Kingdom: Mythmaking on the Saudi Oil Frontier.* London: Verso Books, 2009.

———. "Black Gold, White Crude: An Essay on American Exceptionalism, Hierarchy and Hegemony in the Gulf." *Diplomatic History* 26, no. 2 (2002): 185–213.

Voltaire. *Candide, ou l'optimisme.* Paris: Le Livre de Poche, 1983.

Vora, Neha. "Domestic Work, Affective Labor, and Social Reproduction in South Asian America: A Tribute to Laxmi Soni." *Feminist Formations* 26, no. 2 (2014): 162–85.

———. *Impossible Citizens: Dubai's Indian Diaspora.* Durham, NC: Duke University Press, 2013.

———. "Producing Diasporas and Globalization: Indian Middle-Class Migrants in Dubai." *Anthropological Quarterly* 81, no. 2 (2008): 377–406.

Weber, Max. *The Protestant Ethic and the Spirit of Capitalism.* New York: Routledge, [1930] 2001.

Weeks, Kathi. "Life within and against Work: Affective Labor, Feminist Critique, and Post-Fordist Politics." *Ephemera: Theory and Politics in Organization* 7, no. 1 (2007): 233–49.

———. *The Problem with Work: Feminism, Marxism, Antiwork Politics and Postwork Imaginaries.* Durham, NC: Duke University Press, 2011.

Wohlrab-Sahr, Monika. "Symbolizing Distance: Conversion to Islam in Germany and the United States." In *Women Embracing Islam*, ed. Karin van Nieuwkerk. Austin: University of Texas Press, 2006.

Yan, Hairong. *New Masters, New Servants: Migration, Development, and Women Workers in China.* Durham, NC: Duke University Press, 2008.

Yapp, Malcolm. "The Nineteenth and Twentieth Centuries." In *Persian Gulf States: A General Survey*, ed. Alvin J. Cottrell. Baltimore: Johns Hopkins University Press, 1980.

———. "British Policy in the Persian Gulf." In *Persian Gulf States: A General Survey*, ed. Alvin J. Cottrell. Baltimore: Johns Hopkins University Press, 1980.

Zdanowski, Jerry. "'Saving Sinners, Even Moslems': The Arabian Mission in the Arabian Gulf." In *Conversion and Continuity: Indigenous Christian Communities in Islamic Lands 8th to 18th Centuries*, ed. Mercedes Garcia-Arenal. Paris: Maisonneuve, 2001.

Zipes, Jack. "Traces of Hope: The Non-Synchronicity of Ernst Bloch." In *Not Yet: Reconsidering Ernst Bloch*, ed. Jamie Owen Daniel and Tom Moylan. New York: Verso Books, 2007.

exploitation of domestic workers, 11, 54–55, 60–62, 105, 106, 110

familial relations, 40, 71–72, 84–86, 90, 100, 178–82, 193. *See also* pseudokinship relations

feminization of transnational migration. *See under* transnational migration

Filipina women, 118–20

fitra, 157, 167–73, 180–81, 189

foreign residents, 51, 53, 55, 73–74, 162. *See also* noncitizens

foreign workers, 11, 12, 45, 47, 162. *See also* domestic work sector; migrant domestic workers; noncitizens

Foucault, Michel, 22, 138, 226n114

Freeman, Carla, 27

GCC. *See* Gulf Cooperation Council

gender relations, 2, 6, 16, 20, 26, 83

gifting, 42, 57, 84, 88–90, 114

globalization, 27, 31, 240n10, 241n19

Gulf Cooperation Council (GCC), 49–50, 62, 152

habitus, concept of, 138

hadith, 17

halaqa, 4–5, 140, 167

Hashmi, Farhat, 3, 4–5

Hezb al-Da'wa al-Islamiyya, 16–17

hierarchical relations, 11, 13–14, 18–20, 31, 40, 69, 79–80, 83, 87, 100, 110, 139–50

hijab, 2, 3–4, 146, 151–54, 157, 191

Hirschkind, Charles, 180

households: confluence in, 128–30; disciplining in, 25, 26, 129; everyday conversion and, 20, 30–31, 128–29, 199; globalization and, 31; hierarchies, 139–50; intimacy in, 14, 20, 37–41, 64–65, 69–74, 79–80, 84–85, 89, 114, 127, 128, 138–39, 177, 192; nation-building and, 26, 29; policing, 93–99; protection, 91–93

housetalk, 73–74, 124, 127, 128–30, 139, 154, 194

Ikhwan Muslimin. See Muslim Brotherhood

Indian Ocean: colonial state-building, 26; interrelations, 41–48; Islamic reform movements, 3; religious traditions, 24–25; state policies, 28; transnational processes, 6, 26–27, 29–30, 33, 39

Indo-Pakistani Employees Association, 49

intimacy, 184–88; criticism of, 93; difference and, 29; in households, 14, 20, 37–41, 64–65, 69–74, 79–80, 84–85, 89, 114, 127, 128, 138–39, 177, 192; romantic, 184–88. *See also* housetalk

Islamic conversions. *See* everyday conversions

Islamic Guidance Society, 16

Islamic piety, 8, 9, 14, 17, 21, 22–23, 33, 138, 146–48, 151, 152

Islamic reform movements, 3, 16–17, 21; explanation of conversions, 14–18. *See also* specific movements

Israel, creation of, 12, 162

Jamaat-i-Islam, 162–63

jinsiyya, 43, 47. *See also* nationality

jus soli/jus sanguinis, 47

kafala system, 12–13, 41, 51–56, 58–60, 66

kafeel, 13, 50, 51, 53–56, 60–61, 113–14, 176

Khaliji, use of term, 12

kinship relations, 12, 14, 20, 41–43, 57, 79, 128, 141, 159, 193. *See also* pseudokinship relations

Kuwait Oil Company (KOC), 49

Labor Law (1964), 55–56

labor laws, 14, 55–56, 59–61, 64, 221n32

labor migration bans, 28, 63–64, 103, 106–7

labor strikes, 49

Lamb, Christopher, 109

Latour, Bruno, 129

leftist movements, 16

legal codes, Kuwaiti, 17

liberalism, 9, 16, 192; explanations of conversion, 11–14; use of term, 240n10

transnational migration: belonging and, 166, 177; displacement and, 12, 29, 39–40, 66, 69, 93, 99–100, 109; feminization of, 6, 25, 27–28, 107–9, 138–39, 144, 193; households and, 26–27, 128; programs for, 106; reasons for, 28; sex work and, 186

transnational scholarship, 9, 24–26, 39–40, 138

umma, 17–18, 31, 166

veiling. *See hijab*

wages, 49, 61, 88, 91, 113, 232n90

Wahhabi form of Islam, 2–3, 14–15, 17, 163

women's center. *See da'wa* movement

world religions, 24

zakat, 17